Intellectual Property Misuse
Licensing and Litigation

Section of Antitrust Law

Defending Liberty
Pursuing Justice

This volume should be officially cited as:

ABA SECTION OF ANTITRUST LAW,
INTELLECTUAL PROPERTY MISUSE:
LICENSING AND LITIGATION (2000)

Library of Congress Catalog Card Number: 00-044753
ISBN:1-57073-836-X

Discounts are available for books ordered in bulk. Special consideration is given to state bars, CLE programs, and other bar-related organizations. Inquire at Publications Planning and Marketing, American Bar Association, 750 North Lake Shore Drive, Chicago, Illinois 60611.

05 04 03 02 01   5 4 3 2 1

CONTENTS

iii

FOREWORD

The Section of Antitrust Law is pleased to publish *Intellectual Property Misuse: Licensing and Litigation*. This work is one of a series of handbooks prepared by Section members. Through the publication of handbooks such as this, the Section hopes to provide both practical guidance to attorneys and a valuable reference source for scholars, judges, and policymakers.

Misuse is an especially timely topic because of the increasingly central role intellectual property has come to play in our economy at the beginning of a new century. The misuse defense—a complete defense to an infringement suit or suit to recover royalties—has continued to arise in patent cases, has led to the dismissal of several recent copyright cases, and is even being asserted in trademark cases.

Because misuse impacts both licensing and litigation, we believe that this volume will be extremely useful to both transactional lawyers and litigators. We also hope that it contributes to framing correctly the issues for the future evolution and application of the misuse doctrine.

Janet McDavid
Chair, Section of Antitrust Law
American Bar Association
1999-2000

PREFACE

Misuse has always been an intriguing, slightly mysterious subject to many antitrust and intellectual property lawyers. It is neither fish nor fowl: not quite "antitrusty" enough to be a hard-core concern of the antitrust lawyer, and also likely to remain a somewhat peripheral concern of those who concentrate on obtaining, interpreting, and litigating patents or other forms of intellectual property. Yet recent developments show that misuse questions continue to arise and that these questions may have serious consequences for intellectual property owners and practitioners, and for public policy. For example, courts have continued to apply the doctrine to bar claims for injunctive relief or to overturn infringement damages awards. Moreover, as the length of Chapter VII on copyright misuse attests, the doctrine has spread like wildfire into computer copyright cases since the *Lasercomb* decision in 1990. More recently, it has begun to be asserted in trademark cases as well.

Intellectual Property Misuse: Licensing and Litigation is designed to educate and inform practitioner and policymaker alike about the misuse doctrine: its scope, its origins, its practical effects, and the criticisms and justifications that have been adduced for and against its existence in its present form.

We who wrote and edited the chapters in the handbook hope that it will alert practitioners to the issues involved and quickly add focus and depth to their analysis. But we hope these chapters will serve another purpose as well: drawing attention to the doctrine and providing fodder for debate about its proper role in the intellectual property system, a system of increasing importance as we find ourselves in the twenty-first century. We hope we have subjected the obscure, sometimes crotchety notion of misuse to the full multidimensional glare of practical, historical, and even economic analysis.

This work begins with a chapter written by George Gordon and Robert J. Hoerner providing an overview of the misuse doctrine and its historical development. A chapter written by Nick Coch and Heidi Chen then describes and assesses the present status of each practice that has ever been considered or suggested to be misuse.

Sheilah McCartney and John Fry together with Jim Kobak analyze how the doctrine affects licensing practices and litigation in the next two chapters, respectively, and present some potential strategies for dealing with the resulting problems and opportunities. A chapter prepared by the antitrust economists David Teece and Edward Sherry brings current economic analysis to bear on the misuse doctrine. Another chapter, contributed chiefly by the British barrister Christopher Tootal, with assistance from Jim Kobak, looks briefly, by way of comparison, to what appears to be the only international analogue to misuse, a now-repealed British statutory provision dealing with tie-ins. A chapter prepared principally by the late Ralph Jonas and his colleague, Michele Beuerlein, together with Charles Cohen and George Gordon, examines the case law and policy bearing on copyright and trademark misuse. Our handbook concludes with a brief evaluation of the doctrine and suggestions for possible approaches in the future, prepared by Mark Ostrau.

The task force that edited and assisted in the research and analysis underlying these chapters was formed under the auspices of the ABA Section of Antitrust Law's Intellectual Property Committee. Its members contributed—almost always cheerily—not only substantial writing and research but a wealth of experience and insight over a substantial period of time. They include Elizabeth Benton, Heidi Chen, Michele Beuerlein, Nick Coch, Charles Cohen, John Fry, George Gordon, Robert J. Hoerner, Ralph Jonas, Jim Kobak, Sheilah McCartney, Professor Richard Nelson, Mark Ostrau, Ella Roberts, and the late William Webb. A final editing committee consisted of Jennifer Alpern, Charles Cohen, George Gordon, and Jim Kobak. We also express our appreciation to Kevin Grady, Christopher Hockett, Howard Morse, Keith Shurgarman, Alan Silverstein, Katherine Surprenant, Don MacOdrum, and James Musgrove, who reviewed the manuscript and provided helpful suggestions for its improvement. Finally, we would like to thank Pauline McQuillen, Dolores Noufal, and Maryann Longo, our able word processors, and Anne Spencer Ellis of ABA Publishing.

James B. Kobak, Jr.
Task Force Chair

CHAPTER I

OVERVIEW AND HISTORICAL DEVELOPMENT OF THE MISUSE DOCTRINE

by George Gordon and Robert J. Hoerner

The misuse doctrine has been subject to a great deal of scrutiny in the courts and academic literature. Nevertheless, substantial confusion and disagreement remain over its roots, rationales, and the role it should play in contemporary intellectual property law. Various aspects of the doctrine are explored more fully in later chapters. This chapter provides a basic overview of the scope and historical development of the patent misuse doctrine, which is the genesis of the modern-day misuse doctrine that today encompasses copyrights and trademarks as well.[1]

A. Patent Misuse Generally

Conduct found to be patent misuse typically has fallen into at least one of two categories: (1) improper attempts to "extend" the scope of the patent and (2) violations of the antitrust laws. These two categories are not synonymous, as courts have upheld a misuse defense based on an attempt to extend the scope of the patent, even if that attempt does not also have an unreasonable competitive effect or otherwise contravene antitrust law.

The term "patent misuse" refers to an affirmative defense to an action for patent infringement or for royalties under a license. While conduct constituting patent misuse may sometimes form the basis for an affirmative counterclaim,[2] patent misuse in itself is not an actionable

---

1. Chapter VII contains a separate discussion of the development of the copyright and trademark misuse doctrines.
2. *See* Senza-Gel Corp. v. Seiffhart, 803 F.2d 661, 668 (Fed. Cir. 1986) (stating that an act constituting misuse "may also serve as an element in a complaint charging [an] antitrust violation").

tort.[3] If an accused infringer bases a counterclaim on conduct also alleged to be misuse, the counterclaim must also satisfy all the elements of the independent tort for which the counterclaim is brought. For example, if an alleged infringer brings a counterclaim for attempted monopolization, the conduct claimed to be misuse may also satisfy the anticompetitive conduct element of the attempted monopolization counterclaim. To succeed on the counterclaim, however, the counterclaiming defendant must also establish the additional elements of specific intent to monopolize, dangerous probability of monopolization, and all the other elements of a private antitrust cause of action.

The burden of establishing misuse lies with the alleged infringer or defaulting licensee. If misuse is found, the patent is rendered unenforceable until the misuse is "purged." A finding of misuse precludes prospective injunctive relief and eliminates any damage award (either lost profits or reasonable royalties) for the period during which the misuse occurred. Thus, if misuse is found, an alleged infringer or defaulting licensee, as well as any third party, would enjoy free use of the patented technology for the period prior to successful purging of the misuse.

Although much of the current focus in the debate over the misuse doctrine has been on the role of antitrust principles, the doctrine emerged not from antitrust law, but from the patent law doctrine of contributory infringement. In fact, courts almost universally rejected

---

3. *See, e.g.,* B. Braun Med. Inc. v. Abbott Lab., 124 F.3d 1419, 1427 (Fed. Cir. 1997) ("Patent misuse [is an] equitable defense available to the accused infringer, from the desire 'to restrain practices that did not in themselves violate any law, but that drew anticompetitive strength from the patent right, and thus were deemed to be contrary to public policy.'" (citations omitted)); CMI, Inc. v. Intoximeters, Inc., 918 F. Supp. 1068, 1090 (W.D. Ky. 1995) (citing *Transitron* and holding that there is no cause of action for misuse); Transitron Elec. Corp. v. Hughes Aircraft Co., 487 F. Supp. 885, 893 (D. Mass. 1980) ("On the basis of the history and application of the doctrine, and the availability of other grounds on which plaintiff licensees may seek damages in the context of patent misuse, we conclude that patent misuse of itself is not an actionable tort."), *aff'd*, 649 F.2d 871 (1st Cir. 1981).

early attempts at developing a defense to patent infringement claims based on alleged antitrust violations by the patent holder.

This chapter reviews these early "antitrust defense" cases, charts the development of the misuse defense from the doctrine of contributory infringement, and discusses more recent case law and legislative developments emphasizing antitrust principles in misuse analysis. The chapter also briefly covers the issues of standing in misuse cases and the purge doctrine. The concluding section attempts to summarize what the case law history of misuse teaches us about its doctrinal underpinnings.

B. The Early Cases

Early efforts at developing a defense to patent infringement suits based on the patent holder's conduct relied primarily on the antitrust laws. Almost immediately after the passage of the Sherman Act in 1890, alleged infringers began trying to use this new statute as a defense to patent infringement suits. Patent infringement defendants would plead that the plaintiff was an illegal trust, or that the plaintiff acquired title from an illegal trust, or that the patent infringement suit was part and parcel of a conspiracy to restrain trade, the terms of which were often said to include price stabilization agreements. With little exception, these efforts at developing an antitrust-based defense to patent infringement claims failed.[4]

---

4.   *See, e.g.*, Edison Elec. Light Co. v. Sawyer-Man Elec. Co., 53 F. 592, 598 (2d Cir. 1892); Strait v. National Harrow Co., 51 F. 819, 820 (C.C.N.D.N.Y. 1892); American Soda Fountain Co. v. Green, 69 F. 333 (C.C.E.D. Pa. 1895); Bonsack Co. v. Smith, 70 F. 383, 385-87 (C.C.W.D.N.C. 1895); Columbia Wire Co. v. Freeman Wire Co., 71 F. 302, 306-07 (C.C.E.D. Mo. 1895); Brown Saddle Co. v. Troxel, 98 F. 620 (C.C.N.D. Ohio 1899); National Folding-Box & Paper Co. v. Robertson, 99 F. 985 (C.C.D. Conn. 1900); Otis Elevator Co. v. Geiger, 107 F. 131, 132 (C.C.D. Ky. 1901); Cimiotti Unhairing Co. v. American Fur Ref. Co., 120 F. 672, 673 (C.C.D.N.J.), *rev'd on other grounds*, 123 F. 869 (3d Cir. 1903), *aff'd*, 198 U.S. 399 (1905); Johns-Pratt Co. v. Sachs Co., 176 F. 738, 739-40 (C.C.D. Conn. 1910); Motion Picture Patents Co. v. Ullman, 186 F. 174, 175 (C.C.S.D.N.Y. 1910); United States Fire Escape Counterbalance Co. v. Joseph Halsted Co., 195 F. 295

For example, *Strait v. National Harrow Co.*[5] involved an action by an alleged infringer to enjoin the patent holder from instituting an infringement suit. The alleged infringer asserted that the patent holder had entered into an improper combination for the purpose of acquiring a monopoly in the market for spring-tooth harrows and, as an incident to this combination, had acquired all the relevant patent rights from other manufacturers. The court rejected this assertion, observing that "[e]ven a gambler, or the keeper of a brothel, cannot be deprived of his property because he is an obnoxious person or a criminal; and it is no defense to the trespass upon it . . . that it was used in carrying on the unlawful occupation."[6]

Similarly, in *Brown Saddle Co. v. Troxel,*[7] a direct infringement case, the defendant alleged by way of an affirmative defense that the patent at issue was being used as part of an illegal combination. The trial court struck these allegations as impertinent. Then Circuit Judge Taft upheld the trial court's action, holding that the manner in which a patent is used is immaterial in a suit to enforce it: "[The plaintiff] is merely seeking by its bill to preserve its rights in its own property. What it may do with that property . . . cannot deprive it of its right to invoke the protection of the court against trespass and infringement."[8]

Perhaps the most explicit rejection of a defense based on the patent holder's use of the patent is found in *United States Fire Escape Counterbalance Co. v. Joseph Halsted Co.*[9] There, the court stated that an alleged attempt to extend the patent "monopoly" to cover unpatented products—conduct that would become the very epitome of patent

---

(N.D. Ill. 1912); Western Elec. Co. v. Wallerstein, 48 F.2d 268, 269 (W.D.N.Y. 1930); Western Elec. Co. v. Pacent Reproducer Corp., 53 F.2d 639, 640 (S.D.N.Y. 1930); Radio Corp. of America v. Duovac Radio Tube Corp., 6 F. Supp. 275 (E.D.N.Y. 1931); Radio Corp. of America v. Majestic Distribs. Inc., 53 F.2d 641, 642-44 (D. Conn. 1931); Radio Corp. of America v. Hygrade Sylvania Corp., 10 F. Supp. 879, 881 (D.N.J. 1934).

5.   51 F. 819.
6.   *Id.* at 820-21.
7.   98 F. 620.
8.   *Id.* at 621.
9.   195 F. 295.

misuse—was not a defense to an infringement action, even though it was possibly an antitrust violation:

> The sole value of patent property resides in monopoly. Within certain limits this monopoly may be made to extend to nonpatentable property as just decided by the Supreme Court in Henry v. Dick, 224 U.S. 1.... If the patentee attempts still further to extend his monopoly by occupying unpatented territory, and thus brings himself within the civil and criminal provisions of the Sherman Act, he is amenable under that Statute, but his property rights secured by the patent remain. He is not to be indirectly punished in an infringement action for his breach of an independent statute.[10]

Only one early decision, *National Harrow Co. v. Quick,*[11] appears to counter this authority rejecting an antitrust-based defense to a patent infringement action. In that case, the defendant alleged that the plaintiff was an unlawful "combination or trust attempting to hold and use its naked legal title as assignee [of the patent in suit] for purposes contrary to public policy, and that a court of equity ought not to aid its unlawful purposes by entertaining the present bill."[12] Foreshadowing the reasoning that the Supreme Court would apply some forty-seven years later in *Morton Salt Co. v. G.S. Suppiger Co.,*[13] the court agreed with the defendant:

> It seems to me that the court cannot sustain the present bill without giving aid to the unlawful combination or trust represented by the complainant. The question is not free from doubt, but in a case of doubt I feel it my duty to resolve it in such a way as will not lend the countenance of the court to the creation of combinations, trusts, or monopolies.[14]

---

10. *Id.* at 299.
11. 67 F. 130 (C.C.D. Ind. 1895), *aff'd on other grounds*, 74 F. 236 (7th Cir. 1896).
12. *Id.* at 130-31.
13. 314 U.S. 488 (1942).
14. 67 F. at 132; *see also* National Harrow Co. v. Hench, 76 F. 667 (C.C.E.D. Pa. 1896) (refusing to enforce a price-fixing agreement in two patent licenses), *aff'd*, 83 F. 36 (3d Cir. 1897).

The Seventh Circuit affirmed on other grounds, refusing to consider whether this defense was viable.[15] Several early opinions cite, but refuse to follow, the *National Harrow v. Quick* decision.[16]

C. Contributory Infringement

Thus, the early case law, almost without exception, exhibited overwhelming hostility toward defenses to patent infringement suits based on a patent holder's allegedly unlawful use of the patent. Given this hostility, the patent misuse doctrine was destined to evolve not from the antitrust laws, but primarily from courts' attempts to limit the doctrine of contributory infringement. A thorough understanding of the roots of the patent misuse defense requires some background in the development of the contributory infringement doctrine.

"Contributory infringement" refers generally to a situation where an entity supplies alleged infringers with unpatented components or inputs with the intent that these goods be used with a patented product, combination, or process. The theory is that the entity supplying the alleged infringer with such products is contributing to, or inducing, the infringement. Typically, intent could be shown where the inputs or components had no use other than as part of the patented good, combination, or process, or where the inputs or components were supplied with instructions to use them in an infringing manner.[17]

The concept of contributory infringement arose from attempts by patent holders to protect their patents from the kind of joint infringement activity at issue in *Wallace v. Holmes*.[18] There, the patent involved an improved coal oil lamp apparatus. The patent claims, however, required the presence of a traditional glass chimney. The alleged infringer attempted to avoid an infringement claim by manufacturing the

---

15.   74 F. at 239.
16.   *See, e.g.,* National Folding-Box and Paper Co. v. Robertson, 99 F. 985, 987-88 (C.C.D. Conn. 1900); Columbia Wire Co. v. Freeman Wire Co., 71 F. 302, 306 (C.C.E.D. Mo. 1895).
17.   See cases collected in Robert W. Steele, Comment, *Regulation of Business—Patents—Effect of Section 271 on the Doctrine of Contributory Infringement,* 55 MICH. L. REV. 1151, 1153-54 nn. 5-8 (1957).
18.   29 F. Cas. 74 (C.C.D. Conn. 1871) (No. 17,100).

apparatus only and not supplying the glass chimney (which was a staple item available from other sources). When sued for infringement, the defendant claimed that he had not practiced the claims of the patent and, consequently, was not liable. The court disagreed, holding that if they acted in concert, the defendant and a supplier of glass chimneys could be deemed joint infringers:

> If, in actual concert with a third party, with a view to the actual production of the patented improvement in lamps, and the sale and use thereof, they consented to manufacture the burner, and such other party to make the chimney, and, in such concert, they actually make and sell the burner, and he the chimney, each utterly useless without the other, and each intended to be used, and actually sold to be used, with the other, it cannot be doubtful, that they must be deemed to be joint infringers of the complainants' patent.[19]

After the notion of contributory infringement gained acceptance, patent owners would sometimes insert provisions in a license agreement requiring a licensee to buy a useful or necessary input to the patented product from the patent owner. Such an input was often an element of the patent claim, but not necessarily. If the licensee failed to abide by the provision, the patent owner would contend that the unauthorized use of the patented product with input obtained from a third party constituted patent infringement and sue for infringement remedies in the federal courts.

For example, in *Heaton-Peninsular Button Fastener Co. v. Eureka Specialty Co.,*[20] a patented button fastening machine was always sold with a metal plate containing a notice that the patented machine could be used only with fasteners made by the plaintiff. Despite the fact that the fasteners were not patented, this restraint was upheld. The court concluded that the plaintiff had "chosen to fix the price for the right of use at the profit resulting from the sale of staples."[21] According to the

---

19.   *Id.* at 80.
20.   77 F. 288 (6th Cir. 1896).
21.   *Id.* at 296.

court, the plaintiff could control the market for staples for so long as its invention "control[led] the market for button fastening appliances."[22]

This type of restraint first reached the Supreme Court in *Henry v. A.B. Dick Co.*[23] There, the two patents in suit covered a rotary mimeograph machine which had been sold to a Miss Skou with an attached legend stating that the machine could only "be used with the stencil paper, ink and other supplies" made by the plaintiff, A.B. Dick Co. The Sixth Circuit certified the question whether the defendant, who had sold an unauthorized can of ink to Miss Skou, was a contributory infringer.

The answer to that question turned on whether the legend itself was valid. If Miss Skou had not infringed the patent by using the unauthorized ink, then the defendant could not be liable for contributory infringement. By a four to three vote, the Court held that the legend was valid.[24] In essence, the Court saw no difference between "a sale subject to specific restrictions as to the time, place or purpose of use and restrictions requiring a use only with other things necessary to the use of the patented article purchased from the patentee."[25] Moreover, the majority saw no problem with the patent holder taking its profit through ink sales instead of charging a higher price for the machine itself. According to the majority, "[h]ad [the patentee] kept his invention to himself, no ink could have been sold by others for use upon machines embodying that invention."[26]

Justice White disagreed and filed a lengthy dissent. He did not believe that a patent owner who has sold an invention and not "kept his invention to himself" could necessarily place restrictions on postsale use.[27] Also, in a time of much more limited federal jurisdiction, Justice White was concerned that the enforcement of such restrictions through infringement suits would convert state court breach of contract actions into federal patent infringement cases. Finally, Justice White thought it

---

22.   *Id.*
23.   224 U.S. 1 (1912).
24.   *See id.* at 35-36.
25.   *Id.*
26.   *Id.* at 32.
27.   *Id.* at 69-70 (White, C.J., dissenting).

inconsistent to allow patent holders to bring infringement suits concerning items not covered by the patent when the claims of the patent itself were subject to rigorous examination to prevent the patenting of items in the public domain. According to Justice White, the majority's position would improperly allow the patent holder to extend its patent by contract "without any of the precautions for the benefit of the public which limit the right to obtain a patent."[28]

Justice White's view soon prevailed, as *Henry v. A.B. Dick* was explicitly overruled five years later in *Motion Picture Patents Co. v. Universal Film Co.*,[29] the first of a trio of contributory infringement cases in which the foundations of the patent misuse doctrine were laid. *Motion Picture Patents* involved a patent that covered "a part of the mechanism used in motion picture exhibiting machines for feeding a film through the machine."[30] The licenses granted by the patent holder allowed licensees to sell motion picture projectors incorporating the patented mechanism on the condition that the projectors be used solely for exhibiting films covered by a separate film patent owned by the plaintiff. After this film patent had expired, the patent holder discovered that a theater which had purchased a projector incorporating the patented mechanism was using the projector with unauthorized film and sued the theater for infringement and the suppliers of the film for contributory infringement of the projector patent.

The Supreme Court found that the license provision restricting the type of film that could be used with the projectors was invalid:

> Such a restriction is invalid because such a film is obviously not any part of the invention of the patent in suit; because it is an attempt, without statutory warrant, to continue the patent monopoly in this particular character of film after it has expired, and because to enforce it would be to create a monopoly in the manufacture and use of moving picture films, wholly outside of the patent in suit and of the patent law as we have interpreted it.[31]

---

28.   *Id.* at 70 (White, C.J., dissenting).
29.   243 U.S. 502 (1917).
30.   *Id.* at 505.
31.   *Id.* at 518.

According to the Court, the patent holder's restriction allowed it to benefit "not from the invention on which the law gives it a monopoly but from the unpatented supplies with which it is used and which are wholly without the scope of the patent monopoly."[32] The effect of this "extension" of the patent gave the plaintiff "a potential for evil over an industry which must be recognized as an important element in the amusement life of the nation."[33] Thus, the Court held that there could be no claim for infringement against either (1) the supplier for selling film for use in the patented projectors or (2) the theater for using the patented projectors with unauthorized film. In reaching this conclusion, the Court noted that only two years after its *A.B. Dick* decision, the Congress passed Section 3 of the Clayton Act, which specifically mentioned tying of patented articles as a potential antitrust violation.

The next case in this trio was *Carbice Corp. of America v. American Patents Development Corp.*[34] In *Carbice*, a plaintiff held an exclusive license to a patent on refrigerated "transportation packages," which used unpatented dry ice as a refrigerating element. The plaintiff granted licenses to use the patented transportation package with dry ice purchased from the plaintiff; it granted no other licenses. The plaintiff brought a contributory infringement action against the supplier of unpatented dry ice which was sold with knowledge that it would be used in refrigerated transportation packages like those described in the plaintiffs' patent. The Court, relying in large part on *Motion Picture Patents*, held that such a suit could not be maintained because the plaintiffs were attempting to use the patent "to secure a limited monopoly of unpatented material [dry ice] used in applying the invention."[35] The Court also suggested that the plaintiff's conduct may have violated the antitrust laws: "The present attempt [to secure a monopoly over unpatented dry ice] is analogous to the use of a patent as an instrument for restraining commerce, which was condemned, under

---

32.   *Id.* at 517.
33.   *Id.* at 518-19.
34.   283 U.S. 27, *supplemental op.,* Carbice Corp. of Am. v. American Patents Dev. Corp., 283 U.S. 420 (1931).
35.   *Id.* at 33-34.

the Sherman Anti-Trust Law, in *Standard Sanitary Manufacturing Co. v. United States*"[36]

The final case of the trio was *Leitch Manufacturing Co. v. Barber Co.*[37] The patent involved in *Leitch* concerned a method of applying bituminous emulsion to wet concrete to retard evaporation while curing. The patent holder did not grant any licenses conditioning the use of its method on purchasing the emulsion from it. Rather, it simply sued a competing supplier of bituminous emulsion that allegedly delivered the emulsion to a road builder, knowing that it was to be used for infringing purposes.

Justice Brandeis found the fact that the plaintiff had not issued restrictive notices or licenses immaterial. According to Justice Brandeis, the point was that the plaintiff was trying to extend the scope of its patent; it did not matter whether the plaintiff relied on notices, restrictive license provisions, or contributory infringement suits.[38] Relying on *Carbice*, Justice Brandeis concluded that the lawsuit could not be maintained because the patent did not confer upon the plaintiff the right to be free from competition in supplying the unpatented emulsion used in practicing its invention.[39]

The teachings of *Motion Picture Patents*, *Carbice*, and *Leitch*—that the patentee may not use the patent to restrict trade in unpatented products—contained the seeds of the misuse doctrine. Yet none of these decisions used the term "misuse," and none involved a suit against a direct infringer. In short, the holdings of these cases did not provide defendants accused of direct infringement with a defense. They merely restricted the ability of patentees to sue for contributory infringement.

It was not at all clear that these contributory infringement cases would lead to the patent misuse doctrine as a defense to direct infringement suits. As discussed above, the lower courts were consistently hostile to defenses to direct infringement claims based on the patent holder's conduct. In his concurring opinion in *B.B. Chemical Co. v.*

---

36. *Id.* at 34 (citing Standard Sanitary Mfg. Co. v. Barber Co., 226 U.S. 20 (1912)).
37. 302 U.S. 458 (1938).
38. *See id.* at 463.
39. *See id.* at 461.

Ellis,[40] Judge Magruder of the First Circuit suggested that the cases rejecting defenses to infringement claims based on the patent holder's conduct might be inconsistent with the Supreme Court's contributory infringement decisions, although he declined to resolve the issue: "[t]here is no present need to inquire how far the doctrine of the *Leitch* case squares with earlier lower court holdings that violation of the antitrust laws by a patentee is no defense to a suit for patent infringement."[41] Nevertheless, Judge Magruder predicted that the *Carbice* doctrine would be applied to preclude recovery from a direct infringer.

Interestingly, prior to *Leitch*, at least one court attempted to reconcile *Carbice* with the established precedent rejecting antitrust-based defenses to direct infringement suits. In *Radio Corp. of America v. Majestic Distributors, Inc.*,[42] a direct infringement action, the defendant, relying on *Carbice*, argued that the plaintiffs could not prevail because they were "employing some or all of the patents in suit to attempt, without sanction of law, to secure a monopoly of unpatented material."[43] The court rejected this defense and distinguished *Carbice* on the grounds that, as a contributory infringement case, it was simply not relevant to an action for direct infringement:

> [*Carbice*] as I read it, has no bearing upon the right of an owner of a patent to sue for its infringement. It simply holds, in effect, that *Carbice* did not infringe. *Carbice* was not charged with direct infringement but only contributory infringement. It could not be guilty of contributory infringement otherwise than by aiding the licensee to violate a condition attached to the License. The condition was manifestly void and so there could be no contributory infringement.[44]

---

40.   117 F.2d 829 (1st Cir. 1941), *aff'd*, 314 U.S. 495 (1942).
41.   *Id.* at 836.
42.   53 F.2d 641 (D. Conn. 1931).
43.   *Id.* at 642.
44.   *Id.* at 644. *But see* American Lecithin Co. v. Warfield Co., 105 F.2d 207, 211-12 (7th Cir. 1939) (applying *Carbice* to preclude recovery from direct infringer).

D. *Morton Salt* and the Birth of the Patent Misuse Doctrine

Any question of conflict between the contributory infringement cases and the authority rejecting defenses based on the patent holder's use of the patent was resolved by the Supreme Court's opinion in *Morton Salt Co. v. G.S. Suppiger Co.*,[45] where the Court first applied the teachings of *Motion Picture Patents, Carbice,* and *Leitch* to a direct infringement suit. In *Morton Salt*, the Court effectively extended the contributory infringement case holdings to direct infringement activity and created a new defense for the alleged direct infringer based on the patent holder's use of the patent.

The facts of the *Morton Salt* case are relatively straightforward. The plaintiff owned the patent on a machine for depositing salt tablets in food cans and leased machines to commercial canners on the condition that the lessees only buy salt tablets from the plaintiff's subsidiary. The defendant made and leased salt depositing machines which the plaintiff claimed infringed its patent.

Relying on the *Motion Picture Patents-Carbice-Leitch* trio, the Supreme Court held that the plaintiff's requirement that lessees buy salt tablets from its subsidiary was an improper attempt to obtain a monopoly over the unpatented salt tablets.[46] On this point the Court was relying on what had become relatively well-settled law. However, the Court then took the additional step that created the patent misuse doctrine as we know it. Vindicating the trial court in *National Harrow v. Quick*, the Court held that, because the plaintiff had used its patent to restrain competition in an unpatented product, the patent could not be enforced until the misuse was purged:

> Equity may rightly withhold its assistance from such a use of the patent by declining to entertain a suit for infringement, and should do so at least until it is made to appear that the improper practice has been abandoned and that the consequences of the misuse of the patent have been dissipated.[47]

---

45.   314 U.S. 488 (1942).
46.   *See id.* at 491-92.
47.   *Id.* at 493.

The defendant asserting the misuse doctrine was an alleged infringer of the machine and not a party to any contract containing the tie. The Court held that patent-extending conduct, such as a tying contract, disqualifies a plaintiff from bringing suit, "regardless of whether the particular defendant has suffered from the misuse of the patent."[48] The Court determined that proof of a contract with the tying provision entitled the defendant to summary judgment, specifically holding that the infringement suit should be dismissed without further proof of market power or adverse effect on competition.

The reasoning behind the *Morton Salt* decision reflects a convergence of three related strands of public policy: equity policy, patent policy, and competition policy. The Court viewed the threshold question before it as one concerning the appropriate exercise of a court's equitable powers.[49] According to the Court, courts of equity "may appropriately withhold their aid where the plaintiff is using the right asserted contrary to the public interest."[50] For this reason, the doctrine is often referred to as being rooted in the traditional equity doctrine of unclean hands.[51]

In determining that the patent holder in *Morton Salt* was asserting its patent right in a manner contrary to the public interest, the Court also looked to the patent policy underlying that right. The Court concluded that the patent policy expressed in the Constitution and the Patent Code—the promotion of the useful arts—allows inventors to secure an exclusive right in "new and useful" inventions.[52] By the same token, that policy also excludes from the exclusive right "all that is not embraced in the invention" (such as the salt tablets).[53] Thus, the patent holder's lease restriction violated patent policy by improperly extending the exclusionary effect of the patent beyond the invention claimed.

---

48.   *Id.* at 494.
49.   *See id.* at 490.
50.   *Id.* at 492.
51.   *See* United States Gypsum Co. v. National Gypsum Co., 352 U.S. 457, 465 (1957) ("The [patent misuse doctrine] is an extension of the equitable doctrine of 'unclean hands' to the patent field.").
52.   314 U.S. at 490.
53.   *Id.* at 492.

The Court also expressed a third concern: that the patent holder might be using the patent "as a means of restraining competition" in the market for unpatented salt tablets.[54] Yet, despite this concern over competition, the Court found no need to consider whether the patent holder had actually violated the antitrust laws,[55] specifically reversing the Seventh Circuit on this point.

The companion case of *B.B. Chemical Co. v. Ellis*[56] applied the *Morton Salt* rule to a case involving a patent on a method for reinforcing insoles. The patent holder did not license its patent, but rather sold material for use with its patent process in a manner "that operated as a license to use the patent with that material alone."[57] The patent was held unenforceable even though the patent holder argued that it had no practical alternative for obtaining a reward under its patent: "The patent monopoly is not enlarged by reason of the fact that it would be more convenient to the patentee to have it so, or because he cannot avail himself of its benefits within the limits of the grant."[58]

E. The *Mercoid* Cases

The high-water mark of the patent misuse doctrine was reached two years after *Morton Salt* in the two *Mercoid* decisions, authored by Justice Douglas. The first of these decisions, *Mercoid Corp. v. Mid-Continent Investment Co.*,[59] involved a combination patent for a domestic heating system and one particular unpatented component, a combustion stoker switch, which had no use other than as part of the patented combination. The patent holder brought an action for contributory infringement based on the defendant's sale of the unpatented combustion stoker switches for use in the patented combination.

---

54.   *Id.* at 493.
55.   *See id.* at 490.
56.   314 U.S. 495 (1942).
57.   *Id.* at 497.
58.   *Id.* at 498.
59.   320 U.S. 661 (1944).

The controversy in this case centered on the license agreement between the patent holder and its exclusive licensee (joined as a plaintiff in the infringement suit) to make, use, and sell the patented combination. That license provided for royalties based on sales of the unpatented stoker switch, and therefore the right to use the patented system was only granted when the unpatented stoker switch was purchased from the licensee. Relying on *Motion Picture Patents, Carbice, Leitch,* and *Morton Salt,* the Court found that, by using the patent to try to restrain trade in the unpatented stoker switch, the licensee had misused the patent and could not maintain an action for contributory infringement.[60]

As in *Morton Salt,* the Court's decision was based on both patent and competition policies. The Court was concerned that the patent was "employed to protect the market for a device on which no patent has been granted."[61] According to Justice Douglas, allowing patent holders to expand the reach of the patent by contract (for example, through license agreements) would also permit "private business" to "function as its own patent office and impose its own law upon its licensees."[62] The Court noted that a result permitting circumvention of the Patent Office would also give businesses wide latitude to violate the antitrust laws: "Such a vast power 'to multiply monopolies' at the will of the patentee ... would carve out exceptions to the anti-trust laws which Congress has not sanctioned."[63]

Significantly, the Court rejected any distinction between the case before it and prior cases based on the fact that the unpatented stoker switch had no use other than as part of the patented combination.[64] There is little doubt that the Court realized that this decision was a death blow to the contributory infringement doctrine. Justice Douglas concluded his opinion with these remarks: "The result of this decision, together with those which have preceded it, is to limit substantially the

---

60.   *See id.* at 667-69.
61.   *Id.* at 667.
62.   *Id.*
63.   *Id.* (quoting Henry v. A.B. Dick Co., 224 U.S. 1, 53 (1912) (White, C.J., dissenting)).
64.   *See id.* at 665.

doctrine of contributory infringement. What residuum may be left we need not stop to consider."[65]

The second *Mercoid* case, *Mercoid Corp. v. Minneapolis-Honeywell Regulator Co.*,[66] involved a patent covering a heating system. The patent holder, Minneapolis-Honeywell, licensed five competitors under the patent to make, use, and sell a key component. The component was unpatented but was designed for use with the patented system and could be used for no other purpose. Minneapolis-Honeywell required its licensees to attach notices to the unpatented component stating that it included a license for one installation of the patented system. These notices, in effect, tied the granting of a license for the furnace system to the purchase of the unpatented component from a Minneapolis-Honeywell licensee. The licenses also contained various provisions fixing the minimum price at which the component could be sold.

The defendant in the second *Mercoid* case was a competitor that had refused to enter into such a license. The Court found (1) that the licenses were an improper attempt to gain control over the use and sale of an unpatented component of the patented system, and (2) that, because it had misused its patent, the patent holder could not maintain its infringement suit. Confusingly, Justice Douglas pointed to the antitrust laws, not the patent laws, as the basis for his decision: "The legality of any attempt to bring unpatented goods within the protection of the patent is measured by the antitrust laws not by the patent law."[67] This statement is perplexing because the Court in *Morton Salt* had expressly refused to base its holding on the finding of an antitrust violation. Moreover, it is the first suggestion by the Supreme Court that the misuse doctrine ought to be rooted in the antitrust laws per se, as opposed to the somewhat looser concerns over the competitive effects incident to violations of patent policy expressed in *Morton Salt*.

---

65.   *Id.* at 669.
66.   320 U.S. 680 (1944).
67.   *Id.* at 684.

F. The 1952 Patent Act Amendments

The *Mercoid* cases effectively eliminated a patent holder's ability to prevent a competitor from making and selling a component that had no use other than as part of a patented invention. As a result, Congress stepped in to breathe new life into the doctrine of contributory infringement and to push back the borders of the patent misuse doctrine. In 1952, Congress enacted 35 U.S.C. § 271(c), which created a cause of action for contributory infringement against parties making unauthorized sales of goods that have no use other than as part of a patented device or combination ("nonstaple" goods). Congress also added Sections 271(d)(1)-(3), expressly excepting from the patent misuse doctrine efforts to protect against contributory infringement as defined in Section 271(c).

The Supreme Court considered the effect of the 1952 amendments in its five to four decision in *Dawson Chemical Co. v. Rohm & Haas Co.*[68] In *Dawson Chemical*, Rohm & Haas granted licenses to use its patented process for applying herbicide only to those who purchased propanil, an unpatented chemical herbicide which had no use other than as part of the patented process, from Rohm & Haas. Dawson Chemical Company, an alleged contributory infringer, claimed that Rohm & Haas had misused its patent by conveying the right to practice the patent only to purchasers of its own propanil and by refusing to grant licenses to others, including Dawson.

In the *Dawson Chemical* opinion, the Court recognized that the 1952 amendments reflect a compromise between the doctrines of patent misuse and contributory infringement based on the distinction between staple and nonstaple articles.[69] According to the Court, "the provisions of § 271(d) effectively confer upon the patentee, as a lawful adjunct of

---

68.   448 U.S. 176 (1980). *See also* Giles S. Rich, *Infringement Under Section 271 of the Patent Act of 1952*, 21 GEO. WASH. L. REV. 521 (1953); L. James Harris, *Some Aspects of the Underlying Legislative Intent of the Patent Act of 1952*, 23 GEO. WASH. L. REV. 658, 689-98 (1955); Peter W. Hogg, *Patent Misuse Before and After Section 271*, 42 J. PAT. [& TRADEMARK] OFF. SOC'Y 683 (1960); and Robert J. Hoerner, *Is Activity Within the Subsections of 35 U.S.C. § 271(d) Protected from a Finding of Antitrust Violation?* 74 J. PAT. [& TRADEMARK] OFF. SOC'Y 283 (1992).

69.   *See* 448 U.S. at 200.

his patent rights, a limited power to exclude others from competition in non-staple goods."[70] Yet the Court noted that, while the tying alleged by Dawson Chemical did not appear to go beyond what was allowed by Section 271(d), the language of the statute did not resolve the question.[71] After a review of the legislative history, however, the Court concluded that Rohm and Haas did nothing "that would extend its right of control over unpatented goods beyond the line that Congress drew."[72] Moreover, the Court expressly noted that Rohm and Haas's method of doing business was "essentially the same as the method condemned in the *Mercoid* decisions, and the legislative history reveals that § 271(d) was designed to retreat from *Mercoid* in this regard."[73]

G. Development of the Patent Misuse Doctrine after the *Mercoid* Decisions

In the years since *Mercoid*, courts have held that in addition to the conduct at issue in *Morton Salt, B.B. Chemical,* and the *Mercoid* cases, other types of conduct may constitute improper attempts to extend the scope of the patent.[74] This conduct has included coercing a licensee to take unwanted licenses,[75] conditioning a license on payment of royalties

---

70. *Id.* at 201.
71. *See id.* at 202.
72. *Id.* at 214.
73. *Id.* In *Mercoid*, the owner of the patent had been willing to grant a license to the competitor it sued, and the competitor had refused the license; the patentee in *Dawson Chemical* had gone one step further by both suing for contributory infringement and refusing to license other suppliers. This was the point of the four dissenters.
74. Chapter II contains an extensive discussion of the individual practices condemned as misuse.
75. *See* Hazeltine Research, Inc. v. Zenith Radio Corp., 388 F.2d 25, 33-34 (7th Cir. 1967), *aff'd in part, rev'd in part,* 395 U.S. 100 (1969); American Sec. Co. v. Shatterproof Glass Corp., 268 F.2d 769, 777 (3d Cir. 1959).

based on sales of unpatented goods,[76] and prohibiting licensees from manufacturing competing, unpatented goods.[77]

Along with the extension of the patent misuse doctrine to other forms of conduct, there has been a continuing debate over what role antitrust law should play in the misuse analysis. Despite the statement by Justice Douglas in the second *Mercoid* opinion that the legality of an attempt to extend the scope of the patent should be judged under the antitrust laws, the Supreme Court continued thereafter to refuse to equate misuse and antitrust standards.[78] More recent decisions from the Seventh and Federal Circuits, however, have essentially limited the applicability of Supreme Court precedent to the particular practices at issue in those cases. This more recent case law, in combination with legislative developments,[79] has merged some antitrust principles into misuse analysis. We will turn first to the post-*Mercoid* Supreme Court cases.

Shortly after the *Mercoid* decisions, the Court decided *Hartford Empire Co. v. United States*,[80] a case that involved a request by the government for royalty-free licensing to remedy patent-based antitrust violations.[81] The government relied, in part, on *Morton Salt* and *B.B. Chemical* in support of its request. While the Court did distinguish those cases, it interpreted them as applying "the doctrine that so long as the patent owner is using his patent in violation of the antitrust laws, he cannot restrain infringement of it by others,"[82] lending support to Justice Douglas's view in the second *Mercoid* decision that the patent misuse doctrine was at least in part rooted in antitrust law. However, in neither *Morton Salt* nor *B.B. Chemical* did the Court base its decision on the

---

76. *See* Zenith Radio Corp. v. Hazeltine Research, Inc., 395 U.S. 100, 135 (1969).

77. *See* National Lockwasher Co. v. George K. Garrett Co., 137 F.2d 255, 257 (3d Cir. 1943).

78. *See* Zenith Radio Corp., 395 U.S. at 140; Transparent-Wrap Mach. Corp. v. Stokes & Smith Co., 329 U.S. 637, 641 (1947).

79. *See* 35 U.S.C. § 271(d)(4)-(5) (1988).

80. 323 U.S. 386, *clarified*, 324 U.S. 570 (1945).

81. Compulsory royalty-free licensing is tantamount to nonenforceability without any opportunity to purge.

82. *Hartford Empire*, 323 U.S. at 416.

finding of an antitrust violation. In fact, in *Morton Salt*, it expressly refused to do so.

Two years later, in *Transparent-Wrap Machine Corp. v. Stokes & Smith Co.*,[83] Justice Douglas again wrote on the subject of *Morton Salt*, the *Mercoid* cases, and the patent misuse doctrine. *Transparent-Wrap* involved the legality of a license provision requiring the licensee to assign all future improvement patents to the licensor. The Court did not extend the misuse doctrine to licenses requiring grantbacks of future improvement patents because both basic patents and improvement patents were sanctioned by the patent laws; there was, by definition, no assertion of infringement remedies against the unauthorized sale or use of something in the public domain. Justice Douglas contrasted this situation to tying a patent license to the use or purchase of an unpatented product. While noting that this patent-extending behavior "might" be an antitrust violation, Justice Douglas further explained that no antitrust violation needed to be found for such a practice to be condemned as misuse:

> Though control of the unpatented article or device falls short of a prohibited restraint of trade or monopoly, it will not be sanctioned. For it is the tendency in that direction which condemns the practice and which, if approved by a court either through enjoining infringement or enforcing the covenant, would receive a powerful impetus.[84]

As clarified in *Transparent-Wrap*, Justice Douglas's view appears to be that an antitrust violation is a sufficient but not a necessary condition for a finding of misuse.

Similarly, in *Zenith Radio Corp. v. Hazeltine Research Inc.*,[85] the Supreme Court again distinguished between patent misuse and antitrust violations. *Zenith* involved a license that coerced royalty payments based on total sales of a class of items rather than on those items that actually used the teachings of the patent. The Court made clear that such conduct can be deemed misuse even if it does not rise to the level of an

---

83.   329 U.S. at 641.
84.   *Id.*
85.   395 U.S. 100.

antitrust violation: "And if there was such patent misuse, it does not necessarily follow that the misuse embodies the ingredients of a violation of either § 1 or § 2 of the Sherman Act."[86] Rather, the Court found misuse in *Zenith* because of concerns about unfair leverage and the use of the patent "to derive a benefit not attributable to use of the patent's teachings."[87]

Nonetheless, in the face of these rather clear statements from the Supreme Court that conduct need not constitute an antitrust violation to be deemed misuse, more recent case law tends to emphasize antitrust principles in misuse analysis. This trend began with Judge Posner's opinion in *USM Corp. v. SPS Technologies Inc.*,[88] which involved the implications of a discriminatory royalty scheme in a patent license. Under that license, USM, the licensee, had to remit to SPS, the licensor, 25 percent of any royalties it received by sublicensing SPS's patent. However, USM had to remit 75 percent of any royalties received by sublicensing SPS's patent to four specific companies that SPS had previously licensed directly. In an action for the return of royalties previously paid out under this license, USM claimed that this scheme was patent misuse.

The Seventh Circuit found that the discriminatory royalty scheme could not be said to "enlarge the licensee's obligations beyond the limits of the patent grant" in the same manner as the practices condemned in previous Supreme Court precedent.[89] However, the court found it necessary to "consider whether the patent-misuse doctrine goes beyond these specific practices and constitutes a general code of patent licensing distinct from antitrust law."[90]

Judge Posner distinguished practices within the "conventional, rather stereotyped boundaries" of the misuse doctrine (i.e., tying and resale price maintenance) from those outside these boundaries.[91] While recognizing that practices in the former group need not rise to the level

---

86.   *Id.* at 140.
87.   *Id.* at 136.
88.   694 F.2d 505 (7th Cir. 1982).
89.   *Id.* at 511.
90.   *Id.*
91.   *Id.*

of an antitrust violation to constitute misuse, Judge Posner found in the latter group an "increasing convergence of patent-misuse analysis with standard antitrust analysis."[92]

Judge Posner conceded that "[o]ne still finds plenty of statements in judicial opinions that less evidence of anticompetitive effect is required in a misuse case than in an antitrust case," but concluded that "apart from the conventional applications of the doctrine we have found no cases where standards different from those of antitrust law were actually applied to yield different results."[93] Accordingly, the court analyzed the discriminatory royalty scheme under antitrust principles and held that it did not constitute patent misuse.[94]

The *USM* opinion has had significant influence on the Federal Circuit's thinking. In *Windsurfing International, Inc. v. AMF Inc.*,[95] the Federal Circuit took the Seventh Circuit's analytical distinction between practices inside the traditional boundaries of the patent misuse doctrine and those outside one step further, holding: "To sustain a misuse defense involving a licensing arrangement *not held to have been* per se *anticompetitive by the Supreme Court*, a factual determination must reveal that the overall effect of the license tends to restrain competition unlawfully in an appropriately defined relevant market."[96] Moreover, in a now famous footnote, the Federal Circuit added: "Recent economic analysis questions the rationale behind holding any licensing practice per se anticompetitive [citing to *USM*]."[97] This language clearly takes issue with Supreme Court precedent, suggesting that no licensing practice should be deemed misuse unless it violates an antitrust-type rule of reason.

Less than ten months later, in *Senza-Gel Corp. v. Seiffhart*,[98] the Federal Circuit stepped back a bit from the full implications of the *Windsurfing* footnote. In *Senza-Gel*, the plaintiff, Senza-Gel, refused to

---

92.   *Id.*
93.   *Id.* at 512.
94.   *See id.* at 512-14.
95.   782 F.2d 995 (Fed. Cir. 1986).
96.   *Id.* at 1001-02 (emphasis added) (footnote omitted).
97.   *Id.* at 1001 n.9.
98.   803 F.2d 661 (Fed. Cir. 1986).

permit use of the process patent in suit unless the user also leased its "macerator" machine. The trial court found that Senza-Gel's practice was patent misuse but certified for appeal the question of the proper elements of a misuse claim in the tying context. Conspicuously absent from the elements set forth in the trial court's certification was any requirement of market power in the tying product, an essential element of a per se antitrust tying violation.[99]

Relying on *Dawson Chemical Co. v. Rohm & Haas Co.*,[100] the Federal Circuit held that the elements set forth in the certification were proper despite the absence of a market power requirement.[101] In its opinion, the court noted the ongoing dispute concerning the proper role of per se analysis in the misuse context:

> Commentators and courts have questioned the rationale appearing in Supreme Court opinions dealing with misuse in view of recent economic theory and Supreme Court decisions in non-misuse contexts. We are bound, however, to adhere to existing Supreme Court guidance in the area until otherwise directed by Congress or by the Supreme Court.[102]

---

99.   Specifically, the court questioned:
   1. Is the proper mode for analysis of a claim of patent abuse [sic, misuse] in a tying context the three step analysis undertaken by this court, namely:
   First: Determine whether there are two things tied, i.e., whether there are separable or inseparable items; if so
   Second: Determine whether the "thing" which is assertedly tied to the patented item is a staple or non-staple item in commerce; if staple
   Third: Determine whether in fact they are tied.
   Id. at 664.
100.   448 U.S. 176 (1980).
101.   This holding in *Senza-Gel* has since been legislatively overruled with the passage of the 1988 amendments to 35 U.S.C., which require proof of market power in the tying product market to sustain a misuse defense based on tying. *See* 35 U.S.C. § 271(d)(5) (1988).
102.   *Senza-Gel*, 803 F.2d at 665 n.5 (footnote omitted).

The *Senza-Gel* court also noted that, under Supreme Court precedent, certain conduct "may constitute patent misuse without rising to the level of an antitrust violation."[103] Accordingly, the court found that the trial court had not committed an error by granting the defendant's motion for summary judgment on misuse but denying it on the antitrust counterclaims.[104]

While the Federal Circuit bowed to Supreme Court precedent in *Senza-Gel*, the opinion is not inconsistent with the *Windsurfing* approach of analyzing practices not previously found per se unlawful by the Supreme Court differently from those that have been found per se unlawful. The practice involved in *Senza-Gel*, tying, clearly fell into the "traditional" boundaries of per se patent misuse. Indeed, the *Windsurfing* approach was confirmed by the Federal Circuit in *Mallinckrodt, Inc. v. Medipart, Inc.*[105]

Mallinckrodt involved a patent misuse defense based on a "single use only" restriction on a medical device designed to diagnose and treat respiratory ailments. The restriction on reuse was printed on a label affixed to the device itself. The defendant, Medipart, sterilized used devices and sent them back to hospitals for reuse, in violation of the label license.

Mallinckrodt sued Medipart for infringement. In defense, Medipart claimed that the restriction on reuse was an unenforceable postsale restriction. Mallinckrodt argued that the restriction was nothing more than a valid license to less than all uses of the patent. The district court agreed with Medipart that the restriction was unenforceable and granted summary judgment in its favor. The Federal Circuit reversed.

In its opinion, the Federal Circuit first acknowledged Supreme Court precedent (upon which the lower court had relied) holding per se illegal price-fixing and tying arrangements accompanying the sale of patented goods.[106] However, the court noted that these cases did not establish that all restrictions accompanying the sale of patented goods were illegal.[107]

---

103. *Id.* at 668.
104. *See id.*
105. 976 F.2d 700 (Fed. Cir. 1992).
106. *See id.* at 704.
107. *See id.*

The court also held that while "unconditional sale of a patented device exhausts the patentee's right to control the purchaser's use of the device," this principle did not apply when the sale was a conditional one.[108] The court also rejected as "formalistic line drawing" the lower court's holding that the restraint was an unlawful postsale restriction because hospitals purchased the device from Mallinckrodt directly and not from a manufacturer's licensee.[109]

In *Mallinckrodt*, the Federal Circuit established a two-pronged test for determining whether a practice not previously held to be per se illegal constitutes misuse: "The appropriate criterion is whether Mallinckrodt's restriction is reasonably within the patent grant, or whether the patentee has ventured beyond the patent grant and into behavior having an anticompetitive effect not justifiable under the rule of reason."[110] Under this test, if the restriction is found to be within the scope of the patent grant, there is no misuse and the inquiry is over.[111] However, if the restriction is found to have "anticompetitive effects extending beyond the patentee's statutory right to exclude, these effects do not automatically impeach the restriction."[112] Any anticompetitive effects not per se illegal must be reviewed under the rule of reason.[113] This two-part approach requiring some proof of unreasonable anticompetitive effect, as well as patent-extending conduct, has now been reiterated and applied in a series of Federal Circuit cases.[114] The Federal Circuit has acknowledged, however, that misuse is a "broader

---

108. *Id.* at 706.
109. *Id.* at 705.
110. *Id.* at 708.
111. *See id.*
112. *Id.*
113. *See id.*
114. C.R. Bard, Inc. v. M3 Systems, Inc., 157 F.3d 1340 (Fed. Cir. 1998); Virginia Panel Corp. v. MAC Panel Co., 133 F.3d 860 (Fed. Cir. 1997); B. Braun Med. Inc. v. Abbott Lab., 124 F.3d 1419 (Fed. Cir. 1997). District courts are following this formulation. *See* Texas Instruments, Inc. v. Hyundai Elec. Indus. Co., 49 F. Supp. 2d 893 (E.D. Tex. 1999); PSC Inc. v. Symbol Tech. Inc., 26 F. Supp. 2d 505 (W.D.N.Y. 1998).

wrong than [an] antitrust violation" and "may arise when the conditions of antitrust violation are not met."[115]

Unfortunately, the *Mallinckrodt* opinion does not give much guidance on what practices or restrictions should be considered "reasonably within the patent grant." In some contexts (i.e., tying or extension of royalties beyond the life of the patent) the relevant parameters of the patent grant (product and time) are readily observable.[116] However, the "reasonably within the patent grant" test loses its utility when applied to arrangements that do not involve such easily observable physical or temporal dimensions. The first prong of the *Mallinckrodt* test is therefore unlikely to provide prospective licensors with much guidance. Nevertheless, *Mallinckrodt* does indicate that a finding that a practice or restriction falls outside the "scope" of the patent grant does not doom the plaintiff.

H. The 1988 Patent Act Amendments

The judiciary has not been the only branch of government paring back the scope of the patent misuse doctrine. The doctrine has come under attack in Congress as well. In 1988, Congress amended 35 U.S.C. § 271(d) for the first time since 1952. The 1988 amendments added Sections 271(d)(4) and (5), under which it may not be deemed patent misuse if a plaintiff

> (4) has refused to license or use any rights to the patent; or
> (5) has conditioned the license of any rights to the patent or the sale of the patented product on the acquisition of a license to rights in another patent or purchase of a separate product, unless, in view of the circumstances, the patent owner has market power in the relevant market for the patent or patented product on which the license or sale is conditioned.

---

115. *C.R. Bard*, 157 F.3d at 1372 (citing *Zenith Radio Corp.*, 395 U.S. 100, 140-41).

116. See Blonder-Tongue Lab., Inc. v. University of Ill. Found., 402 U.S. 313 (1971), where the Supreme Court phrased the misuse question as whether an arrangement "attempts to broaden the physical or temporal scope of the patent monopoly." *Id.* at 343.

Because it is not bound by Supreme Court precedent, Congress was able to go further than the Federal Circuit in limiting the misuse doctrine. For example, Section 271(d)(5) trumps a significant aspect of *Morton Salt* in that it requires market power for a finding of misuse based on tying and clearly overrules the Federal Circuit's decision in *Senza-Gel*. At least two courts have held that 35 U.S.C. § 271(d) applies to "tie-out" provisions, where a licensee is prohibited from using the products of the licensor's competitors, as well as to "tie-in" provisions.[117] Significantly, however, Congress did not go as far as suggested by the Federal Circuit in *Windsurfing* (or by some of the draft bills which preceded the actual legislation) and mandate a rule of reason inquiry in every licensing misuse case, whether based on tying or some other provision.[118]

In sum, recent developments, both in leading federal cases and in Congress, have gone a long way toward merging antitrust and patent misuse analysis. While it remains true that a practice need not rise to the level of an antitrust violation to be considered misuse, any practices that appear likely to be patent extending are increasingly likely to be analyzed under antitrust rule of reason principles.

---

117. *In re* Recombinant DNA Tech. Patent & Contract Litig., 850 F. Supp. 769 (S.D. Ind. 1994); *Texas Instruments*, 49 F. Supp. 2d at 909, n. 22.

118. *See* Robert J. Hoerner, *Patent Misuse: The Law Changes*, 1 J. PROPRIETARY RTS. 10 (Feb. 1989); Thomas M. Susman & Elizabeth R. Krentzman, *Congressional Reform of Patent Misuse Doctrine Benefits High Technology Innovators*, 5 COMPUTER LAW. 8 (1988); Richard Calkins, *Patent Law: The Impact of the 1988 Patent Misuse Reform Act and Noerr-Pennington Doctrine on Misuse Defenses and Antitrust Counterclaims*, 38 DRAKE L. REV. 175, 193-96 (1989); James B. Kobak, Jr., *The New Patent Misuse Law*, 71 J. PAT. [& TRADEMARK] OFF. SOC'Y 859 (1989); Jere M. Webb & Lawrence A. Locke, *Intellectual Property Misuse: Recent Developments in the Misuse Doctrine*, 75 J. PAT. [& TRADEMARK] OFF. SOC'Y 339 (1991).

I. Standing and Patent Misuse

Although the patent misuse doctrine has evolved to take into account some antitrust principles, it retains distinctive features. One particularly distinctive feature is that the party complaining of misuse need not satisfy the traditional standing or injury requirements: a defendant in an infringement suit need not show that it was the target of, or harmed by, the alleged misuse to take advantage of the defense. The doctrine developed as a deterrent measure rather than a compensatory one.

In *Morton Salt*, the defendant who asserted the misuse defense was allegedly a competitor of the patent owner in the sale of machines. The defendant was not a party to any of the tying agreements that were held to involve a misuse of the patent, and no harm or nexus between the defendant and the misuse of the patent was alleged or held to be necessary by the Supreme Court. Rather, the Court stated: "It is the adverse effect upon the public interest of a successful infringement suit in conjunction with the patentee's course of conduct which disqualifies him to maintain the suit, regardless of whether the particular defendant has suffered from the misuse of the patent."[119]

Courts have required that the conduct complained of bear some relation to the patent in suit,[120] although the alleged misuse need not even directly involve conditions in a patent license. For example, in *Ansul Co. v. Uniroyal Inc.,*[121] the alleged infringer, Ansul, claimed that the patentee, Uniroyal, had misused the patent in suit by imposing a territorial restriction and resale price maintenance scheme on distributors through sales transactions, not patent licenses. Uniroyal argued that an antitrust violation was not patent misuse merely because it involved patented products and that there was not a sufficient nexus between the antitrust violation and the patent in suit.

---

119. Morton Salt Co. v. G.S. Suppiger Co., 314 U.S. 488, 494 (1942). *See also* Noll v. O.M. Scott & Sons Co., 467 F.2d 295 (6th Cir. 1972); Blohm & Voss AG v. Prudential-Grace Lines, Inc., 346 F. Supp. 1116 (D. Md. 1972), *rev'd on other grounds*, 489 F.2d 231 (4th Cir. 1973).

120. *E.g.,* Kolene Corp. v. Motor City Metal Treating, Inc., 440 F.2d 77, 84 (6th Cir. 1971) ("The misuse must be of the patent in suit.").

121. 448 F.2d 872 (2d Cir. 1971).

Both the trial court and the Second Circuit disagreed with Uniroyal.[122] In the words of the Second Circuit, the application of the misuse doctrine "depends upon whether the patent itself significantly contributes to the unlawful antitrust practice."[123] According to the court, "since [the product at issue] was an easily formulated commercial chemical, the only reason that Uniroyal was able to impose the restraints it did with any degree of success was that it owned the patent on [the product at issue] and thus had a monopoly on its sale."[124] The fact that the unlawful scheme was implemented through sales transactions, not patent licenses, was immaterial.

J. Purging Misuse

A finding of misuse does not render the patent forever unenforceable. In the words of *Morton Salt*, the misuse can be purged, and the patent rendered enforceable for the future, if the patentee demonstrates that "the improper practice has been abandoned and that the consequences of the misuse of the patent have been dissipated."[125] The combination of abandonment and dissipation are known as "purging" the misuse. In *B.B. Chemical*, the Supreme Court reiterated its purging criteria with little, if any, elucidation: "It will be appropriate to consider petitioner's right to relief when it is able to show that it has fully abandoned its present method of restraining competition in the sale of unpatented articles and that the consequences of that practice have been fully dissipated."[126] As a result, no test has been consistently applied in the relatively few lower court cases dealing with purge. Most courts acknowledge the possibility of purging misuse, but this is usually only in the form of a paraphrase or a citation to the general definition set forth in *Morton Salt*.[127]

---

122. See *id.* at 879-82.
123. *Id.* at 879.
124. *Id.* at 880.
125. 314 U.S. at 493.
126. 314 U.S. 495, 498 (1942).
127. See, e.g., United States Gypsum Co. v. National Gypsum Co., 352 U.S. 457, 465 (1957); *In re* Yarn Processing Patent Validity Litig., 472 F. Supp 180, 183 (S.D. Fla. 1979); Rohm & Haas Co. v. Dawson Chem.

In practice, some courts have been willing to find purge with little more than a cursory analysis of whether the practice has been abandoned and with no analysis of dissipation. For example, in *McCullough Tool Co. v. Well Surveys, Inc.*,[128] the court held that Well Surveys had misused its patent by entering into an agreement with a licensee that effectively coerced any additional licensees to buy particular instruments from Well Surveys. The court affirmed the trial court's finding that the misuse was purged on the date that the contract providing for the prohibited practices no longer had legal effect. The court was persuaded that the effects of the misuse had dissipated because Well Surveys had "notified its licensees and potential licensees by letter and public notice that it would enter into new agreements or renegotiate old agreements on reasonable terms under any or all of its patents."[129] Similarly, in *Shea v. Blaw-Knox Co.*,[130] a purge was effected when the patent holder sent letters to its licensees waiving provisions that precluded the licensees from dealing in certain unpatented goods.[131] Thus, in cases where there

---

Co., No. CIV.A. 74-H-790, 1976 U.S. Dist. LEXIS 12167, at *8 (S.D. Tex. Nov. 23, 1976). *See also* Practice Management Info. Corp. v. AMA, 121 F.3d 516 (9th Cir. 1997) (copyright case).

128. 343 F.2d 381 (10th Cir. 1965).

129. *Id.* at 407-08.

130. 388 F.2d 761 (7th Cir. 1968).

131. *Id.* at 765. *See also* Metals Disintegrating Co. v. Reynolds Metals Co., 228 F.2d 885, 889 (3d Cir. 1956) (misuse purged by licensor's attempt, albeit unsuccessful, to obtain defendant's formal agreement to eliminate price-fixing clause from their license and licensor's abrogation of its only other license containing a price-fixing clause); Eastern Venetian Blind Co. v. Acme Steel Co., 188 F.2d 247, 252-54 (4th Cir. 1951) (misuse purged when licensor changed second stage licenses and sent letter which made clear that second stage licensees did not have to purchase the previously tied product from the defendant or the first stage licensees); Westinghouse Elec. Corp. v. Bulldog Elec. Prods. Co., 179 F.2d 139, 145 (4th Cir. 1950) (licensor's letter written during pendency of action waiving its rights under price maintenance provisions purged any possible misuse); *In re* Independent Serv. Orgs. Antitrust Litig., 964 F. Supp. 1479, 1483 (D. Kan. 1997) (misuse purged by change in policy prior to filing copyright infringement claim). *But see* Berlenbach v. Anderson & Thompson Ski Co., 329 F.2d 782, 784-85 (9th Cir. 1964) (mere failure to enforce

was no showing that the misuse caused significant unlawful effects, courts have not seemed to require additional proof of dissipation.[132]

Some courts, however, have found that abandonment is not enough. For example, in *Koratron Co. v. Lion Uniform Inc.*,[133] the court held that merely giving licensees the option to switch to new agreements without tying provisions and then allowing the remaining old agreements to expire was not sufficient to dissipate the effect of the misuse. Similarly, the court in *Ansul* found that the mere cessation of overt acts in furtherance of an unlawful scheme to enforce resale prices and territorial restrictions did not dissipate the effects of the misuse.[134]

The holdings in *Koratron* and *Ansul*, however, were based on particularly striking examples of patent misuse. In *Koratron*, the tying provisions were only one of a "multiplicity of misuses," and the court did not believe that a passive approach would effectively dissipate the "far reaching effects" of the misuse.[135] The *Ansul* court concluded that the patentee's behavior subsequent to the claimed abandonment,

---

objectionable provision would not preclude finding of misuse if illegal clause still existed).

132. *See* Sylvania Indus. Corp. v. Visking Corp., 132 F.2d 947 (4th Cir. 1993) (court in supplemental proceedings found misuse had ceased after trial and enjoined further infringement); White Cap Co. v. Owens-Illinois Glass Co., 203 F.2d 694, 698 (6th Cir. 1953) (court found that no showing of dissipation was necessary because there was no evidence that an unlawful tying provision ever affected customer's choice of products); Gray Tool Co. v. Humble Oil & Ref. Co., 186 F.2d 365 (5th Cir. 1951) (permitting plaintiff to purge after trial, seemingly assuming cessation would constitute purge). *See also Yarn Processing*, 472 F. Supp at 190-91 (abandonment of illegal rebate arrangements was effective purge when there was no evidence that the rebates had any effect on the incentive to patronize alternative technology).

133. 409 F. Supp. 1019 (N.D. Cal. 1976).

134. *See also* Preformed Line Prods. Co. v. Fanner Mfg. Co., 225 F. Supp. 762, 797 (N.D. Ohio) (without any substantive discussion of its reasoning the court held that purging efforts commenced on January 12, 1960 were completed on June 15, 1961, the date of the purge hearing), *aff'd*, 328 F.2d 265 (6th Cir. 1962).

135. 409 F. Supp. at 1028.

including holding meetings with distributors to discuss prices and "orderly marketing," actually may have prolonged the unlawful effects of the misuse.[136]

Finally, while the ability to purge misuse may weaken the penalty for patent misuse in some cases, it is not a panacea. The patent is unenforceable, and damages for infringement are unavailable to the patentee, for the period prior to purge. From the patentee's perspective, the usefulness of the opportunity to purge turns primarily on three factors: (1) the significance of the infringement remedy sought by the patentee, (2) the remaining life of the patent, and (3) how the court applies the dissipation requirement. Purging misuse does not entitle a patentee to damages for past infringement; it only permits prospective enforcement. Thus, the ability to purge may be of little use to a patentee who is seeking a significant damage award or whose patent is close to the end of its statutory life. Additionally, if the objectionable practice is shown to have significant effects on the relevant market, a court may require affirmative acts beyond abandonment of the objectionable practice to effect dissipation.

K. Conclusion: Public Policy Underlying the Patent Misuse Doctrine

The history of the patent misuse doctrine makes clear that it has evolved from three related areas of public policy: the prevention of anticompetitive effects, protection of licensees from overreaching by patentees, and ensuring compliance with the purposes of the patent laws. The doctrine cannot be understood by analyzing it from any one of these perspectives alone. This section will summarize the several rationales expressed by the courts at various times during the evaluation of the misuse doctrine.

First, one concern expressed in the early contributory infringement cases, *Morton Salt,* and the *Mercoid* decisions is that attempts to extend the exclusive effect of the patent grant beyond the narrow claims of the patent may have a tendency to produce anticompetitive effects in markets for goods not covered by the patent. The rationale for not

---

136.   Ansul Co. v. Uniroyal Co., 448 F.2d 872, 881-82 (2d Cir. 1971).

requiring this competitive effect to rise to the level of an antitrust violation was articulated in *Transparent-Wrap* as a concern that any attempted extension of the patent will have a tendency in that direction and should be nipped in the bud.[137] In *Transparent-Wrap* and *Morton Salt*, the Court also concluded that judicial intervention and enforcement of the patent would enhance the patent holder's ability to extend the exclusionary effect of the patent through its licensing arrangements.[138] This appears to be the rationale for holding the patent unenforceable rather than merely voiding the challenged provision.

Second, in *Zenith*, the Court also recognized that allowing patent holders to extend the scope of the patent to include nonpatented items would give the patent holder undue leverage over potential licensees in negotiating license terms. This leverage would allow patent holders to extract benefits that are unrelated to their contribution to the art as embodied in the claims of the patent. Specifically, the Court in *Zenith* pointed to the fact that the patent holder was able to obtain royalties on unpatented items.[139]

Third, permitting patent holders to extend this privilege by contract would allow them to sidestep the procedures of the Patent Office, an issue raised in the first *Mercoid* decision and in Justice White's influential dissent in *Henry v. A.B. Dick & Co.*[140] An additional patent law-based rationale for the misuse doctrine has been suggested in cases involving restrictions on a licensee's ability to make, use, sell, or buy a product that competes with the licensed product. Such restrictions prevent innovation and the invention of patentable improvements—the

---

137. *See* Transparent-Wrap Mach. Corp. v. Stokes & Smith Co., 329 U.S. 637, 641 (1947).
138. *See id.*; Morton Salt Co. v. G.S. Suppiger Co., 314 U.S. 488, 492-93 (1942).
139. *See* Zenith Radio Corp. v. Hazeltine Research, Inc., 395 U.S. 100, 135 (1969).
140. 224 U.S. 1, 70 (1912) (White, C.J., dissenting). Justice White explained at length how permitting the patent holder to tie the grant of a license to the use or purchase of nonpatented goods would allow the patent holder to extend the patent by contract "without any of the precautions for the benefit of the public which limit the right to obtain a patent."

very thing the patent laws are designed to encourage. As was stated by the Ninth Circuit in *McCullough v. Kammerer Corp.:*

> We hold that the evidence establishes that the licensing contract and the operations thereunder substantially prejudiced the public interest in that they stifled new competitive invention and suppressed competitive forces which stimulate newer and better products, and that the contract's covenants strike at the very purpose of the statute and its constitutional basis.[141]

Recent decisions of the Federal Circuit view the patent misuse doctrine as designed primarily to prevent anticompetitive effects resulting from improper patent licensing and largely ignore the equity and patent law-based rationales that gave rise to the doctrine. While the Federal Circuit does not require conduct constituting patent misuse to rise to the level of an antitrust violation, it does often look to antitrust law to supply at least general standards for determining when a practice should be considered misuse.[142]

---

141. 166 F.2d 759, 764 (9th Cir. 1948). *See also* Berlenbach v. Anderson & Thompson Ski Co., 329 F.2d 782 (9th Cir. 1964); National Lockwasher Co. v. George K. Garrett Co., 137 F.2d 255 (3d Cir. 1943). As discussed in detail in Chapter VII, this rationale has now been applied on a per se basis by at least two courts of appeal in cases involving copyrights. *See* Practice Management Info. Corp. v. AMA, 121 F.3d 516 (9th Cir. 1997); Lasercomb Am., Inc. v. Reynolds, 911 F.2d 970 (4th Cir. 1990).

142. *See, e.g.,* Virginia Panel Corp. v. MAC Panel Co., 133 F.3d 860 (Fed. Cir. 1997); Mallinckrodt, Inc. v. Medipart, Inc., 976 F.2d 700 (Fed. Cir. 1992); Windsurfing Int'l, Inc. v. AMF, Inc., 782 F.2d 995 (Fed. Cir. 1986).

CHAPTER II

SPECIFIC PRACTICES THAT HAVE BEEN CHALLENGED AS MISUSE

by Nicholas Coch and Heidi Chen

While the intellectual property misuse doctrine is conceptually broad, over the years only a relatively finite set of practices has been held to constitute misuse. Some practices condemned as misuse are potentially anticompetitive, and may also constitute an antitrust violation; other practices merely enable a patent owner to extend its patent beyond the scope of the official grant. This chapter summarizes the practices that have been challenged and the reasons why they have or have not been considered misuse.

A. Refusal to License

A patent owner has the discretion whether and to whom it will grant a license to its patented product or process.[1] Therefore, a patent owner who unilaterally determines simply not to license a patented invention should not be guilty of patent misuse. The Supreme Court implicitly so held in its five to four *Rohm & Haas*[2] decision; it approved Rohm & Haas's practice, challenged as misuse, of licensing the use of its patented process only with an unpatented chemical manufactured by Rohm & Haas, but not with the unpatented chemical if produced by third parties. Section 271(d) of the Patent Act, added by the Patent Misuse Reform Act of 1988, now explicitly provides that, "No patent owner otherwise entitled to relief for infringement or contributory infringement of a patent shall be denied relief or deemed guilty of misuse or illegal extension of the patent right by reason of his having . . . (4) refused to license or use any rights to the patent." The Federal Circuit has held that

---

1.   *See* Continental Paper Bag Co. v. Eastern Paper Bag Co., 210 U.S. 405, 424-30 (1908); Cataphote Corp. v. DeSoto Chem. Coatings, Inc., 450 F.2d 769, 774 (9th Cir. 1971).

2.   Dawson Chem. Co. v. Rohm & Haas Co., 448 U.S. 176 (1980).

a refusal to sell patented products or license a patent falls within the statutory patent grant and cannot constitute an antitrust violation or patent misuse.[3]

B. Tying Arrangements

The patent misuse doctrine originated in the context of tie-ins. A "tie-in" (or "tying") is an arrangement in which a patent owner conditions the grant of a patent license or the sale or lease of a patented product (the "tying product") upon the purchase of materials, supplies, components, or other items not covered by the patent (the "tied product"), or upon the contracting party's promise not to purchase the tied product from any other supplier.[4] The classic example of a situation that raises tying concerns is the patentee's sale or lease of a patented machine subject to an obligation on the part of the purchaser or lessee who uses the machine to procure supplies, maintenance services, or component repair parts for the machine from the patentee.[5] In these circumstances, the courts have historically found misuse, faulting the

---

3.   *See In re* Independent Serv. Orgs. Antitrust Litig., 203 F.3d 1322, 1328 n.2 (Fed. Cir. 2000). In *Allied Research Prods. Inc. v. Heatbath Corp.*, 300 F. Supp. 656 (N.D. Ill. 1969), a patent owner had already licensed its patent to competitors of the defendant when it refused to license the defendant solely because of a "personal dispute" between the two individuals. The court did not formulate the issue in terms of patent misuse, but awarded a misuse-like remedy by not requiring the defendant to pay damages for past infringement. A literal construction of 35 U.S.C. § 271(d)(4) would now prevent this result.

4.   *See* Morton Salt Co. v. G.S. Suppiger Co., 314 U.S. 488 (1942); *see also* Northern Pac. Ry. Co. v. United States, 356 U.S. 1, 5-6 (1958), *cited in* Eastman Kodak Co. v. Image Tech. Servs., Inc., 504 U.S. 451, 461 (1992).

5.   *E.g.*, Carbice Corp. of Am. v. American Patents Dev. Corp., 283 U.S. 27 (1931) (conditioning the grant of a license for a patented refrigerating transportation apparatus upon the purchase of unpatented dry ice characterized as an improper attempt to extend the "patent monopoly"); *Morton Salt*, 314 U.S. 488 (requiring the lessee of a patented salt canning machine to purchase the unpatented salt tablets used in the machine only from the lessor-patentee found to be misuse).

patent owner for extending the scope of its patent to encompass products or services not covered by the patent.[6]

In early misuse cases, courts did not examine the tied product market but simply observed that the patent owner obtained (or at least was in a position to obtain or otherwise benefit from)[7] sales of the tied product. The courts also did not inquire into the ability of the patentee to coerce these transactions; the necessary power was assumed from the presence of the patent on the tying product. Since many of the earlier cases involved tied products that were staples (like salt tablets), the patentee's tied product clearly had no merit over competitive products and was not closely related to or especially adapted for the patented invention. Thus, it was reasonable for the courts to conclude that the patentee's sales of the tied product were attributable to its exploitation of the leverage of its patent on the tying product.

Today, a tying arrangement is patent misuse if the claimant establishes the following elements in any license, contract, or other arrangement between the patent owner and even one other party:[8]

1. two separate items are involved,
2. the tied product is a staple article,
3. the items are in fact tied, and
4. the licensor or seller has market power.

These four elements will be separately described.

1. *The two purportedly tied items are separate.* While antitrust law uses a more complex test for separability of tied products that is

---

6.   *See, e.g.,* Senza-Gel Corp. v. Seiffhart, 803 F.2d 661, 667 (Fed. Cir. 1986).
7.   As in *Morton Salt,* 314 U.S. 488, a defendant may not be subject to or damaged by the misuse, but may rely on the mere presence of a tying arrangement in the contract of another.
8.   *See Senza-Gel,* 803 F.2d at 661; 35 U.S.C. § 271(d)(5) (1988). *Senza-Gel* sets out the law of misuse for tying as it existed prior to the enactment of the Patent Misuse Reform Act of 1988, which added Section 271(d)(5).

market-oriented and based on consumer demand, the patent misuse test looks simply for physical separateness to determine whether the tied product is a necessary concomitant.[9]

2. *The tied product is a staple article.* Congress enacted a law in 1952 that provides that misuse does not exist where the tied product is a nonstaple article, i.e., an article that has no substantial noninfringing use.[10]

3. *There is in fact a tie.* For misuse to be found, the availability of the tying item must be conditioned on taking the tied item. The condition requiring use of the tied item may be express, as in a contract term, or implied. An example of an implied condition is where a staple product that is an ingredient in a patented process is sold with a package label that licenses the use of the patented process only with the contents of the package; a tie may be found if the patented process is not otherwise licensed. Tying may also be inferred from the fact that the licensee or purchaser had no realistic economic choice.[11]

4. *The licensor or seller has sufficient power to compel or coerce the licensee or buyer to accept the tie-in.* The gist of a tying arrangement is that the licensee or buyer desires the tying product, but not the tied product, or at least prefers to have a choice as to

9. See Ricoh Co. v. Nashua Corp., No. 97-1344, 1999 WL 88969 (Fed. Cir. Feb. 18, 1999) (misuse claim failed because Nashua could not show that toner was separate from patented toner cartridge); *Senza-Gel,* 803 F.2d at 670 n.14; Micro Chem., Inc. v. Great Plains Chem. Co., 900 F. Supp. 1386, 1404 (D. Colo. 1995), *aff'd in part and rev'd in part,* 103 F.3d 1538 (Fed. Cir. 1997).

10. Patent Act § 271(d)(1); *see also* Hodosh v. Block Drug Co., 833 F.2d 1575 (Fed. Cir. 1987) (toothpaste actually sold by patentee was a specially formatted nonstaple even though key ingredient was a staple); Hilleby v. FMC Corp., No. C. 91-0568 FMS, 1993 WL 83417 (N.D. Cal. Jan. 20, 1993); Rohm & Haas Co. v. Owens-Corning Fiberglas Corp., 196 U.S.P.Q. 726 (N.D. Ala. 1977).

11. *See Micro Chem., Inc.,* 900 F. Supp. at 1404-05 (no tie where contracts permitted choice of other products). *See also* Engel Indus., Inc. v. Lockformer Co., 96 F.3d 1398, 1409 (Fed. Cir. 1996) (no tie where license recited it was entered into for the mutual convenience of the parties).

supplier of the tied product, and that the patent owner forces the undesired transaction on the unwilling licensee or buyer. In the Patent Misuse Reform Act of 1988, Congress made a finding of market power essential to a decision that a tie-in is misuse.[12] Before the Patent Misuse Reform Act of 1988, courts found misuse when actual purchases of the tied product by the contracting party had occurred, presuming that the patent on the tying product vested in the patent owner the requisite power to force the purchasers. Courts simply examined whether the licensee or purchaser accepted the tying arrangement voluntarily,[13]

---

12. *See* Schlafly v. Public Key Partners, 1998-1 Trade Cas. (CCH) ¶ 72,138 (Fed. Cir. Apr. 28, 1998); Nihon Keizai Shimbun, Inc. v. Comline Bus. Data, Inc., 98 Civ. 641 DLC, 1998 U.S. Dist. LEXIS 6806 (S.D.N.Y. Apr. 14, 1998) (copyright case requiring copyright that confers "market dominance"). The terms "market power" and "relevant market" are antitrust concepts; see the legislative history of the Patent Misuse Reform Act of 1988 for Congress's intent in this regard (134 Cong. Rec. S17148 (daily ed. Oct. 21, 1988)).

   Market power must be evaluated "in view of the circumstances." Some commentators and one district court believe that Congress intended by this phrase to subject a misuse claim to a full rule of reason inquiry, as that approach has developed under antitrust law, and therefore to eliminate a per se analysis and permit the patent owner to provide a business justification defense. *See, e.g.,* Texas Instruments, Inc. v. Hyundai Elecs. Indus. Co., 49 F. Supp. 2d 893, 907-13 (S.D. Tex. 1999); House and Senate Action on Patent Misuse in PTO Authorization Bill (HR 4972), *reprinted in* 36 Pat. Trademark & Copyright J. (BNA) 774, 776 (1988); Jere M. Webb & Lawrence A. Locke, *Intellectual Property Misuse: Developments In The Misuse Doctrine,* 4 HARV. J.L. & TECH. 257, 265 (1991). Others believe that Congress had a more limited purpose: to eliminate the presumption in tying/misuse law that market power arises from the fact that the tying product is intellectual property, by requiring the existence of market power to be gleaned from "all the circumstances." *See, e.g.,* Kenneth J. Burchfiel, *Patent Misuse and Antitrust Reform: "Blessed Be The Tie?"* 4 HARV. J.L. & TECH. 1, 9 (1991).

13. *See Senza-Gel,* 803 F.2d at 668 (after finding that the tied product, a macerating machine, was a staple article of commerce and that the patentee refused a request to license the patented process—the tying

apparently assuming that the presence of sufficient power to force the arrangement on the licensee existed because the tying product was patented.[14] The patent misuse test for the requisite power to compel or coerce as now codified in Patent Act Section 271(d)(5) requires that, when all the circumstances are evaluated, the patent owner have market power in the relevant market for the tying product, either the technology market or the market for the product protected by the licensed patent.

---

product—for producing whole boneless hams without leasing the machine, the Federal Circuit observed that the patent owner had "submitted no evidence of voluntariness").

14.   Under antitrust tying law, the presumption that the patent on the tying product confers market power may still have some legitimacy. Supreme Court precedent invokes a presumption that the requisite power exists when the licensor/seller has a patent or other intellectual property right in the tying product. *See* Jefferson Parish Hosp. Dist. No. 2 v. Hyde, 466 U.S. 2, 16 (1984) (dictum in 5-4 majority opinion); United States v. Loew's, Inc., 371 U.S. 38, 45 (1962); Town Sound & Custom Tops, Inc. v. Chrysler Motors Corp., 959 F.2d 468, 479 (3d Cir. 1992). The original rationale for such a presumption was that a statutory monopoly (e.g., a patent or copyright) provided the licensor sufficient leverage to compel licensees or purchasers to accept burdensome terms. In the mid-1980s, however, some courts began to question this tradition and apply an economics, market-based approach. A.I. Root Co. v. Computer Dynamics, Inc., 806 F.2d 673 (6th Cir. 1986); Nobel Scientific Indus., Inc. v. Beckman Instruments, 670 F. Supp. 1313 (D. Md. 1986), *aff'd*, 831 F.2d 537 (4th Cir. 1987). Support for this change continues to build, and many believe that the market power presumption is no longer the law. *See* U.S. DEP'T OF JUSTICE & FEDERAL TRADE COMM'N, ANTITRUST GUIDELINES FOR THE LICENSING OF INTELLECTUAL PROPERTY § 2.2 (1995), *reprinted in* 4 Trade Reg. Rep. (CCH) ¶ 13,132; Virtual Maintenance, Inc. v. Prime Computer, Inc., 957 F.2d 1318 (6th Cir. 1992), *vacated*, 506 U.S. 911 (1992), *on remand*, 995 F.2d 1324, *superseded*, 11 F.3d 660 (6th Cir. 1993). Congress, however, has failed to enact legislation abolishing the presumption, which some courts continue to apply. *See* MCA Television, Ltd. v. Public Interest Corp., 171 F.3d 1265 (11th Cir. 1999) (applying presumption in copyright block-booking case similar to *Loew's*).

C. Package Licensing

A package license occurs when a patent owner simultaneously licenses two or more patents. Licensing multiple patents in a package is not unusual. In fact, it is common for a licensor to grant a single licensee the right to use all patents relating to a particular product or applicable to a particular field of use. In some instances, the licensee chooses each of the patents it wishes to license; in other instances, the licensor may condition the license of one patent on the license of related patents.

As a general rule, voluntary package licenses are legal, whereas mandatory, compulsory, or coercive package licenses may raise misuse issues absent some inseparable relationship between the licensed patents.[15] In *American Security Co. v. Shatterproof Glass Corp.*, the court explained:

> Mandatory package licensing is no more than the exercise of the power created by a particular patent monopoly to condition the licensing of that patent upon the acceptance of another patent, but that is too much; the protection, or monopoly, which is given to the first patent stops where monopoly of the second begins.[16]

---

15. *Compare* Zenith Radio Corp. v. Hazeltine Research Inc., 395 U.S. 100 (1969), *with* Automatic Radio Mfg. Co. v. Hazeltine Research, Inc., 339 U.S. 827 (1950) ("conditioning the granting of a license under one patent upon the acceptance of another and different license" is misuse). *See* Western Elec. Co. v. Stewart-Warner Corp., 631 F.2d 333 (4th Cir. 1980) ("Stewart-Warner must have shown that Western did not give it a choice to take a license under the . . . patent alone or in combination with other patents on reasonable terms"); McCullough Tool Co. v. Well Surveys, Inc., 343 F.2d 381 (10th Cir. 1965) (to find patent misuse "there must be an element of coercion, such as where there has been a request by a prospective licensee for a license under less than all of the patents and a refusal by the licensor to grant such a license").

16. 268 F.2d 769, 777 (3d Cir. 1959).

Thus, the practice of mandatory or coercive package licensing is a special form of tying arrangement in which both the tying and the tied products are patents.[17]

Forced package licensing is objectionable as misuse because it enables an extension of the scope of the tying patent. For example, a licensor may extend the term of a valuable, about-to-expire tying patent by licensing it in a bundle with some insignificant, newly issued tied patents with no provision for reducing royalties as the patents in the package expire.[18] On the other hand, a showing that the package license was entered into for the mutual convenience of the parties (for example, to settle disputes about the scope of patents as applied to particular products) typically will defeat a claim of misuse.[19]

The elements of separability and conditioning required for patent misuse in the tying context are not present when the packaged patents are blocking (interlocking) patents, which are essentially interdependent such that one patent alone cannot be practiced without infringing the others.[20] As the Ninth Circuit explained in *International Manufacturing Co. v. Landon, Inc.*:

---

17.   *See id. See also Zenith Radio Corp.*, 395 U.S. 100.
18.   Mandatory package licensing may also be objectionable under antitrust law because it permits the licensor to exploit the market power of the tying patent in the field of the tied patent. A licensor with a seminal or basic patent in one technological field may use a package license to gain a competitive advantage in another technological area where the licensor's patented approach faces competition from more desirable alternatives or may be easily designed around. Grid Systems Corp. v. Texas Instruments Inc., 771 F. Supp. 1033 (N.D. Cal. 1991), *amended by* 91 Daily Journal D.A.R. 9374 (N.D. Cal. 1991).
19.   *See* Engel Indus, Inc. v. Lockformer Co., 96 F.3d 1398, 1409 (Fed. Cir. 1996); Construction Tech., Inc. v. Cybermation, Inc., 91 CIV 7474 (JSM), 1996 WL 44430 (S.D.N.Y. Feb. 2, 1996); Texas Instruments, Inc. v. Hyundai Elecs. Indus. Co., 49 F. Supp. 2d 893 (E.D. Tex. 1999).
20.   *See, e.g.,* Carpet Seaming Tape Licensing v. Best Seam, Inc., 694 F.2d 570 (9th Cir. 1982); International Mfg. Co. v. Landon, Inc., 336 F.2d 723, 730 (9th Cir. 1964).

The evil of mandatory package licensing [is] that the prospective licensee, in order to obtain a license under one patent, would be compelled to accept licenses under patents that [are] not necessarily needed. The same evil does not arise in mandatory package licensing of blocking patents. In such a case, the prospective licensee is being compelled to accept no more than he would, in any event, have to obtain in order to make worthwhile a license under any of the patents.[21]

As with other tying arrangements, the conditioning of the licensee's use of the tying item on taking the tied item may be express or implied. A licensor may explicitly state that only the package is available and that it will not license the patents separately. Similarly, conditioning occurs if the licensor refuses the licensee's request for a license under a smaller number of patents. Finally, conditioning may be implied where the licensee has no realistic economic choice. For example, a court characterized the following rate structure as a refusal to license less than the package: $150,000 for a package consisting of all black and white and all color television patents; $500,000 for all color patents and future applications; and $435,000 for nine color patents.[22]

Package licensing of patents, like other tying arrangements, is now subject to the requirement of Section 271(d)(5) of the Patent Act (added by the Patent Misuse Reform Act of 1988) that the patent owner must have market power in the tying product market. Thus, the capacity to coerce must be established by proof that the licensor has, "in view of the circumstances," market power in the relevant market for the tying patent or patented product. Even when market power exists, however, some evidence may be required that the licensee accepted the package involuntarily.

D. Covenants Not to Deal in Competing Products or Technologies (Tie-Outs)

A clause in a license agreement precluding the licensee from dealing in other noninfringing products or technologies that may compete with the licensed product or technology is frequently referred to as a "tie-

---

21.   336 F.2d at 729-30.
22.   *See* Hazeltine Research, Inc. v. Zenith Radio Corp., 388 F.2d 25 (7th Cir. 1967), *aff'd and modified on other grounds*, 395 U.S. 100 (1969).

out."[23]   However, the analogy of such clauses to tie-ins may be somewhat misleading because only one market is involved: the market for the licensed product or technology. In the past, such clauses were declared patent misuse because the power to enforce the arrangement was presumed from the existence of the patent.[24] Such a limitation was offensive as misuse because it violated the public policy of the patent laws by extending the scope of the patent to cover noninfringing products and frustrated the use or development of other technologies.

Two courts have held that Patent Act Section 271(d)(5), which eliminates in tie-in cases the presumption of market power from the existence of the patent, applies to patent tie-out as well.[25] Underlying these decisions is the premise that without market power, the licensee's acquiescence in the restriction is essentially voluntary, and the licensor may not in fact be using the power of the patent to acquire more than the patent grants.

---

23.   Covenants not to deal in *infringing* products that compete with the patented product have been upheld as within the scope of the patent right. *See* Bela Seating Co. v. Poloron Prods., Inc., 438 F.2d 733, 739 (7th Cir. 1971); North Drive-In Theatre Corp. v. Park-In Theatres, 248 F.2d 232, 236-38 (10th Cir. 1957).

24.   *See, e.g.*, Compton v. Metal Products, Inc., 453 F.2d 38 (4th Cir. 1971); Berlenbach v. Anderson & Thompson Ski Co., 329 F.2d 782 (9th Cir. 1964); Preformed Line Prod. Co. v. Fanner Mfg. Co., 328 F.2d 265 (6th Cir. 1964); Zajicek v. Koolvent Metal Awning Corp., 283 F.2d 127 (9th Cir. 1960); F.C. Russell Co. v. Consumers Insulation Co., 226 F.2d 373 (3d Cir. 1955); National Lockwasher Co. v. George K. Garret Co., 137 F.2d 255 (3d Cir. 1943) ("[a] patentee's right does not extend to the use of the patent to purge the market of competing non-patented goods except, of course, through the process of fair competition"). *See also* Stewart v. Motrim, Inc., 192 U.S.P.Q. 410, 412 (S.D. Ohio 1975) (finding that the anticompetition clause of the license agreement was an example of misuse).

25.   *See In re* Recombinant DNA Tech. Patent & Contract Litig., 850 F. Supp. 769 (S.D. Ind. 1994); Texas Instruments, Inc. v. Hyundai Elecs. Indus. Co., 49 F. Supp. 2d 893 (E.D. Tex. 1999).

Competitive effect as well as market power may be necessary for a tie-out to be considered patent misuse. In *Keystone Retaining Wall Systems, Inc. v. Westrock, Inc.*,[26] a series of licensing agreements "prohibit[ed] licensees from dealing in products having a 'substantially similar design to,' or 'characteristics substantially similar to,' [the] patented products."[27] The Oregon district court relied on the Federal Circuit's *Windsurfing* decision to add the element of anticompetitive effects to the other requirements for finding a tie-out to constitute misuse.[28] (In *Windsurfing*, the Federal Circuit stated, "To sustain a misuse defense involving a licensing arrangement not held to have been per se anticompetitive by the Supreme Court, a factual determination must reveal that the overall effect of the license tends to restrict competition unlawfully in an appropriately defined relevant market."[29])

The tie-out misuse theory has now been extended to copyright licenses by *Lasercomb America, Inc. v. Reynolds* and subsequent cases from within the Fourth, Seventh, and Ninth Circuits.[30] In *Lasercomb*, a licensor of a copyrighted software program extracted a promise from its licensee not to develop or sell a competing program. The court upheld a defense of copyright misuse because this limitation extended the scope of the copyright beyond the licensor's particular expression to the ideas in the program (or other new, independent, and noninfringing expressions of the same ideas). According to the *Lasercomb* court, inclusion of a long-term noncompete clause in a licensing agreement is

26.   792 F. Supp. 1552 (D. Or. 1991), *aff'd in part and rev'd in part*, 997 F.2d 1444 (Fed. Cir. 1993).
27.   *Id.* at 1559.
28.   *Id.* at 1559-60, citing Windsurfing Int'l, Inc, v. AMF, Inc., 782 F.2d 995 (Fed. Cir. 1986). *See also Texas Instruments*, 49 F. Supp. 2d 893 (applying rule of reason approach to alleged tie-out).
29.   782 F.2d at 1002.
30.   Lasercomb Am., Inc. v. Reynolds, 911 F.2d 970 (4th Cir. 1990). *Accord* Practice Mgt. Info. Corp. v. AMA, 121 F.3d 516 (9th Cir. 1997); Service & Training, Inc. v. Data Gen. Corp., 963 F.2d 680 (4th Cir. 1992); Tamburo v. Calvin, No. 94 C5206, 1995 WL 121539 (N.D. Ill. Mar. 15, 1995); PRC Realty Sys., Inc. v. National Ass'n of Realtors, Inc., 766 F. Supp. 453 (E.D. Va. 1991), *aff'd in part, rev'd in part, without op.*, 972 F.2d 341 (4th Cir. 1992).

an attempt to use a copyright in a manner adverse to the public policy embodied in copyright law. Unlike recent patent cases, however, *Lasercomb* and other recent copyright cases condemning broad noncompete or tie-out provisions as misuse have presumed anticompetitive effects from the nature of the restriction and have not required additional proof of such effects.[31]

E. Excessive Royalties

Generally, a patent owner—and presumably a copyright holder as well[32]—may set a price for a protected product, or a royalty rate for the use of a protected invention, at a level which will maximize the return on the intellectual property embodied therein.[33] According to the Supreme Court: "A patent empowers the owner to exact royalties as high as he can negotiate with the leverage of that monopoly."[34]

There is only one case where a court suggested that "exorbitant and oppressive" royalty rates are patent misuse. In *American Photocopy Equipment Co. v. Rovico Inc.*,[35] the Seventh Circuit reversed the lower court's grant of a preliminary injunction favoring the patent owner by restraining the defendant from making, using, or selling certain photocopy machines that allegedly infringed the plaintiff's patent. The

---

31.   *See Lasercomb*, 911 F.2d 970; *Tamburo*, 1995 WL 121539. *See also Practice Management Info. Corp.*, 121 F.3d at 520-21 (reasoning that adverse effects of contractual restrictions were "apparent"). Tie-outs or covenants not to compete are also regarded with some suspicion for antitrust purposes under Section 5.4 of the U.S. Dep't of Justice & Federal Trade Comm'n, Antitrust Guidelines for the Licensing of Intellectual Property (1995), *reprinted in* 4 Trade Reg. Rep. (CCH) ¶ 13,132.

32.   *See In re* Independent Serv. Orgs. Antitrust Litig., 964 F. Supp. 1479 (D. Kan. 1997) (rejecting misuse claim based on alleged excessive prices of copyrighted parts) (alternative holding).

33.   *See* Brulotte v. Thys Co., 379 U.S. 29 (1964); W.L. Gore & Assocs., Inc. v. Carlisle Corp., 381 F. Supp. 680 (D. Del. 1974), *aff'd in part, rev'd in part*, 529 F.2d 614 (3d Cir. 1976).

34.   *Brulotte*, 379 U.S. at 33 (dictum).

35.   359 F.2d 745 (7th Cir. 1966).

patent owner had charged a royalty of 6 percent of the net retail selling price of a copying machine, which was equivalent to about 12 percent of the manufacturer's selling price. According to the Seventh Circuit, the defendant in its answer made an "undisputed showing of an exorbitant, oppressive royalty, involving the bulk of the industry, with a corresponding raise of the manufacturer's and retailer's selling prices of the licensed machines."[36] The Court of Appeals was troubled by the possibility that the royalty caused licensees to increase their prices and compared the situation to minimum price fixing.

Dissenters of this view have argued that since a royalty payment usually equates to a cost of manufacturing a product, it is not surprising if a licensee has to increase its prices to cover the additional cost. Furthermore, the decision is of doubtful precedential value.[37] On remand, the trial court found as a matter of fact that the plaintiff's royalties were not exorbitant or oppressive and observed that it is a patent owner's prerogative to set whatever royalty rate it wishes; the Seventh Circuit subsequently affirmed this decision.[38] In a subsequent case, the Seventh Circuit endorsed the general rule that royalty charges are within the patentee's discretion.[39]

F. Postexpiration Royalties

In some pre-World War II decisions, courts assumed that a licensee of a patent could agree by contract to pay royalties for use of a patented machine or process after the patent expired. For example, in *Pressed Steel Car Co. v. Union Pacific Railroad Co.*[40] and *Sproull v. Pratt & Whitney Co.*,[41] the Second Circuit stated that, although liability to pay royalties terminates upon the expiration of the patent, the parties may contract to the contrary.

---

36. *Id.*
37. 5 DONALD S. CHISUM, PATENTS § 19.04[3], at 19-337 (1993).
38. *See* American Photocopy Equip. Co. v. Rovico, Inc., 257 F. Supp. 192 (N.D. Ill. 1966), *aff'd*, 384 F.2d 813 (7th Cir. 1967).
39. *See* LaSalle St. Press, Inc. v. McCormick & Henderson, Inc., 445 F.2d 84 (7th Cir. 1971).
40. 270 F. 518 (2d Cir. 1920).
41. 108 F. 963 (2d Cir. 1901).

However, without reaching the issue of patent misuse, the Supreme Court subsequently held that a patentee's use of a royalty term that projects beyond the expiration date of the patent is unenforceable per se. The Court in its 1964 decision in *Brulotte v. Thys*[42] held that "leverag[ing] . . . royalty payments beyond the life of the patent is analogous to an effort to enlarge the monopoly of the patent by tieing [sic] the sale or use of the patented article to the purchase or use of unpatented ones."

In *Brulotte*, the plaintiff sold a patented machine to the defendant for a fixed amount and issued a license for its use. Under the license, the patentee charged a royalty for each hop-picking season. The license by its terms continued for seventeen years from the date the machine was sold, thus extending beyond the patent term. When the defendant refused to make royalty payments accruing both before and after expiration of all the patents, the patent owner sued. The trial court viewed the royalty period as simply "a reasonable amount of time over which to spread the payments for the use of the patent."[43]

The Supreme Court disagreed. Comparing the royalty provision to a tying arrangement, the Supreme Court held that the royalty clause was an attempt to extend the terms of the patent beyond the limited period prescribed by the patent statute and refused to enforce the contract provision requiring postexpiration royalties:

> The present licenses draw no line between the term of the patent and the post-expiration period. The same provisions as respects both use and royalties are applicable to each. The contracts are, therefore, on their face a bald attempt to exact the same terms and conditions for the period after the patents have expired as they do for the monopoly period.[44]

However, the Court left open the question whether such a provision constitutes patent misuse, thereby also failing to resolve the issue of the patent's enforceability, including whether the patent itself is rendered

---

42.   379 U.S. 29, 33 (1964).
43.   *Id.* at 31.
44.   *Id.* at 32.

unenforceable prior to its expiration (as opposed to nonenforcement of the contractual royalty provision postpatent expiration). Furthermore, the Court defined two exceptions to the per se rule: (1) situations involving a package license where the parties agree for their mutual convenience to a royalty rate that does not diminish as each patent in the package expires[45] and (2) deferred royalty payments. Both of these exceptions relate to the intent of the parties to the licensing negotiation and whether the patent owner used the power of its patent to force a postexpiration royalty provision on the licensee.

While courts have refused to give effect to postexpiration royalty clauses, the circuits have split on whether a postexpiration clause constitutes misuse rendering the patent unenforceable even before its expiration.[46] At least one district court has held that postexpiration royalties constitute patent misuse. In *Sanford Redmond, Inc. v. Mid-America Dairymen, Inc*,[47] the patent owner leased patented machines and required lease payments beyond the date of the patent's expiration.

45.　See Automatic Radio Mfg. Co. v. Hazeltine Research, Inc., 339 U.S. 827 (1950).

46.　*Compare* Agrashell, Inc. v. Hammons Prods. Co., 479 F.2d 269, 283 (8th Cir. 1973) (contract in its entirety violated the antitrust laws), Rocform Corp. v. Acitelli-Standard Concrete Wall, Inc., 367 F.2d 678, 681 (6th Cir. 1966) (clause providing for postexpiration royalties renders patent unenforceable at all times until purge), *and* Sanford Redmond, Inc. v. Mid-America Dairymen, Inc., 29 U.S.P.Q.2d 1222 (S.D.N.Y. Mar. 2, 1992), *aff'd without op.*, 993 F.2d 1534 (2d Cir. 1993), *with* Modrey v. American Gage & Mach. Co., 478 F.2d 470 (2d Cir. 1973) (patent enforceable until expiration but postexpiration royalty clause given no effect), *and* Atlas-Pacific Eng'g Co. v. Geo. W. Ashlock Co., 339 F.2d 288, 289 n.1 (9th Cir. 1964). Similarly, several cases have held "no contest" clauses which prevented the licensee from challenging the validity of licensed technology unenforceable but have not considered them a misuse which would bar recovery from third-party infringers. See Panther Pumps & Equip. Co. v. Hydrocraft, Inc., 468 F.2d 225, 232 (7th Cir. 1972); Robintech, Inc. v. Chemidus Wavin, Ltd., 450 F. Supp. 817, 821 (D.D.C. 1978); Congoleum Indus., Inc. v. Armstrong Cork Co., 366 F. Supp. 220, 233 (E.D. Pa. 1973).

47.　29 U.S.P.Q.2d 1222 (S.D.N.Y.), *aff'd without opinion*, 993 F.2d 1534 (1993).

Citing earlier precedent, the court ruled that an arrangement extracting royalty payments beyond a patent's expiration "'constitutes patent misuse even in the absence of evidence demonstrating that the patent holder used the leverage of the patent coercively to impose an extended term on the licensee.'"[48] As discussed in the sections of this chapter on tying, package licensing, and total sales royalties, some courts might reach a different result if confronted with proof that the postexpiration royalties were agreed to by the licensee as a convenient means for spreading out royalty payments.

G. Royalties Based on Total Sales

Generally, royalty provisions requiring a patent licensee to pay the licensor a percentage of total sales or revenue, regardless of which products sold actually incorporated the invention of the licensed patent, are suspect as patent misuse. Misuse is customarily found if the patent owner refused to license on any other terms, so that the questionable provision was not a voluntary agreement for the convenience of the parties.[49]

The Supreme Court has spoken twice on this issue. In 1950, in *Automatic Radio Manufacturing Co. v. Hazeltine Research, Inc.*,[50] the Court upheld a total sales royalty provision:

> We cannot say that payment of royalties according to an agreed percentage for the licensee's sales is unreasonable. Sound business judgment could indicate that such payment represents the most convenient method of fixing the business value of the privileges granted by the licensing agreement. We are not unmindful that convenience cannot justify an extension of the monopoly of the patent. . . . But . . . there is in this royalty provision no inherent extension of the monopoly of the patent. . . . What [the licensee] acquired by the agreement into which it entered was the privilege to use any or all of the patents and developments as it desired to use them. If it chooses to use none of

---

48.   *Id.* at 1226, *quoting* Leesona Corp. v. Varta Batteries, Inc., 522 F. Supp. 1304, 1342 (S.D.N.Y. 1981).

49.   5 DONALD S. CHISUM, PATENTS § 19.04[3][e] at 19-330 (1993).

50.   339 U.S. 827, 834 (1950).

them, it has nevertheless contracted to pay for the privilege of using existing patents plus any developments resulting from respondent's continuous research. We hold that in licensing the use of patents to one engaged in a related enterprise, it is not per se a misuse of patents to measure the consideration by a percentage of the licensee's sales.[51]

Later, in 1969, in *Zenith Radio Corp. v. Hazeltine Research, Inc.*, the Supreme Court elaborated on its decision in *Automatic Radio*, noting that the earlier case "is not authority for the proposition that patentees have *carte blanche* authority to condition the grant of patent licenses upon the payment of royalties on unpatented articles."[52] There is misuse if the patentee uses "its patent leverage to coerce a promise to pay royalties on [items] not practicing the learning of the patent."[53] Thus, "misuse inheres in a patentee's insistence on a percentage-of-sales royalty, regardless of use, and his rejection of licensee proposals to pay only for actual use."[54] Here again, market power sufficient to force the objectionable provision on the licensee was presumed from the existence of the patent. Nevertheless, the Court declined to declare that total sales royalty provisions are per se unlawful, since there is no misuse when the licensing parties voluntarily agree to such a contract clause. Finally, the Court indicated that a patentee could charge a minimum royalty figure "to insure the patentee against loss in negotiating and administering his monopoly, even if in fact the patent is not used at all."[55]

Lower court cases after *Zenith Radio* have treated as a question of fact whether a patent owner has impermissibly used the leverage of its patent to insist on a royalty provision based on total revenue.[56] Relevant criteria these courts have considered include the bargaining positions of the licensing parties, whether the licensor offered reasonable alternative

---

51.   *Id.*
52.   395 U.S. 100, 137 (1969).
53.   *Id.* at 138.
54.   *Id.* at 139.
55.   *Id.* at 140.
56.   *See* Hull v. Brunswick Corp., 704 F.2d 1195 (10th Cir. 1983); Glen Mfg. Inc. v. Perfect Fit Indus., Inc., 420 F.2d 319 (2d Cir. 1970); Lightwave Techs., Inc. v. Corning Glass Works, 19 U.S.P.Q.2d 1838, 1840 (S.D.N.Y. 1991).

royalty terms, and whether the licensor insisted on the royalty provision despite objections by the licensee.[57]

In *Engel Industries, Inc. v. Lockformer Co.*,[58] the Federal Circuit rejected charges that a license constituted patent misuse because royalty payments were based on sales of unpatented components that the licensee had the option of purchasing from the patent owner. The Federal Circuit found that the licensee could have chosen not to buy unpatented components from the licensor, thereby voluntarily accepting the royalty payments as recited in the license agreement. The Federal Circuit relied heavily on contractual language reciting that the royalty provision had been inserted for the mutual convenience of the parties. Although it does not appear that the licensee was offered the choice of not paying royalties on unpatented items, the Federal Circuit found that there had been no conditioning of the license of the patented items on the purchase of the unpatented items, and therefore no misuse as defined in *Zenith*.[59]

H. Discriminatory Royalties

Historically, a patentee had absolute discretion to set royalty rates at different levels for different licensees or different uses. Nevertheless, in a group of cases in the 1960s involving a patented shrimp-peeling machine (the so-called "Shrimp Peeler cases"), several courts found that the royalty rate structure for the machine was innately discriminatory and anticompetitive, and constituted either patent misuse or an antitrust violation.

The facts of the Shrimp Peeler cases are as follows. The patentee leased peeling machines to canners in the Gulf Coast at the rate of 55 cents per 100 cycles of the machine's roller, but leased the same

---

57.   *See Glen Mfg.*, 420 F.2d at 321; *Lightwave*, 19 U.S.P.Q.2d at 1840.

58.   96 F.3d 1398, 1408-09 (Fed. Cir. 1996).

59.   *See* Zenith Radio Corp. v. Hazeltine Research, Inc., 395 U.S. at 138. *See also* Construction Tech., Inc. v. Cybermation, Inc., 91 CIV 7474 (JSM), 1996 WL 44430, at *4 (S.D.N.Y. Feb. 2, 1996) (citing *Zenith* as support for the proposition that "the tying of sales of infringing items to non-infringing items [does] not constitute a misuse of the patent if it is done for the convenience of the parties").

machines to canners in the Northwest United States at double that rate. The patent owner justified the difference on the ground that the machine was more valuable to the Northwest canners because the Northwest shrimp were smaller and required more hand labor, which the machine eliminated. The owner, however, was itself a Gulf Coast canner that benefited from the high royalty rate that limited price competition from the Northwest shrimp.

In *Laitram Corp. v. King Crab, Inc.*,[60] the district court in Alaska ruled that this discrimination in rates that allegedly disadvantaged competitors was patent misuse. The Washington district court in *Peelers Co. v. Wendt*[61] reached the same conclusion. In *LaPeyre v. FTC*,[62] the Fifth Circuit affirmed an administrative finding that the rate structure was an unfair method of competition under Section 5 of the Federal Trade Commission Act because it was "innately discriminatory and anticompetitive in its effect."[63]

Commentators have criticized the Shrimp Peeler cases for thwarting the patent policy of encouraging dissemination of inventions through licensing. For example, one court said that a licensor's natural conclusion from these cases is to grant only one license at as high a rate as possible.[64] Furthermore, the circumstances in which misuse may be predicated on discriminatory royalties are rare:[65] the licensees must be similarly situated competitors, and the royalty rate must have a significant impact on competition among them (e.g., it must be a significant cost factor or have a significant effect on profit).

Subsequent to the Shrimp Peeler cases, the Federal Circuit has upheld royalties that vary with the use to which a process is put or the field in which its output is sold as presumptively competitive and within

---

60.   245 F. Supp. 1019 (D. Alaska 1965).
61.   260 F. Supp. 193 (W.D. Wash. 1966).
62.   366 F.2d 117 (5th Cir. 1966).
63.   *Id.* at 121.
64.   *See* Carter-Wallace, Inc. v. United States, 167 U.S.P.Q. 667, 673 (Ct. Cl. 1970), *modified*, 449 F.2d 1374, 1386-88 (Ct. Cl. 1971).
65.   *See* Christopher B. Roberts, *Antitrust and Patent Misuse Considerations of Royalty Rate Differences Among Patent Licensees*, 65 J. PAT. [& TRADEMARK] OFF. SOC'Y 344 (1983).

the patentee's rights.[66] In *USM Corp. v. SPS Technologies Inc.*,[67] the Seventh Circuit, in an opinion by Judge Posner, rejected the Shrimp Peeler cases and held that differential royalty schedules should not constitute patent misuse unless "competitive effects in the market of the patentee's customers have been shown."[68] In *USM*, the licensor permitted the licensee to grant sublicenses to the patented products so long as the licensee remitted 75 percent of its returns on sublicenses with four specific companies that were existing customers of the licensor, but only 25 percent on all other sublicenses. In upholding this rate structure, the court observed: "USM has made no offer to prove that competition in the manufacture or sale of the products made by SPS's licensee and sublicensees would be greater but for the royalty differential; and it is unlikely that it would."[69]

I. Field of Use and Customer Limitations in Licenses

Field of use restrictions in a patent license limit the licensed products a licensee is permitted to make, use, or sell. The limitation may be worded in terms of specified products (e.g., certain types of products, where the patent is applicable to a number of products, or certain styles of one product type), or specified product markets, or customer sets

---

66.   *See* Akzo N.V. v. United States Int'l Trade Comm'n. 808 F.2d 1471 (Fed. Cir. 1986); *accord* Carter-Wallace, Inc. v. United States, 449 F.2d 1374 (Ct. Cl. 1971); Bela Seating Co. v. Poloron Prods., Inc., 438 F.2d 733 (7th Cir. 1971). *See generally* William F. Baxter, *Legal Restrictions on Exploitation of the Patent Monopoly: An Economic Analysis*, 76 YALE L.J. 267, 339-47 (1966).

67.   694 F.2d 505 (7th Cir. 1982).

68.   *Id.* at 513. *Accord In re* Independent Serv. Orgs. Antitrust Litig., 964 F. Supp. 1479 (D. Kan. 1997).

69.   *Id. See also* Western Elec. v. Stewart-Warner Corp., 631 F.2d 333, 339 (4th Cir. 1980) (unequal treatment of potential licensees is not necessarily a discriminatory practice); Honeywell Inc. v. Sperry-Rand Corp., 180 U.S.P.Q. 673 (D. Minn. 1973) (must show actual difference in treatment offered to one licensee compared to that given a similarly situated licensee); *Bela-Seating Co.*, 438 F.2d 733 (showing of intent to cause substantial impairment of competition required).

(e.g., products for commercial use as distinguished from residential or home use). In 1938, the Supreme Court held that field of use restrictions were not patent misuse in *General Talking Pictures Co. v. Western Electric Co.*[70]

The plaintiff in *General Talking Pictures* owned various patents for vacuum tube amplifiers that were useful in two distinct fields: (1) the commercial field, including talking picture equipment for theaters, and (2) the private field, embracing reception for radio broadcast, radio amateur, and radio experimental. The plaintiff granted several exclusive licenses to manufacture and sell amplifiers for use in various portions of the commercial field. Additionally, the plaintiff issued a number of nonexclusive licenses for the manufacture and sale of amplifiers only for private or home use. As early as 1938, the Supreme Court stated:

> That a restrictive license is legal seems clear. . . . [T]he patentee may grant a license "upon any condition the performance of which is reasonably within the reward which the patentee by the grant of the patent is entitled to secure." The restriction here imposed is of that character. The practice of granting [patent] licenses for restricted use is an old one. . . . So far as it appears, its legality has never been questioned.[71]

General Talking Pictures involved a product patent. Later decisions have diverged on whether unpatented products manufactured using a patented process or machine may be the subject of a field of use restriction.[72]

---

70.   305 U.S. 124 (1938).
71.   *Id.* at 127 (quoting United States v. General Elec. Co., 272 U.S. 476, 489 (1926)).
72.   Compare the D.C. Circuit's opinions, issued just months apart, in *United States v. Studiengesellschaft Kohle, m.b.H.*, 670 F.2d 1122 (D.C. Cir. 1981) (no antitrust violation found), and *Robintech, Inc. v. Chemidus Wavin, Ltd.*, 628 F.2d 142 (D.C. Cir. 1980) (misuse found). These cases are discussed in the following section dealing with territorial limitations. *See also* Amgen, Inc. v. Chugai Pharm. Co., 808 F. Supp 894, 903-04 (D. Mass. 1992) (ban on exports of products made under U.S. process patent

Field of use limitations imposed on purchasers of patented products were often treated as misuse, although the Federal Circuit's *Mallinckrodt* case has modified this result, as discussed in Section II.L of this chapter.[73]

J. Territorial Limitations in Licenses

Section 261 of the Patent Act[74] expressly authorizes territorial limitations on the manufacture, sale, or use of a patented product, and on the use of a patented process, in the United States. Section 261 provides that "[t]he . . . patentee . . . may . . . grant . . . an exclusive right under his patent[ ] to the whole or any specified part of the United States." Because courts have construed Section 261 to apply to licenses as well as assignments, they have held that territorial allocations in patent licenses are not misuse. For example, in *Brownell v. Ketcham Wire & Manufacturing Co.*,[75] a case in which the patent owner limited the licensee's activities to the United States and agreed not to import into the United States, the court held: "It is a fundamental rule of patent law that the owner of a patent may license another and prescribe territorial limitations. . . . Exclusive territorial licenses granted under patents are old in the law. Unless they run afoul of the antitrust laws for other reasons, and based on additional facts . . . they are legal."[76]

Section 261 does not automatically protect territorial restraints that take effect after patent rights have been exhausted, such as restrictions on the sale of an unpatented item produced by a patented process or

---

exceeded scope of patent; misuse cases discussed by analogy), *aff'd sub nom.* Ortho Pharm. Corp. v. Genetics Inst., 52 F.3d 1026 (Fed. Cir. 1995).

73. *See* Mallinckrodt, Inc. v. Medipart, Inc., 976 F.2d 700 (Fed. Cir. 1992).

74. 35 U.S.C. § 261 (1988).

75. 211 F.2d 121 (9th Cir. 1954).

76. *Id.* at 128-29. *See also* United States v. Crown Zellerbach Corp., 141 F. Supp. 118 (N.D. Ill. 1956); Security Materials Co. v. Mixermobile, 72 F. Supp. 450 (S.D. Cal. 1947). *But see* Baxter, *supra* note 66, at 349-51 (1966) (taking the position that Section 261 should not apply to licenses in light of considerations under the Sherman Act). *See also* Gerald R. Gibbons, *Domestic Territorial Restrictions in Patent Transactions and the Antitrust Laws*, 34 GEO. WASH. L. REV. 893, 894-96 (1966).

machine. In *Robintech, Inc. v. Chemidus Wavin, Ltd.*,[77] the D.C. Circuit Court held that an export restraint on the licensee's products, which were staples derived from a patented method, was patent misuse. According to the court, the patent rights were exhausted with the practice of the process, so the patentee could not lawfully restrict the products of the process under Section 261. Less than a year later, however, another panel of the same circuit, without citing *Robintech*, criticized as artificial the distinction between limitations based on a process patent and a product patent, and sustained use limitations in a license of the same patent against an antitrust challenge.[78] Today, territorial limitations clearly imposed at the time of sale would probably be analyzed under the rule of reason, as discussed in Section II.L of this chapter.

K. Price Limitations and Minimum Resale Price Maintenance

Limiting the minimum price a licensee may charge when it sells a patented product is per se misuse, with one extremely narrow exception. The exception derives from the 1926 decision in *United States v. General Electric Co.*,[79] in which the Supreme Court upheld a price restraint against antitrust challenge where the licensor and licensee both manufactured the patented product and were direct horizontal competitors. The Supreme Court analyzed a situation of this sort as within the inherent rights of the patent as long as it was intended to maximize the patentee's reward. On two occasions, *General Electric* barely escaped being overruled by virtue of an equally divided Supreme Court.[80] Repeated challenges to the holding in *General Electric* have resulted in the following additional limitations on the rights considered

---

77.   628 F.2d 142 (D.C. Cir. 1980).
78.   *See* United States v. Studiengesellschaft Kohle, m.b.H., 670 F.2d 1122 (D.C. Cir. 1981).
79.   272 U.S. 476 (1926).
80.   *See* United States v. Huck Mfg. Co., 382 U.S. 197 (1965); United States v. Line Material Co., 333 U.S. 287 (1948). *See also* Robert Taylor, *Analyzing Licensor-Licensee Relationships: The Methodology Revisited*, 53 ANTITRUST L.J. 577, 581-92 (1985).

inherent in the patent: only one such license is permissible,[81] and the price restraints may apply only to the first sale by the licensee.[82] Furthermore, the *GE* rationale also does not apply to price restrictions on the output of a patented process or machine, or on products containing unpatented components.[83]

An agreement between a patent owner and its licensee as to the royalties to be paid by sublicensees may not constitute misuse.[84] However, restrictions on minimum resale prices imposed after the first sale remain strictly forbidden under both the misuse doctrine and antitrust law.[85] Maximum resale price restrictions, however, are now subject to rule of reason treatment under the antitrust laws.[86] While there is no case law on maximum resale price restrictions in the misuse context, this recent antitrust law development is likely to influence the misuse analysis.

Given the history of antagonism toward the *General Electric* exception, many attorneys are skeptical of relying on it. Nevertheless, in a 1993 copyright case, a price limitation in a copyright license was

---

81.   *See* United States v. New Wrinkle, Inc., 342 U.S. 371 (1952); Newburgh Moire Co. v. Superior Moire Co., 237 F.2d 283 (3d Cir. 1956).

82.   *See, e.g.,* United States v. Univis Lens Co., 316 U.S. 241, 252 (1942).

83.   *See* Cummer-Graham Co. v. Straight Side Basket Corp., 142 F.2d 646 (5th Cir. 1944); Barber-Coleman v. National Tool Co., 136 F.2d 339 (6th Cir. 1943); United States v. General Elec. Co., 80 F. Supp. 989 (S.D.N.Y. 1948).

84.   *See* Congoleum Indus. v. Armstrong Cork Co., 366 F. Supp. 220 (E.D. Pa. 1973), *aff'd*, 510 F.2d 334 (3d Cir. 1975). It should also be noted that, although the economic effects of quantity or output limitations are ultimately the same as price restraints, license restrictions on output or quantity of production have generally been enforced. Rubber Tire Wheel Co. v. Milwaukee Rubber Works Co., 154 F. 358 (7th Cir. 1907); Q-Tips, Inc. v. Johnson & Johnson, 109 F. Supp. 657 (D.N.J. 1951), *modified*, 207 F.2d 509 (3d Cir. 1953); United States v. General Elec. Co., 82 F. Supp. 753 (D.N.J. 1949).

85.   *See* United States v. Univis Lens Co., 316 U.S. 241 (1942); Ethyl Gasoline Corp. v. United States, 309 U.S. 436 (1940).

86.   *See* State Oil Co. v. Kahn, 522 U.S. 3 (1997).

sustained at the trial court level against a misuse challenge.[87] The restriction provided that a computerized game incorporating a copyrighted feature could not be sold at a price below 75 percent of prevailing price levels. The court relied on the *GE* rationale and the special nature of intellectual property as involving marginal costs of zero to hold that the restrictions could encourage licensing and were not per se misuse.

L. Nonprice Resale Restrictions: Restrictions after the First Sale

Field of use, territorial, and other licensing restrictions typically have been held not to constitute patent misuse only insofar as they apply to the first sale of a patented product.[88] However, patent owners may now in some circumstances perpetuate some limitations beyond the first sale.[89] In *Mallinckrodt, Inc. v. Medipart, Inc.*,[90] the Federal Circuit held, on appeal from a decision granting a motion to dismiss a patent infringement case, that a "single use only" restriction by the patentee could be enforced against a secondary purchaser who acquired the product from the original purchaser and reconditioned the product so that it could be reused. The court's analysis included the following points: (1) the doctrine of exhaustion did not operate to extinguish the use condition because the device had never been sold without restriction; (2) the label may have served as notice to the second transferee; and (3) the use restriction itself, although not within the scope of the patent

---

87. *See* LucasArts Entertainment Co. v. Humongous Entertainment Co., 815 F. Supp. 332 (N.D. Cal. 1993) (cross-motion for summary judgment striking the defense granted).

88. *See, e.g.,* General Talking Pictures Corp. v. Western Elec. Co., 305 U.S. 124 (1938) (field of use); Brownell v. Ketcham Wire & Mfg. Co., 211 F.2d 121 (9th Cir. 1954) (territorial); American Indus. Fastener v. Flushing Enterprises, Inc., 362 F. Supp. 32 (N.D. Ohio 1973).

89. *See, e.g.,* Mallinckrodt, Inc. v. Medipart, Inc., 976 F.2d 700 (Fed. Cir. 1992); B. Braun Med. Inc. v. Abbot Lab., 124 F.3d 1419 (Fed. Cir. 1997).

90. 976 F.2d 700.

grant, could be justified by a valid business purpose and could be sustained if not unreasonable or in violation of the antitrust laws.

The Federal Circuit has held that nonprice resale restrictions are not per se misuse and, based on *Mallinckrodt*, has developed a two-part test for determining whether a particular postsale restriction constitutes patent misuse.[91] The first step is to determine "whether, by imposing the condition, the patentee has impermissibly broadened the 'physical or temporal scope' of the patent grant with anticompetitive effect."[92] If that question is answered affirmatively, then the second step is to employ the rule of reason, taking into account business justifications and other circumstances.[93]

Applying these principles, the Western District of New York recently held that a licensor's practice of charging "double royalties" for license of the same patents both to a direct licensee and to a downstream purchaser constituted misuse.[94] The downstream purchaser incorporated a component purchased from the licensee (on which a royalty to the patent owner had been paid) in a system it sold; the system was also licensed and subject to a second royalty to the patent owner under the same (and some additional) patents. The court held this conduct to be patent-extending because it allowed a second royalty to be charged after all patent rights in the component had been exhausted through its sale. Because the court found no evidence of voluntariness, it further held that the downstream purchaser was coerced. The court found that the effect of the double royalty was anticompetitive and unreasonable because it

---

91.   *See B. Braun*, 124 F.3d at 1426; *Mallinckrodt*, 976 F.2d at 706; Virginia Panel Corp. v. MAC Panel Co., 133 F.3d 860 (Fed. Cir. 1997); C.R. Bard, Inc. v. M3 Sys., Inc., 157 F.3d 1540 (Fed. Cir. 1998).

92.   *B. Braun*, 124 F.3d at 1426 (citing Windsurfing Int'l, Inc. v. AMF, Inc., 782 F.2d 995, 1001-02 (Fed. Cir. 1986)).

93.   *See B. Braun*, 124 F.3d at 1426 (reversing a decision that assumed all resale restrictions are per se misuse). *See also* James B. Kobak, Jr., *Contracting Around Exhaustion: Some Thoughts About the CAFC's Mallinckrodt Decision*, 75 J. PAT. [& TRADEMARK] OFF. SOC'Y 550 (1993).

94.   PSC Inc. v. Symbol Tech. Inc., 26 F. Supp. 2d 505, 510-11 (W.D.N.Y. 1998).

gave the patent owner, which already dominated the market for component sales, a considerable cost advantage over its licensee.

M. Grantback Clauses

A grantback clause in a patent license relates to the licensee's future inventions, whether or not patented, and its obligation to assign or license them to the licensor. There are many varieties of grantback, based on the following elements:

1. The scope of the grantback may be narrowly confined to improvements on the licensor's licensed patent, or may relate to the field of the licensor's patent, or be even broader.
2. The time period for determining which of the licensee's future inventions are subject to the grantback clause may be limited or unlimited.
3. The licensor may be entitled to an assignment or exclusive license, or a nonexclusive license, or an option to one of these.
4. In the case of an assignment or exclusive license back, the licensee may or may not retain some rights to practice its own patented inventions granted back.
5. If the licensee does retain rights to its own inventions, the licensee may or may not have to pay royalties to the licensor; similarly, the licensor may or may not have to pay royalties to the licensee, and the royalty rates for the patents granted back may be different from the rates for the patents licensed by the licensor.
6. The licensor may or may not be able to sublicense the patents granted back, and the licensee may or may not be entitled to license them.

In contrast to the potential variety and breadth of grantback clauses, a few narrow legal principles apply to misuse allegations against grantback clauses. The leading case is the 1947 Supreme Court decision in *Transparent-Wrap Machine Corp. v. Stokes & Smith Co.*[95] The defendant in *Transparent-Wrap* owned patents on a machine that made, filled, and sealed

---

95.   329 U.S. 637 (1947).

transparent packages. The defendant granted a fixed-term exclusive license to the plaintiff with territorial limits and grantback provisions. The plaintiff agreed to submit any discoveries or inventions relating to "an improvement which is applicable to the Transwrap Packaging Machine and suitable for use in connection therewith and applicable to the making and closing of the package, but not the filling nor to the contents of the package" to the patentee, who could then apply for patent rights.[96] In addition, the parties provided that all improvements or new inventions during the term of the license, "whether made by the Licensor or by the Licensee, shall be deemed included within the terms of this license" without additional royalty.[97] Subsequently, the plaintiff applied for and obtained a number of patents which it declined to assign to the defendant. When the defendant attempted to terminate the license, the plaintiff sought a declaratory judgment that the grantback provision was illegal and unenforceable.

After inconsistent rulings by the lower courts,[98] the Supreme Court held that a grantback clause consisting of an assignment back of improvement patents was not per se misuse. Disputing the Second Circuit's finding that an assignment back was analogous to a tying arrangement, the Supreme Court viewed the grantback as simply consideration for the licensor's grant of patent rights. The Court pointed out that, by statute, patents are both assignable and a species of property which "is, for purposes of the assignment statute, of the same dignity as any other property which may be used to purchase patents."[99] Thus, the licensee was using one so-called legal monopoly to acquire another legal monopoly, not to acquire rights over something in the public domain.[100]

---

96. *Id.* at 637 n.1.
97. *Id.*
98. The district court dismissed the licensee's complaint, declared the agreement terminated, and ordered the respondent to assign the petitioner the improvement patents. Subsequently, the Second Circuit reversed, finding that the grantback clause was per se misuse under the principle of the tying cases.
99. 329 U.S. at 643.
100. *See id.* at 644 ("One who uses one patent to acquire another is not extending his patent monopoly to articles governed by the general law and as respects which neither monopolies nor restraints of trade are

Because the Supreme Court viewed a grantback as consideration and not comparable to a tying arrangement, it could be argued that a grantback can never be misuse. Courts, however, have reached inconsistent conclusions when examining grantbacks covering intellectual property that is broader in scope than that covered by the licensed patents. In *Duplan Corp. v. Deering Milliken, Inc.*,[101] the grantback clause required an assignment back of the licensee's inventions in the field of the licensor's patent. The court observed that the licensor's patent, which covered one feature in a manufacturing process, was not widely used in the industry because it did not address a frequently occurring problem. Furthermore, it was the licensee, not the licensor, that was in the business of manufacturing and thus the one most likely to originate inventions. In fact, a large number of the licensee's inventions were subject to the grantback clause. The court viewed the grantback as obvious overreaching.

The court in *Robintech, Inc. v. Chemidus Wavin, Ltd.*[102] reached a contrary result with a similar grantback. In that case, however, the clause was never enforced, and the licensor ultimately notified the licensee that the clause was canceled. In addition, the court distinguished *Duplan v. Deering Milliken* because the contract provision was "not so drafted as clearly to evidence an attempt to expand the licensor's entitlement beyond the scope of the patent."[103]

N. Use of Patents Contributing to an Antitrust Violation

Apart from the specific practices listed above, which can all be seen in large part as extensions of patent type misuse, a number of cases have also indicated that misuse could be found from use of a patent as a substantial part of an antitrust violation.[104] Typically these cases have

---

sanctioned. He is indeed using one legalized monopoly to acquire another legalized monopoly.").

101. 444 F. Supp. 648, 699-701 (D.S.C. 1977), *aff'd in part, rev'd in part*, 594 F.2d 979 (4th Cir. 1979).

102. 450 F. Supp. 817 (D.D.C. 1978), *aff'd*, 628 F.2d 142 (D.C. Cir. 1980).

103. *Id.* at 822.

104. *See* United States Gypsum Co. v. National Gypsum Co., 352 U.S. 457 (1957); Hartford Empire Co. v. United States, 323 U.S. 386 (1945),

addressed situations where a patent was believed to serve as a vehicle for implementing a cartel. These cases afford little explanation beyond generalized public policy for applying the misuse doctrine in this situation, and they offer little concrete guidance on how directly related the use of the patent must relate to the antitrust violation.

O. Bad Faith Enforcement and Litigation of Intellectual Property Rights

A few recent cases have involved contentions that bad faith acquisition and enforcement of intellectual property rights constitute misuse. These contentions have generally been rejected with respect to patent misuse,[105] with one court noting that seeking to enforce a patent does not fall within the categories of conduct capable of constituting misuse under Section 271 of the Patent Act.[106] The Federal Circuit has held that threats to seek injunctions and infringement notices are protected against misuse claims as efforts to enforce patent rights under 35 U.S.C. § 271(d)(3) as long as there is a good faith belief of infringement.[107]

A number of courts have assumed, at least provisionally, that bad faith litigation of patents or copyrights also might be a form of misuse. However, they have applied the Supreme Court's stringent test for what constitutes a "sham" litigation under the *Noerr-Pennington* doctrine, set forth in *Professional Real Estate Investors, Inc. v. Columbia Pictures Industries, Inc.*[108] The *Professional Real Estate* test requires proof both

---

    clarified, 324 U.S. 570 (1945); Ansul Co. v. Uniroyal, Inc., 448 F.2d 872, 879 (2d Cir. 1971); Hensley Equip. Co. v. Esco Corp., 383 F.2d 252 (5th Cir. 1967); PSC Inc. v. Symbol Techs., 26 F. Supp. 2d 505, 511 (W.D.N.Y. 1998)

105. *See, e.g.,* Eastman Kodak Co. v. Goodyear Tire & Rubber Co., 114 F.3d 1547, 1558 (Fed. Cir. 1997), *amended, reh'g, en banc, granted in part* Nos. 95-1511, 95-1512, 95-1532, 95-1533, 1997 U.S. App. LEXIS 17526 (Fed. Cir. July 2, 1997).

106. *See* Raines v. Switch Mfg. Co., 44 U.S.P.Q.2d 1195 (N.D. Cal. 1997).

107. Virginia Panel Corp. v. MAC Panel Co., 133 F.3d 860 (Fed. Cir. 1997); C.R. Bard, Inc. v. M3 Sys., Inc., 157 F.3d 1340 (Fed. Cir. 1998).

108. 508 U.S. 49 (1993).

that a litigation is "objectively baseless" and "subjectively intended to interfere" directly with a competitor's business rather than simply to win the lawsuit.[109] In the misuse cases, the patent or copyright litigation at issue did not meet these requirements.[110]

In *qad, Inc. v. ALN Associates, Inc.*,[111] a district court held that a copyright owner's misrepresentations to the Copyright Office and the courts about its original contributions to a work in order to obtain broad injunctive relief against a competitive product constituted copyright misuse. Although the district court's opinion dissolving a preliminary injunction was affirmed on appeal, the Seventh Circuit did not affirm the copyright misuse holding. Rather, it based its decision on the ground that courts will not sustain an injunction obtained through misrepresentation.[112]

In *DSC Communication. Corp. v. DGI Technologies Corp.*,[113] the Fifth Circuit invoked misuse principles to place reasonable limitations on a copyright's substantive rights. A copyright owner sought to preliminarily enjoin others from copying its copyrighted telephone operating switch system software for purposes of testing independently developed microprocessor cards to assure compatibility with the system. The court held that the possibility of a misuse defense deprived the plaintiff of enough likelihood of success to support a preliminary injunction.[114] Subsequently, the court barred infringement relief after

---

109. *Id.* at 60.
110. *See, e.g.*, Glaverbal Societe Anonyme v. Northlake Mktg. & Supply, Inc., 45 F.3d 1550, 1558-59 (Fed. Cir. 1996); *In re* Independent Serv. Orgs. Antitrust Litig., 964 F. Supp. 1479, 1482 (D. Kan. 1997) (enforcement of copyrights for ulterior motives not patent-extending). *See also* Religious Tech. Center v. Lerma, 40 U.S.P.Q.2d 1569 (E.D. Va. 1996).
111. 770 F. Supp. 1261 (N.D. Ill. 1991), *aff'd*, 974 F.2d 834 (7th Cir. 1992).
112. qad, Inc. v. ALN Assoc., Inc., 974 F.2d 834, 837 (7th Cir. 1992).
113. DSC Communs. Corp. v. DGI Techs., Inc., 81 F.3d 597 (5th Cir. 1996), *injunction granted*, No. 3 94-CV-1047-X, 1997 U.S. Dist. LEXIS 19068 (N.D. Tex. Nov. 17, 1997), *aff'd in part and rev'd in part, vacated in part, remanded in part sub nom.* Alcatel USA, Inc. v. DGI Techs., Inc., 166 F.3d 772 (5th Cir. 1999).
114. *See id.*

trial based on a jury finding of copyright misuse from this conduct.[115] In *DSC* the misuse defense was sustained even though the same conduct was found not to constitute an antitrust violation because of lack of market power.

A district court in another circuit rejected a similar defense of misuse involving the same copyright owner, finding on the summary judgment record before it that the general policy of enforcement of copyright was not "outweighed by any overreaching conduct on the part of plaintiff."[116]

P. Misuse and Inequitable Conduct

The doctrine of inequitable conduct is sometimes confused with the doctrine of misuse. The two doctrines are separate. Inequitable conduct refers to breach of the duty of candor to the Patent Office, involving intentional failure to disclose material facts at all times during the application process.[117] Like misuse, inequitable conduct renders a patent

---

115. *See* Alcatel USA, Inc. v. DGI Techs., Inc., 166 F.3d 772, 792-94 (5th Cir. 1999).

116. DSC Communs. Corp. v. Pulse Communs., Inc., No. 96-1447-A, 1997 U.S. Dist. LEXIS 10104 (E.D. Va. Mar. 21, 1997), *motion granted, count dismissed*, 976 F. Supp. 359 (E.D. Va. 1997), *aff'd in part and rev'd in part, vacated in part, remanded*, 170 F.3d 1354 (Fed. Cir. 1999). *See also In re* Independent Serv. Orgs. Antitrust Litig., 964 F. Supp. 1479 (D. Kan. 1997) (not misuse to enforce patents which can be used to confer market power in more than one market).

117. *See* Precision Instrument Mfg. Co. v. Automotive Maintenance Mach. Co., 324 U.S. 806 (1945) (applicant owes an uncompromising duty to report to the Patent Office all facts concerning possible fraud or inequitableness underlying the application in issue); Paragon Podiatry Lab. Inc. v. KLM Lab., Inc., 984 F.2d 1182 (Fed. Cir. 1993); LaBounty Mfg., Inc. v. U.S. Int'l Trade Comm'n, 958 F.2d 1066 (Fed. Cir. 1992).

(and even any related patents) unenforceable, but, unlike misuse, cannot be purged after the fact.[118]

---

118. *See* Hewlett-Packard Co. v. Bausch & Lomb Inc., 882 F.2d 1556, 1563-64 n.7 (Fed. Cir. 1989) (reissue will not rescue patentee who has committed inequitable conduct during the original prosecution); KangaROOS U.S.A., Inc. v. Caldor Inc., 585 F. Supp. 1516, 1523 (S.D.N.Y. 1984), *vacated, remanded,* 778 F.2d 1571 (Fed. Cir. 1985). There is some possibility that the inequitable conduct may be "cured" at the time of the prosecution of the patent. In *Rohm & Haas Co. v. Crystal Chem. Co.,* 722 F.2d 1556, 1572 (Fed. Cir. 1983), however, the Federal Circuit held that where intentional material misrepresentations have been made, a complete cure must also be demonstrated by clear, unequivocal, and convincing evidence. The court found that the inequitable conduct had not been cured because there was no documentation that the PTO was told that any misrepresentation had been made or precisely where it had been made.

CHAPTER III

PRACTICAL ASPECTS OF THE LAW OF MISUSE: MISUSE IN THE LICENSING CONTEXT

by Sheilah McCartney

Licensing intellectual property rights to third-party entities in the best position to exploit such rights promotes many of the objectives underlying both the intellectual property and antitrust laws. The prospect of licensing revenues stimulates initial expenditures for innovation and authorship by enabling the licensor to recover research and development costs. Any profits resulting therefrom are funds available for future experimentation and creative endeavors. Licensing also accelerates follow-on inventions and expressions by permitting licensees to become intimately familiar with the licensed intellectual property. Finally, by placing new creations and inventions into the hands of companies that can commercialize, expand upon, and publicize them, licensing ensures the dissemination of such intellectual property to the public.

Licensing also supports the objectives of the antitrust laws. Courts, commentators, and enforcement agencies have all increasingly come to recognize the significant procompetitive benefits of licensing in introducing new products, furthering the development of new technologies, and realizing efficiencies from some combinations of complementary components of production.[1]

---

1. "Licensing, cross-licensing, or otherwise transferring intellectual property (hereinafter 'licensing') can facilitate integration of the licensed property with complementary factors of production, which include manufacturing and distribution facilities, workforces, and other items of intellectual property rights. This integration can lead to more efficient exploitation of the intellectual property, benefiting consumers through the reduction of costs and the introduction of new products. Such arrangements increase the value of intellectual property to consumers and to the developers of the technology. By potentially increasing the expected returns from intellectual property, licensing also can increase the incentive for its

In fact, licensing has become of critical importance in the emerging commercial atmosphere of global markets and worldwide communications. In the "new economy," one principal component of the future national competitive advantage of the United States will be innovation, knowledge, and intellectual capital.[2] Interoperability and alliances are the sine qua non of complex services chains like the National and Global Information Infrastructures. Even in international industries where licensing may remain the exception (e.g., certain sectors of the chemical industry), the cost and scale of new product development and other forces may demand joint projects with associated licensing.

While licensing under appropriate terms and conditions enables the foregoing objectives, the exclusive nature of intellectual property protection enables a licensor to overreach and exert some degree of control over a licensee's activities beyond the reasonable scope of the licensed intellectual property. The licensor is able to exercise leverage or market power associated with the licensed intellectual property. Licensing thereby has the potential to discourage innovation or distort the competitive process in defeat of its beneficial attributes.

The law of misuse is intended, in part, to deter licensing practices that will likely have these undesirable effects. However, the misuse doctrine has been applied to desirable as well as undesirable licensing practices because courts have defined inconsistently the requisite elements of the defense and the doctrine's underlying rationale. The risk of illegality deters licensors from entering into certain procompetitive licensing arrangements that would benefit the licensee as well as the licensor.

This chapter first discusses the reasons for the misuse doctrine's lack of clarity and the result of its overreaching applicability to certain

---

creation and thus promote greater investment in research and development. Licensing also may promote the coordinated development of technologies that are in a blocking relationship." U.S. DEPT OF JUSTICE & FEDERAL TRADE COMM'N, ANTITRUST GUIDELINES FOR THE LICENSING OF INTELLECTUAL PROPERTY § 2.3 (1995), *reprinted in* 4 Trade Reg. Rep. (CCH) ¶ 13,132.

2.   *See* MICHAEL E. PORTER, THE COMPETITIVE ADVANTAGE OF NATIONS 723-33 (Free Press 1990); Thomas A. Stewart, *Your Company's Most Valuable Asset: Intellectual Capital,* FORTUNE, Oct. 4, 1994, at 68-74.

licensing arrangements.   It then proposes negotiation and drafting techniques for limiting the risk of a misuse finding in the context of certain beneficial licensing practices.

A. Uncertainty in the Misuse Doctrine's Applicability

The lack of clarity in the law of misuse is attributable primarily to the unsystematic development of the doctrine. Most of the seminal cases are old. *Morton Salt Co. v. G.S. Suppiger* Co.[3] was decided more than half a century ago, and the *Motion Picture Patents Co. v. Universal Film Manufacturing Co.*[4] case more than three-quarters of a century ago. At the time of the misuse doctrine's primary development, intellectual property rights were suspect as "monopolies" and disfavored by the courts.[5]

Legislation and developments in economics and world trade have reduced some of the suspicion regarding intellectual property protection. For example, the Federal Circuit was created to hear all federal patent cases on appeal and, given its specialized focus and expertise, has upheld patent rights that are appropriately obtained and interpreted.[6] In addition, there has been growing recognition that intellectual property not only contributes to dynamic economic growth but has become perhaps the United States' most significant export. Finally, Congress enacted 35 U.S.C. § 271(c) and (d), creating a cause of action for contributory infringement of patents and creating certain exceptions to application of the patent misuse doctrine for tying contracts.[7]

Some of the older misuse decisions have been affected by the foregoing developments, including the enactment of Section 271(d), but

---

3.   314 U.S. 488 (1942).
4.   243 U.S. 502 (1917).
5.   *See* United States v. Loew's, Inc., 371 U.S. 38 (1962); Mercoid Corp. v. Mid-Continent Inv. Co., 320 U.S. 661 (1944); Mercoid Corp. v. Minneapolis-Honeywell Regulator Co., 320 U.S. 680 (1944). Judicial hostility was also demonstrated by the willingness of the Court to invalidate patents on obviousness grounds. *See* Sakraida *v.* Ag Pro, Inc., 425 U.S. 273 (1976); Graham v. John Deere Co., 383 U.S. 1 (1966).
6.   Federal Courts Improvement Act of 1982, Pub. L. No. 97-164, 96 Stat. 25.
7.   *See* Chapter I.F.

others have not. Where a Supreme Court opinion on a particular practice does exist, the holding may only cover a very limited fact pattern and may or may not be readily applicable to the multitude of licensing options available today.

Moreover, some of the cases finding misuse provide little explanation of the rationale for their holdings or consider their impact on future transactions, further encouraging inconsistent outcomes. In the area of grantbacks, for example, lower court decisions are conflicted over the issue of whether the scope of the grantback may be broader than the scope of the patents licensed.[8] The one Supreme Court decision on the subject treats grantbacks as consideration only, not a tying arrangement, suggesting to an unwary reader that grantbacks cannot constitute misuse.[9]

The consequences of a mistaken judgment that a particular licensing practice constitutes misuse are severe. If a court finds misuse, the licensor is unable to enforce its intellectual property rights against third parties. The defendant infringer or licensee who has failed to pay royalties incurs no liability. Other infringers or licensees have carte blanche to infringe the same intellectual property rights or cease making royalty payments.

While it is true that the licensor may eventually restore the enforceability of its patent or other intellectual property protection by a purge of the misuse, the requirements for a purge are obscure.[10] An infringer or defaulting licensee might engage in additional infringing conduct before the licensor can establish the finality of its purge. Before purge occurs, the intellectual property and corresponding right to earn royalties may be unenforceable for a considerable period of time, perhaps for much of the term of the intellectual property protection.

---

8.   *Compare* Duplan Corp. v. Deering Milliken, Inc., 444 F. Supp. 648 (D.S.C. 1977), *aff'd in part, rev'd in part,* 594 F.2d 979 (4th Cir. 1979), *with* Robintech, Inc. v. Chemidus Wavin, Ltd., 450 F. Supp. 823 (D.D.C. 1978), *aff'd,* 628 F.2d 142 (D.C. Cir. 1980).

9.   *See* Transparent-Wrap Machine Corp. v. Stokes & Smith Co., 329 U.S. 637 (1947).

10.   *See* Chapter I.J.

B. Limiting the Risk of Misuse

Given the potential risks of licensing intellectual property under the current misuse doctrine, the licensor and licensee must enter into an arrangement that avoids or reduces the risk of a misuse finding while still achieving their respective commercial objectives. The following sets forth proposals for structuring such a license with respect to potentially beneficial practices that most frequently give rise to misuse concerns.

1. Tying Arrangements

A tie-in occurs when a buyer or licensee, seeking to acquire or license a desired product (the "tying product"), must purchase or license a different product (the "tied product") from the licensor, or at least agree not to purchase or license the tied product from any other supplier.[11] An example would be a manufacturer who licenses another to make and sell its patented product only on the condition that the licensee purchase certain parts or other items from the licensor. In *Morton Salt*,[12] misuse was found when a patentee leased its patented salt canning machine on the condition that the lessee not purchase the salt supplies used in the machine from anyone but the patentee.

The following elements must be shown to establish misuse under current law:

1. The tying and the tied items must be physically separate products.
2. The two separate products must be tied. This means that the availability of the tying item must be conditioned on the purchase of the tied item. The condition may be express, as in a contract term, or implied, as in situations where the licensee or purchaser had no realistic economic choice.
3. The licensor or seller must have the requisite market power in the tying product to force the licensee or buyer to accept the tie.

---

11. *See* Northern Pac. Ry. Co. v. United States, 356 U.S. 1, 5-6 (1958), *cited in* Eastman Kodak Co. v. Image Tech. Servs., Inc., 504 U.S. 451, 461 (1992).
12. Morton Salt Co. v. G.S. Suppiger Co., 314 U.S. 488 (1942).

4. For patent misuse, the tied item must be a staple article of commerce having substantial noninfringing uses.[13]

If the relevant products or services are separate, the simplest way for a seller or licensor to avoid an illegal tie is to refrain from conditioning the sale or license of the alleged tying item upon the purchase or licensing of the purported tied item, and to offer the two products separately. In general, as long as the licensee has an economically realistic choice, the arrangement fails the coercion requirement of a tie. For example, the Federal Circuit has held that a licensor's decision not to provide a warranty for its patented products if used with items not obtained from the patentee does not amount to conditioning and, therefore, misuse, and can be a reasonable precaution for a patent owner to take.[14]

Even where separate staple items are allegedly tied, there may be circumstances in which the licensee in fact wants to license or purchase such items from the licensor or seller in connection with its license of intellectual property rights. If the contract language appears to create a tie, the licensor or seller should document the facts and circumstances that belie coercion as the negotiation proceeds and include them in the agreement preamble and in appropriate contractual representations. This language would notify the defendant infringer or third-party licensee of the licensee's voluntary acquiescence to the tying arrangement. It would also make it more difficult for an alleged infringer or third-party licensee to prove a misuse defense based on the contract. The Federal Circuit recently rejected a misuse defense where the licensee was given a choice of purchasing unpatented components from the licensor or paying royalties on components purchased from third-party suppliers, and the license explicitly stated that the parties' agreement of payment on use of components was an effective means for measuring the value of the patented system.[15]

---

13.   35 U.S.C. § 271(c) and (d)(1) (1988). *See* Hilleby v. FMC Corp., 25 U.S.P.Q.2d 1423 (N.D. Cal. 1992); Alcon Lab., Inc. v. Allergan, Inc., 17 U.S.P.Q.2d 1365 (N.D. Tex. 1990).
14.   *See* Virginia Panel Corp. v. MAC Panel Co., 133 F.3d 860 (Fed. Cir. 1997).
15.   Engel Indus., Inc. v. Lockformer Co., 96 F.3d 1398 (Fed. Cir. 1996).

For an illegal tie-in to exist, the licensor also must have sufficient market power to force the licensee or buyer to do something it would not otherwise do in a competitive marketplace. For patent misuse analysis, unlike antitrust analysis, there is no presumption that the patent conveys market power. The misuse test for market power in tying cases is codified in the Patent Act[16] and requires an evaluation of all the circumstances,[17] which is a rule of reason-type approach.

In gauging the risk that it has enough market power in the tying product for purposes of a misuse defense, the licensor should conduct a careful assessment of the relevant market, taking into account meaningful substitutes. The licensor's percentage of that relevant market and the existence of substitute products or substitute technologies may reveal a lack of economic power.

2. Package and Hybrid Licenses

An intellectual property license that includes more than one item of intellectual property is either a "package license" of the same type of intellectual property or a "hybrid license" of different types of intellectual property (for example, patents and know-how). A package license has the potential to constitute a special form of tying arrangement when both the tying and the tied products are patents. In this case, mandatory package licensing may constitute misuse because it enables an extension of the scope of the tying patents. For example, the term of a valuable, about-to-expire tying patent may be extended by licensing it in a package with some insignificant, newly issued tied patents with no provision for reducing royalties as the patents in the package expire.

Because package and hybrid licensing are forms of tying arrangements, they are governed by the same elements of misuse previously discussed for tying arrangements, including the necessity of proving market power.[18] If the intellectual property at issue takes the

---

16. 35 U.S.C. § 271(d)(5) (1988).
17. According to 35 U.S.C. § 271(d)(5), the existence of "market power" in a "relevant market" must be determined under "all the circumstances."
18. *See, e.g.,* Patent Misuse Reform Act of 1988, which added 35 U.S.C. §§ 271(d)(4) and (5).

form of patents, the licensor might limit the license to blocking patents. The requirement of two separate products is not met for blocking (interlocking) patents because each patent in the package cannot be practiced without infringing the others. It is important to note, however, that a package of complementary patents that cover separate components of a product or steps in a process may not be treated as a license of blocking patents.[19]

A critical issue in evaluating package licenses is often whether the package license is mandatory—whether the licensee is compelled to license patents it does not want. The compulsion may be express or implied. Where the package license serves the mutual convenience of both licensee and licensor, and the licensee accepts the package willingly and voluntarily, there is no compulsion or coercion, and thus no misuse.

Coercion occurs where the rate for a single or a smaller group of tied patents is so high in comparison to the package rate that the licensee has no realistic economic choice. For example, the following rate structure has been considered essentially a refusal to license less than the package: $150,000 for a package consisting of all black and white and all color television patents; $500,000 for all color patents and future applications; and $435,000 for nine color patents.[20]

A licensor may avoid the element of compulsion by negotiating carefully and documenting concessions by both sides.[21] The following points are guidelines for conducting the negotiation:

1. The licensor should indicate a willingness to negotiate in response to a prospective licensee's request to license less than the package.[22]

---

19. *See* WILLIAM C. HOLMES, INTELLECTUAL PROPERTY AND ANTITRUST LAW § 22.01 (1994).

20. *See* Hazeltine Research, Inc. v. Zenith Radio Corp., 388 F.2d 25 (7th Cir. 1967), *aff'd and modified on other grounds*, 395 U.S. 100 (1969).

21. *See* Lightwave Techs. Inc. v. Corning Glass Works, 19 U.S.P.Q.2d 1838, 1840 (S.D.N.Y. 1991) (Corning "convincingly demonstrated . . . that its licensing agreements were the product of mutual negotiations").

2. The licensor should document why the package license is mutually convenient and obtain the licensee's acquiescence. This may require asking the licensee if it wishes to undertake the effort to determine precisely which of the inventions licensed in the package are embodied in its products.[23] Conversely, the licensee may have accepted the package only after a thorough business evaluation.[24] In either case, the licensee's concurrence should be reflected in contemporaneous meeting reports or memoranda, as well as in contract recitals.

3. The licensor may be able to demonstrate a long negotiation in which several alternatives were considered and rejected before the parties finalized their package license agreement. The licensor's position would be particularly strengthened by proof that, during the negotiation, the parties revised the original package offered by the licensor with a result more favorable to the licensee.[25] In fact, the licensor could offer an alternative licensing program with supporting rationale, establishing that the licensee or purchaser was given another economically realistic choice in addition to the bundle.

4. A patent licensor might argue that the package license does not prohibit the licensee from licensing or designing and developing an alternative technology in the tied field. This argument, however, requires a careful assessment of the economic feasibility of such an alternative. If the licensee's product price is barely above its costs, and its low margin is not attributable to the licensee's failure to minimize manufacturing costs but is typical of the industry involved, the licensee probably does not realistically have the financial choice to procure an alternative. The licensee may not be able to justify expending additional

---

22. *See* McCullough Tool Co. v. Well Surveys, Inc., 343 F.2d 381, 407 (10th Cir. 1965).
23. *See* Engel Indus., Inc. v. Lockformer Co., 96 F.3d 1398 (Fed. Cir. 1996); Texas Instruments, Inc. v. Hyundai Elecs. Indus. Co., 49 F. Supp. 2d 893 (S.D. Tex. 1999).
24. *See* ROGER M. MILGRIM, MILGRIM ON LICENSING § 8.27 (1994).
25. *See id.*

funds to acquire different licenses that serve the same purpose as the package license the licensee already has.

5. The terms of the license agreement itself may be structured to preclude a finding of a coercive package license. For example, if the licensee has a unilateral right to terminate licenses to one or more of the licensed patents with some reduction in royalties, there should be no coercion.

6. The licensor may formulate a royalty rate structure that is inconsistent with a finding of coercion. When the package of intellectual property is small (e.g., three patents), the same rate for one as for all is probably acceptable.[26] For a large package, a rate that is the same for the package and for the package minus a couple of patents is also probably lawful.[27] The licensor of a package of patents should provide, in any case, for a rate reduction when a patent in the package expires, is declared invalid, or becomes unenforceable (unless such a result is automatic, as where the base for computing royalties is the element of the product covered by a patent claim).[28]

3. Postexpiration Patent Royalties; Royalties in Hybrid Licenses

Postexpiration royalties. A contract provision exacting royalties beyond the life of a patent is either misuse or simply unenforceable after the patent expires.[29] Clauses requiring payment of postexpiration

---

26. *See* JULIAN O. VON KALINOWSKI, ANTITRUST LAWS AND TRADE REGULATION § 59.06[1][v] (1995).

27. A court found no illegal package license where there was a group rate for nine patents, and individual patents were offered at 50% of the group rate for one patent, 80% of the group rate for two patents, and 100% of the group rate for three or more patents. *See* Hazeltine Research Inc. v. Zenith Radio Corp., 388 F.2d 25, 34 (7th Cir. 1967), *aff'd and modified on other grounds*, 395 U.S. 100 (1969).

28. *See* Lightwave Techs. Inc. v. Corning Glass Works, 19 U.S.P.Q.2d 1838, 1840 (S.D.N.Y. 1991).

29. *See* Brulotte v. Thys Co., 379 U.S. 29 (1964). *Compare* Agrashell, Inc. v. Hammons Prods. Co., 479 F.2d 269, 283 (8th Cir. 1973) (contract in its entirety violated the antitrust laws), Rocform Corp. v. Acitelli-Standard

royalties should be avoided. However, a licensor may not intend to charge royalties beyond a patent's termination. Rather, the licensor and licensee may wish to spread the total payment for the use of the patent over a period of time that extends beyond the patent's expiration date. In such a case, the payments coming due after the patent expires would actually be deferred royalties for the use of the patent during its life. This type of arrangement is possible but requires careful drafting and recitals explaining the calculation of the royalty.

A patent package license for a fixed rate that does not diminish as patents in the package expire may constitute misuse if acceptance of such a royalty obligation is mandatory. However, if such a royalty scheme is mutually agreeable, there may be no misuse,[30] particularly if the licensor:

1. documents contemporaneously any agreement between the parties that the royalty scheme is for their mutual benefit;
2. requires some minimum acceptable annual royalty during the life of all the patents in the package;
3. permits the licensee to terminate the license at will; and
4. defines the royalty base as only those portions of a product or process that infringe an unexpired, licensed patent, in which

---

Concrete Wall, Inc., 367 F.2d 678, 681 (6th Cir. 1966) (clause providing for postexpiration royalties renders patent unenforceable at all times until purge), *and* Sanford Redmond, Inc. v. Mid-America Dairymen, Inc., 29 U.S.P.Q.2d 1222 (S.D.N.Y. Mar. 2, 1992), *aff'd without op.*, 993 F.2d 1534 (2d Cir. 1993), *with* Modrey v. American Gage & Mach. Co., 478 F.2d 470 (2d Cir. 1973) (patent enforceable until expiration but post-expiration royalty clause given no effect), *and* Atlas-Pacific Eng'g Co. v. Geo. W. Ashlock Co., 339 F.2d 288, 289 n.1 (9th Cir. 1964). *See* Chapter II, at note 46, *supra*, for a collection of cases on the issue of the effect of postexpiration royalties and "no contest" clauses on the enforceability of a patent).

30. *See* A.C. Aukerman Co. v. R.L. Chaides Constr. Co., 29 U.S.P.Q.2d 1054 (N.D. Cal. 1993).

case no royalties would even be required in connection with an expired patent.[31]

Hybrid licenses. Hybrid licenses of patents and trade secrets present special problems in connection with postexpiration royalties. If the contract does not allocate royalties between the patents and the know-how, royalties due after the patents expire are normally uncollectable in a suit for breach of contract, even if the trade secret is still valuable. On the other hand, where royalties are allocated in a meaningful manner between the two, the royalties on the trade secrets will continue to be collectable after the patents expire.[32]

The better practice for drafters of hybrid licenses is to prepare separate agreements, one for the patents and another for the know-how. If only one contract document is used, a clear distinction should be drawn between royalties for patents and those for know-how. Finally, if, contrary to the normal presumption, the significant intellectual property being licensed is the know-how, and the patents are only a minor factor in the determination of the royalty to be charged, the parties may establish a royalty for the know-how only and provide for patent rights to flow pursuant to an immunity or covenant not to sue.

4. Covenants Not to Compete (Tie-Outs)

A covenant in a license agreement precluding the licensee from dealing in products that compete with the licensed patented or copyrighted product exposes the licensor to misuse claims. In *Lasercomb* and later cases, courts have found copyright misuse where a license provision extracted a promise from the licensee not to develop or promote computer programs performing the same function as the licensed ones.[33] Such a

---

31. See *Lightwave Techs.*, 19 U.S.P.Q.2d at 1840. See also Well Surveys, Inc. v. Perfo-Log, Inc., 396 F.2d 15 (10th Cir. 1968).
32. See Chromalloy Am. Corp. v. Fischmann, 716 F.2d 683, 685 (9th Cir. 1983).
33. See Practice Management Info. Corp. v. AMA, 121 F.3d 516 (9th Cir. 1997); Lasercomb Am. Inc. v. Reynolds, 911 F.2d 970, 979 (4th Cir. 1990); PRC Realty Sys. Inc. v. National Ass'n of Realtors, 766 F. Supp.

contract clause was deemed to have extended the scope of the copyright beyond expression to ideas and prevented a new and independent expression of those ideas. Similar clauses in patent licenses have also been held to be misuse on the theory that they restrict innovation,[34] although at least two courts have now held such a restriction governed by Section 271(d) of the Patent Act and its market power requirement.[35]

Licensors considering a noncompete clause can minimize the risk of a misuse challenge by restricting the coverage of the clause to infringing goods. If the clause is broader, even exclusive licenses containing such a clause are susceptible to challenge.[36] Special care is warranted when drafting noncompete clauses for copyright licenses because the scope of a copyright's protection, and consequently the range of infringing goods, is often narrower than a patent's.

Alternatively, rather than including an outright noncompete clause, the licensor might provide the licensee with a disincentive for dealing in competing goods. For example, in such a case, an exclusive license could become nonexclusive.[37]

5. *Territorial Restrictions*

Section 261 of the Patent Act expressly authorizes territorial restrictions, which may be imposed on licenses to manufacture, use, and sell a patented product, as well as on the use of a patented process. Thus, territorial allocations in pure patent licenses are normally not misuse.

However, under the doctrine of patent exhaustion, certain types of territorial limitations imposed after the first sale are potentially open to

---

453 (E.D. Va. 1991), *aff'd in part, rev'd in part, without op.*, 972 F.2d 341 (4th Cir. 1992).

34. *See, e.g.,* National Lockwasher Co. v. George K. Garrett Co., 137 F.2d 255, 266 (3d Cir. 1943).

35. *See* Texas Instruments, Inc. v. Hyundai Elecs. Indus. Co., 49 F. Supp. 2d 893 (S.D. Tex. 1999); *In re* Recombinant DNA Tech. Patent & Contract Litig., 850 F. Supp. 769, 777 (S.D. Ind. 1994).

36. *See* HOLMES, *supra* note 19, at § 21.03.

37. *See* Naxon Telesign Corp. v. Bunker Ramo Corp., 517 F. Supp. 804 (N.D. Ill. 1981), *aff'd*, 686 F.2d 1258 (7th Cir. 1982).

challenge as misuse.[38]   The Federal Circuit in *Mallinckrodt, Inc. v. Medipart, Inc.*[39] and *B. Braun Medical Laboratories v. Abbott*[40] has held that patent misuse requires postsale restrictions to be unrelated to the patent and otherwise unreasonable in scope. Thus, a patent holder imposing such resale limitations should document the business reasons for them and the lack of anticompetitive intent. The analysis would be much the same as that undertaken for determining the legality of a restriction under the antitrust laws, and a party with a small market share could be more aggressive in imposing such restrictions than one with a dominant share. This approach should also hold for copyright licenses and sales.[41]

6. Field of Use and Customer Restrictions

Field of use restrictions in an intellectual property license limit the licensed products a licensee is permitted to make, use, or sell. The limit may be worded in terms of specified products (e.g., certain types or styles of products, where the intellectual property is applicable to a number of products), or specified product markets or customer sets (e.g., products for commercial use as distinguished from residential or home use). Field of use restrictions in a license are accepted as a legitimate exercise of the exclusionary right of a patent or copyright.[42] Normally, therefore, misuse problems do not arise. However, courts have diverged on whether unpatented products manufactured using a patented process or machine may be the subject of a field of use restriction.[43]

---

38.   *See* Studiengesellschaft Kohle m.b.H. v. Northern Petrochemical Co., 225 U.S.P.Q. 194, 197 (N.D. Ill. 1984), *aff'd in part, rev'd in part*, 784 F.2d 351 (Fed. Cir. 1986).

39.   976 F.2d 700 (Fed. Cir. 1992).

40.   124 F.3d 1419 (Fed. Cir. 1997).

41.   *See* LucasArts Entertainment Co. v. Humongous Entertainment Co., 815 F. Supp. 332 (N.D. Cal. 1993).

42.   *See* General Talking Pictures Corp. v. Western Elec. Co., 304 U.S. 175 (1938).

43.   For example, the court in *Amgen, Inc. v. Chugai Pharmaceutical Co.*, 808 F. Supp. 894 (D. Mass. 1992), *aff'd sub nom. Ortho Pharmaceutical Corp. v. Genetics Institute, Inc.*, 52 F.3d 1026 (Fed. Cir. 1995), held that

Patentees may also perpetuate field of use limitations beyond the first sale of a patented product in some circumstances.[44] The same considerations that apply to territorial resale restrictions apply to postsale field of use and customer restrictions. If the restraint is related to the claims of the patent and not unreasonably anticompetitive, the licensor should make the restrictions a clear and unambiguous condition of the sale or license. The licensor should also make every effort to ensure that the protected device is never transferred without notice of the restriction to the subsequent purchaser. If the transferee does not receive notice, the licensor's remedy may be confined to damages from the licensee or termination of the license agreement.

7. Output or Quantity Limitations

A licensor, particularly of patents, also may wish to restrict the number of units produced by the licensee through use of the protected process or product. Such a restriction may take various forms: (1) a maximum quantity limit, or cap, which cannot be exceeded; (2) a threshold beyond which higher royalty rates apply, or after which the benefits of a royalty-free cross-license do not extend; or (3) royalties based on a minimum output when the licensor is attempting to encourage exploitation of the licensed patent.

Quantity limits are usually acceptable when a manufacturing machine or process is licensed because the limit relates to the number of times the machine or process is used.[45] Because output constraints are considered to fall within the exclusionary power of a patent, patent misuse is rarely alleged in connection with quantity limits.[46]

---

a license provision limiting the use of a patented machine to make an unpatented product only for sale abroad exceeded the scope of the patent. *Cf.* United States v. Studiengesellschaft Kohle, m.b.H., 670 F.2d 1122 (D.C. Cir. 1981).

44. Mallinckrodt, Inc. v. Medipart, Inc., 976 F.2d 700 (Fed. Cir. 1992).

45. *See* Q-Tips, Inc. v. Johnson & Johnson, 109 F. Supp. 657 (D.N.J. 1951), *modified*, 207 F.2d 509 (3d Cir. 1953).

46. Moreover, such limits have not raised significant antitrust problems. *See, e.g.*, Atari Games Corp. v. Nintendo of Am., Inc., 897 F.2d 1572, 1578 (Fed. Cir. 1990).

8. Grantbacks

A grantback is the licensee's obligation to license back to the licensor intellectual property related to the licensed creation or invention. The grantback may cover the licensee's intellectual property in existence on the date of the license agreement or developed or acquired in the future.

There are numerous ways to structure a grantback, involving variables such as: (1) the relative rights of the licensor and licensee in the licensee's intellectual property, including their respective rights to sublicense; (2) the licensee's rights to practice its own protected creations or inventions, and whether the licensee must pay royalties for rights to its own inventions to the licensor; (3) the scope of the grantback, ranging from mere improvements on the licensed intellectual property to the field of the licensor's licensed intellectual property or beyond; (4) the duration of the grantback; and (5) the licensee's right to receive royalties from the licensor for the licensee's intellectual property and, if so, the relationship of the rates paid by the licensor to those paid by the licensee.

The Supreme Court has held that an assignment back is not patent misuse but simply a consideration for the license.[47] This holding assumed that a grantback would not extend the scope of the licensor's patent over unpatented items in the public domain;[48] rather, it would simply confer a right to another patent as appropriate consideration for a contract. However, where the scope of the grantback is broader than the scope of the licensed patents, courts have reached contrary conclusions, sometimes finding misuse.[49] At the extreme, the licensor may have

---

47. Transparent-Wrap Mach. Corp. v. Stokes & Smith Co., 329 U.S. 637 (1947).
48. *Id.* at 641.
49. *Compare* Duplan Corp. v. Deering Milliken, Inc., 444 F. Supp. 648 (D.S.C. 1977), *aff'd in part, rev'd in part*, 594 F.2d 979 (4th Cir. 1979), *with* Robintech, Inc. v. Chemidus Wavin, Ltd., 450 F. Supp. 823 (D.D.C. 1978), *aff'd*, 628 F.2d 142 (D.C. Cir. 1980); *see also* U.S. DEP'T OF JUSTICE & FEDERAL TRADE COMM'N, ANTITRUST GUIDELINES FOR THE LICENSING OF INTELLECTUAL PROPERTY § 5.6 (1995), *reprinted in* 4 Trade Reg. Rep. (CCH) ¶ 13,132.

engaged in monopolization by using a grantback to funnel back to itself all innovation in the industry.[50]

Reasonableness and business justifications are the key considerations in negotiating a grantback. Few definite rules exist. If possible, licensors should avoid grantbacks in the form of assignments or exclusive licenses. Similarly, the licensor should seek rights of use for itself, without restraining unreasonably the licensee's practice of its own inventions or imposing on the licensee royalty payments for its use of its own intellectual property. A licensor should scrutinize its business reasons for requiring a grantback that is broader in scope than improvements to the licensed patents, as it may be regarded as unreasonably restricting a licensee's incentives to innovate.

9. Total Sales Royalties

Royalty charges in patent licenses may take many forms, the most common being (1) a percentage of the sales price for each patented product (or of the total revenue or profit derived from all sales of patented products) or (2) a fixed sum for each sale. However, where the licensor attempts to charge a royalty based on a percentage of total sales revenue or profit from a licensee's product regardless of whether the product incorporates or uses the patented invention, the licensor risks a misuse claim. A risk still may exist when the royalty is based on the selling price of a product containing only a single patented component.[51]

---

50. In *United States v. General Elec. Co.*, 82 F. Supp. 753 (D.N.J. 1949), *supplemental op.*, 115 F. Supp. 835 (D.N.J. 1952), GE licensed a basic patent that was about to expire and gained the right to sublicense the licensee's improvement patents. Even though the grantback was only a nonexclusive license back, GE effectively funneled all of the industry's innovation back to it and precluded any of its competitors from retaining an industry "exclusive." Therefore, GE was able to extend the power of its basic patent and resulting control of the incandescent lamp industry far beyond its seventeen years' life. *See also* United States v. Aluminum Co. of Am., 91 F. Supp. 333, 410 (S.D.N.Y. 1950) (refusing to permit Alcoa to include even nonexclusive grantbacks in royalty-free licenses to competitors as a proposed cure for the monopolization found in the famous *Alcoa* case, United States v. Aluminum Co. of Am., 148 F.2d 416 (2d Cir. 1945)).

51. MILGRIM, *supra* note 24, at § 8.02 (1994).

Despite these potential risks, so-called "total sales" royalty provisions are employed in some circumstances where patent licenses and cross-licenses are difficult to value. A licensee may actually prefer such a measure of royalties to avoid the arduous task of determining which of its products infringe the licensed patents and which do not, and including the necessary detail in its royalty reports. As long as a total sales royalty provision is clearly and demonstrably entered for the mutual convenience of the parties to the license agreement, there should be no misuse.[52]

The licensor should take care not to insist on using only a royalty base which includes royalty payments based on sales of unpatented items or to demand a fee for every unit produced regardless of infringement. The licensor may approach the situation by offering two or more reasonable royalty schemes. If the parties decide on a total sales formula, then there is strong evidence that the license was not conditioned on the licensee's acceptance of the total sales royalty provision.[53]

Documentation again is critical to the licensor's rebuttal to a misuse defense. Where a number of patents apply to the licensee's product and the licensee does not want to make the effort to determine which patents cover its various products, the licensor should memorialize in a contemporaneous letter or memorandum the inconvenience and uncertainty involved and the licensee's voluntary decision to accept the total sales approach after full disclosure by the licensor. A licensor with market power in the patented technology or product—which implies some power to compel acceptance of a total sales royalty base—should exercise special care.

---

52.   Zenith Radio Corp. v. Hazeltine Research, Inc., 395 U.S. 100 (1969). *See also* Texas Instruments, Inc. v. Hyundai Elecs. Indus. Co., 49 F. Supp. 2d 893 (E.D. Tex. 1999); Engel Indus., Inc. v. Lockformer Co., 96 F.3d 1398 (Fed. Cir. 1996).

53.   In *Engel Indus., Inc. v. Lockformer Co.*, 96 F.3d 1398, 1408-09 (Fed. Cir. 1996), discussed above and under Chapter II.G, the Federal Circuit rejected a misuse challenge to a provision requiring royalty payments on unpatented items because the agreement stated that the method of payment was adopted as a reasonable way to measure the value of the patent, and the licensee had the alternative of buying the unpatented items from the patentee.

Finally, where there is doubt, the licensor should employ a royalty computation that does not raise the total sales issue. For example, the parties could negotiate an annual fee based on reasonable assumptions for production levels and a range of values for each variable in the equation.

10. Discriminatory Royalties

In limited circumstances, licensors might face charges of misuse from imposing discriminatory royalty rates. However, despite the "Shrimp Peeler cases" discussed in Chapter II.H,[54] the courts have upheld royalty schemes involving different rates for different licensees.[55] One court exonerated a licensor who explained that it had simply underestimated the value of its patent in the original license.[56] The Federal Circuit has also vindicated "value in use" royalty systems, where the patent has more value for some uses than others and the royalty rate varies according to use.[57]

Nontheless, a licensor should examine the legitimacy of its business purpose for any difference in rates among similarly situated licensees. In the face of any valid reason for the practice, a discriminatory royalty is unlikely to be held to be misuse.

---

54. The so-called Shrimp Peeler cases (e.g., LaPeyre v. FTC, 366 F.2d 117 (5th Cir. 1966); Peelers Co. v. Wendt, 260 F. Supp. 193 (W.D. Wash. 1966); Laitram Corp. v. King Crab, Inc., 245 F. Supp. 1019 (D. Alaska 1965)) established the concept that different royalties which severely disadvantage the licensor's competitors may result in misuse or a violation of Section 5 of the Federal Trade Commission Act by the licensor who imposes them.

55. *See* USM Corp. v. SPS Techs, Inc., 694 F.2d 505 (7th Cir. 1982); Christopher B. Roberts, *Antitrust and Patent Misuse Considerations of Royalty Rate Differences Among Patent Licensees*, 65 J. PAT. [& TRADEMARK] OFF. SOC'Y 344 (1983).

56. *See* Bela Seating Co., Inc. v. Poloron Prods., Inc., 438 F.2d 733 (7th Cir. 1971).

57. *See* Akzo N.V. v. International Trade Comm'n, 808 F.2d 1471, 1489 (Fed. Cir. 1986) (citing Carter-Wallace Inc. v. United States, 449 F.2d 1374 (Ct. Cl. 1971)).

11. Price Limitations

Limiting the minimum price a patent licensee can charge when it sells a patented product is almost always per se patent misuse, as well as per se illegal under the antitrust laws.[58] In 1926, the Supreme Court in *United States v. General Electric Co.*[59] upheld a price restraint where the licensor and licensee both manufactured and sold a product covered by a dominant GE patent. However, the rule of the *General Electric* case has been repeatedly challenged and confined to its particular, seldom-duplicated facts.[60] Misuse and an antitrust violation are also likely to be found when a price restraint is imposed on an unpatented product either manufactured using a patented process or machine or containing a patented component.[61]

While one district court has upheld a clause severely limiting a reseller's price in a copyright license,[62] most licensors avoid price restraints because of the per se nature of both the antitrust and misuse rules as applied to price-fixing conduct. Possible alternative approaches are either to impose a higher royalty rate on sales of the licensed product that exceed specified volume thresholds or revenue caps or simply to limit the licensee's authorized output.

---

58. Fixing a maximum resale price in a vertical relationship is now subject to the rule of reason. *See* State Oil Co. v. Kahn, 522 U.S. 3, 10 (1997).

59. 272 U.S. 476 (1926).

60. *See* U.S. DEP'T OF JUSTICE & FEDERAL TRADE COMM'N, ANTITRUST GUIDELINES FOR THE LICENSING OF INTELLECTUAL PROPERTY § 5.2 n.33 (1995), *reprinted in* 4 Trade Reg. Rep. (CCH) ¶ 13,132. The facts of *GE* involved a manufacturer with a controlling patent which used the patented technology to produce and sell the patented product and granted a single license to manufacture and sell the product. *See* HOLMES, *supra* note 19, for a thorough discussion of the rule and its limits.

61. *See, e.g.*, Cummer-Graham Co. v. Straight-Side Basket, 142 F.2d 646 (5th Cir. 1964); Mercoid Corp. v. Minneapolis-Honeywell Regulator Co., 320 U.S. 680 (1944).

62. LucasArts Entertainment Co. v. Humongous Entertainment Co., 815 F. Supp. 332 (N.D. Cal. 1993).

C. Conclusion

The parties to an intellectual property license can avoid many misuse issues by considering and documenting alternative arrangements and carefully drafting the documents embodying their agreement. In particular, the licensing parties should tailor restrictions in the license to demonstrably reasonable business needs. They also should document either the licensee's voluntary acceptance of such restrictive provisions or the existence of alternatives to a licensing restriction that might otherwise be susceptible to a misuse characterization.

The poor formulation of the current misuse doctrine produces costs to parties—and to society—because it acts as a trap for the unwary, increases the costs of negotiating and drafting licenses, and sometimes forces the parties to choose a second-best alternative to achieving a desirable goal. Although these costs cannot be entirely eliminated, ingenuity in drafting and prudence in negotiation can minimize many risks for licensors.

CHAPTER IV

PRACTICAL ASPECTS OF THE LAW OF MISUSE: MISUSE IN THE LITIGATION CONTEXT

by James B. Kobak, Jr. and John Fry

The effect of a well-founded misuse defense on an intellectual property litigation can be profound. If the alleged infringer prevails on its misuse defense, it may have a complete defense to a suit for royalties, damages, or an injunction even if the conduct does not affect the alleged infringer. This chapter discusses the procedural issues that are likely to arise when seeking either to raise or defend against misuse claims.

A. Pleading Misuse

Misuse is an affirmative defense that must be pleaded;[1] if not pleaded, it may be waived.[2] Before pleading a misuse defense, however, the

---

1. *See* 35 U.S.C. § 282 (1988). *See generally* 4 CHARLES A. WRIGHT & ARTHUR R. MILLER, FEDERAL PRACTICE AND PROCEDURE §§ 1023, 1257 (1969). The defense is analogous to defenses such as estoppel, fraud, and illegality, all of which must be pleaded under Rule 8(c) of the Federal Rules of Civil Procedure. FED. R. CIV. P. 8(C). *See, e.g.*, My Pie Int'l, Inc. v. Debould, Inc., 687 F.2d 919 (7th Cir. 1982) (estoppel); Stanish v. Polish Roman Catholic Union of Am., 484 F.2d 713 (7th Cir. 1973) (illegality); Hayes v. Irwin, 541 F. Supp. 397, 413 n.19 (N.D. Ga. 1982) (fraud), *aff'd without op.*, 729 F.2d 1466 (11th Cir. 1984).
2. *See* Bio-Rad Lab. v. Nicolet Instrument Corp., 739 F.2d 604, 617-18 (Fed. Cir. 1984) (defense of patent misuse to patent infringement action waived as to patent owner's alleged refusal to sell its product without purchase of a license under the patent where that defense was not pleaded in the answer or presented to the jury); Trio Process Corp. v. L. Goldstein's Sons, Inc., 461 F.2d 66, 74 (3d Cir. 1972) (failure of an alleged infringer to raise misuse defense in its answer resulted in waiver). *See generally* 5 CHARLES A. WRIGHT & ARTHUR R. MILLER, FEDERAL PRACTICE AND PROCEDURE § 1278 (1969). *But see* CMI, Inc. v. Intoximeters, Inc., 866 F. Supp. 342, 347 (W.D. Ky. 1994) (opining that

---

defendant and its counsel must have good ground for believing that a factual basis for the defense exists or face possible Rule 11 sanctions.[3] An alleged infringer may be caught on the horns of a dilemma: wanting to plead misuse so that it can take discovery on the issue, but needing some discovery before it can plead misuse in good faith. This problem is most likely to arise where the misuse is based not on the intellectual property owner's conduct with the defendant but, rather, on its conduct with others.[4]

Courts will often, but not always, grant a Rule 15 motion to amend to assert such a defense where the evidence was unavailable to a party originally, provided that the motion is made promptly upon discovery of the information providing the basis for the defense.[5] Some courts have

---

misuse defense is properly before the court when the court accepts proof of patent misuse despite defendant's failure to plead it) (W.D. Ky. 1995).

3. *Cf.* Lund Indus., Inc. v. Westin, Inc., 764 F. Supp. 1342, 1346-47 (D. Minn. 1990) (court denied Rule 11 motion after finding that defendants' affirmative defense of patent misuse had reasonable ground in fact and law).

4. *See* Noll v. O.M. Scott & Sons Co., 467 F.2d 295 (6th Cir. 1972) (strong public policy underlying misuse doctrine allows alleged infringer to interpose misuse defense without allegation or proof that it was victim of any misuse); Blohm & Voss AG v. Prudential-Grace Lines, Inc., 346 F. Supp. 1116 (D. Md. 1972) (defendant in a suit for patent infringement has standing to raise defense of misuse of patent even though it was not a licensee), *rev'd on other grounds*, 489 F.2d 231 (4th Cir. 1973).

5. *See* Senza-Gel Corp. v. Seiffhart, 803 F.2d 661, 671 (Fed. Cir. 1986) (granting defendant's motion to amend pleading to assert affirmative defense of patent misuse after trial, where no prejudice was likely); Texas Instruments, Inc. v. Hyundai Elec. Indus. Co., 49 F. Supp. 2d 893 (S.D. Tex. 1999) (reluctantly permitting amendment six days before trial). *See also In re* Recombinant DNA Tech. Patent & Contract Litig., 30 U.S.P.Q.2d 1881, 1892-94 (S.D. Ind. 1993) (granting motion to amend pleadings to add a misuse defense seven years after the initial complaint seeking declaratory judgment was filed on the grounds that (1) any additional discovery would not be unduly burdensome and (2) the delay factor must be balanced against the public's interest in assuring that the patentee does not extend its patent beyond the statutory monopoly it has been granted); Key Pharm., Inc. v. Lowey, 373 F. Supp. 1190, 1193-94 (S.D.N.Y. 1974) (granting motion to amend to assert patent misuse

even perceived an important public interest in permitting such defenses to be asserted.[6] Needless to say, courts are more skeptical of such motions the closer they are made to trial and the more likely they are to delay trial and prolong discovery.[7] This skepticism may translate into a hostility for the theory of the defense itself, particularly if the theory is novel or one demanding substantial proof.

The decisions of the Federal Circuit in *Bio-Rad Laboratories v. Nicolet Instrument Corp.*[8] and *Senza-Gel Corp. v. Seiffhart*,[9] two years apart, illustrate how the standards applied to such a motion to amend may vary. In *Bio-Rad*, the Federal Circuit held that a misuse defense was waived because it was not specifically pleaded until the eve of trial.[10] In *Senza-Gel*, by contrast, the Federal Circuit, following Ninth Circuit law on waivers of defenses, permitted the defense to be asserted after the trial.[11] Given the uncertainty surrounding whether a motion to amend will be granted, it will normally behoove the defendant to assert such a motion at the earliest possible time, and with as much factual support as possible.

Because of the need to assert the misuse defense early, the possibility of the defense should be investigated as soon as a serious threat of an infringement suit exists. The time between threat and actual suit may be used to interview industry participants and consult other sources to determine whether a misuse defense exists. Statements by the intellectual property owner itself may prove particularly helpful in conjunction with other information. Because of possible changes in

---

defense after completion of some discovery). *But see* Bio-Rad Lab. v. Nicolet Instrument Corp., 739 F.2d 604, 617 (Fed. Cir. 1984).

6. *See In re Recombinant DNA Tech.*, 30 U.S.P.Q.2d at 1892-94; *Key Pharm.*, 373 F. Supp. at 1193-94.

7. *See* Congoleum Indus., Inc. v. Armstrong Cork Co., 319 F. Supp. 714, 717-18 (E.D. Pa. 1970) (denying defendant's motion to amend answer to plead patent misuse, where information providing basis for such a defense was available for extensive period of time and where case would be substantially delayed); CTS Corp. v. Alloys Unlimited, Inc., No. 69-C-1058, 1972 WL 607 (E.D.N.Y. July 13, 1972).

8. 739 F.2d 604 (Fed. Cir. 1984).

9. 803 F.2d 661.

10. 739 F.2d at 617.

11. 803 F.2d at 671.

testimony and Rule 11 problems, statements by a potential plaintiff or others should be documented and memorialized in memoranda.

If a basis for a misuse defense exists, it may help dissuade the intellectual property owner from suing or persuade it to enter a settlement on reasonable terms. Indeed, a party threatened with suit and concerned with the possibility of an injunction or substantial damages may decide to seek a declaratory judgment that the misuse has rendered the intellectual property unenforceable.[12]

On the other hand, a defendant does have some latitude in its timing in bringing a misuse defense. Under revised Rule 11, a party is not subject to sanctions if it has good reason to believe that a fact is true or false but needs discovery to gather and confirm the evidentiary basis for the allegation. Thus, a defendant asserting a misuse defense in the initial answer may not have to adduce too many specifics in support of that defense until after it has had the opportunity to conduct discovery.

Moreover, at the preliminary stages of a lawsuit, the plaintiff has limited weapons in its arsenal to force the defendant to flesh out the facts supporting the defense or to strike the defense altogether. A plaintiff may not submit a motion for a more definite statement under Rule 12(e), since the answer is not "a pleading to which a responsive pleading is permitted."[13] A motion to strike under Rule 12(f) is a possibility, but not always a realistic one. As one court concluded:

---

12. *See* B. Braun Med., Inc. v. Abbot Lab., 124 F.3d 1419, 1428 (Fed. Cir. 1997). A claim of misuse is sometimes coupled with a claim for affirmative relief under antitrust or unfair competition law. The *B. Braun* decision made clear that an independent ground for damages must exist before monetary relief can be granted; the Declaratory Judgment Act does not alter or expand substantive rights. *Id. See also* Warner/Chappell Music, Inc. v. Pilz Compact Disc, Inc., 52 U.S.P.Q.2d 1942, 1945 n.5 (E.D. Pa. 1999); Juno Online Services, L.P. v. Juno Lighting, Inc., 979 F. Supp. 684, 693 (N.D. Ill. 1997) (dismissing declaratory judgment claim of trademark misuse seeking monetary damages).

13. *See* Goodyear Tire & Rubber Co. v. General Tire, Inc., No. 3:93CV220-MU (W.D.N.C. Sept. 20, 1993) (order denying motion to strike defenses or in the alternative for a more definite statement).

As the defendant contends, motions to strike are disfavored by the federal courts, particularly in the early, prediscovery stage of a case. Whether or not those defenses have merit is a wholly different matter, of course, one which ordinarily cannot be determined until after discovery is completed and perhaps not until after submission to a properly instructed jury. In any event, neither a motion to strike nor a motion for a more definite statement is the proper vehicle for obtaining the results or information sought by the plaintiff in the subject motion.[14]

This position is not surprising since the standard for prevailing on a motion to strike a defense is particularly onerous.[15] Provided at least the basic elements for a misuse defense exist (i.e., the intellectual property owner has licensed its intellectual property on at least superficially restrictive terms and has some market power in the market for the licensed product), it would be difficult, if not impossible, for a plaintiff to show that "it appears to a certainty that plaintiffs would succeed despite any state of facts which could be proved in support of the defense."[16] Where misuse is

---

14. *Id.* at 2.
15. *See* Cipollone v. Liggett Group, Inc., 789 F.2d 181, 188 (3d Cir. 1986) (concluding that a court "should restrain from evaluating the merits of a defense where . . . the factual background for a case is largely undeveloped"); Estee Lauder, Inc. v. The Fragrance Counter, Inc., 189 F.R.D. 269, 271 (S.D.N.Y. 1999) (denying motion to strike a trademark misuse defense; "a motion to strike an affirmative defense under Rule 12(f) for legal insufficiency is not favored." (quotations omitted); Carpenter v. Ford Motor Co., 761 F. Supp. 62, 65 (N.D. Ill. 1991) (affirmative defense "need only apprise a party of the nature of a . . . defense to satisfy the pleading requirements"); United States v. Kramer, 757 F. Supp. 397, 410 (D.N.J. 1991) (concluding that where "there has been little or no opportunity for discovery and hence to develop the factual background [, it] would thus appear premature to strike defenses that have any possible merit.").
16. Essex Music, Inc. v. ABKCO Music and Records, 743 F. Supp. 237, 240 (S.D.N.Y. 1990). In *Astra Aktiebolag v. Genpharm Inc.,* No. 98 Civ. 3657 (BSJ), 2000 WL 257119, at *2 (S.D.N.Y. Mar. 8, 2000), the court dismissed a misuse claim which it described as "nothing more than conclusory allegations . . . ."

based on an improperly pleaded antitrust violation, however, a motion to strike might be granted.[17]

Once a complaint is filed, the defendant may often desire a generous extension of time to answer in order to investigate the possibility of asserting a misuse defense. Even where goodwill among counsel prevails, one cannot count on obtaining a lengthy extension. The intellectual property owner may be seeking a prompt determination of the matter, including a preliminary injunction. Unless the infringement suit is as much settlement device as lawsuit, it is in the intellectual property owner's interest to keep the case moving forward with issues of infringement as its main focus. Finally, in many districts, even complex intellectual property cases may be placed on a rapid docket with timelines that may not permit more than modest extensions of time. The fact that time may be short and occupied by discovery and many other matters is itself an important reason why thorough precomplaint investigation is desirable.

A defendant investigating a misuse defense might consider the opposite strategy of seeking accelerated discovery on the misuse issue. Such discovery might put the defendant in a position to plead the defense or to make a potentially dispositive summary judgment motion. This strategy may be attractive to a defendant to the extent that it permits a quick strike move and shifts much of the focus away from infringement to defensive issues. It could, however, entail substantial expense for what might prove to be a wild goose chase—and lead to a significant loss of credibility with the court.

---

17. *See* Townshend v. Rockwell Int'l Corp., 2000 U.S. Dist. LEXIS 5070, at *45 (N.D. Cal. Mar. 28, 2000) (granting motion to strike antitrust counterclaim and misuse defense with prejudice because "allegations do not state anti-competitive conduct" by plaintiff); Northwestern Corp. v. Gabriel Mfg. Co., No. 95 C 2004, 1996 WL 732519, at *19 (N.D. Ill. Dec. 18, 1996) (granting motion to strike misuse defense based on antitrust violation without prejudice in trademark infringement action for "lack of sufficient allegations of the relevant product and geographic market, the probability of obtaining monopoly power, predatory intent and conduct, and potential harm to consumers").

B. Preliminary Injunctions

Particularly in a patent infringement case, a misuse defense may also be used by a defendant to make it more difficult for a plaintiff to prevail on a motion for a preliminary injunction. To obtain a preliminary injunction in a patent infringement action, the moving party must show "(1) reasonable likelihood of success on the merits; (2) irreparable harm if the injunction is not granted; (3) the balance of hardships tips in its favor; and (4) that a preliminary injunction is in the public's best interest."[18]

Although the ultimate burden of proving invalidity at trial will rest on the defendant, the Federal Circuit has held that a patentee is entitled to a preliminary injunction only if it clearly shows "likelihood of success on the merits with respect to the patent's validity, enforceability, and infringement."[19] In practice, this means that the plaintiff must establish a reasonable likelihood that the defendant's attack on the validity and enforceability of the patent will fail.[20]

This inquiry is necessarily limited. The Federal Circuit has observed that "[a]t this preliminary stage, the trial court does not resolve the validity question but rather must ... make an assessment of the persuasiveness of the challenger's evidence, recognizing that it is doing

---

18. Wang Lab., Inc. v. Chip Merchant, Inc., 28 U.S.P.Q.2d 1677, 1678 (S.D. Cal. 1993); A & E Prods. Group v. California Supply, Inc., 28 U.S.P.Q.2d 1041, 1044 (C.D. Cal. 1993). The Federal Circuit has held that a request for a preliminary injunction in a patent infringement case is so bound up with issues of substantive patent law that Federal Circuit law regarding application of the standards for issuance of a preliminary injunction applies. Chrysler Motors Corp. v. Auto Body Panels of Ohio, Inc., 908 F.2d 951 (Fed. Cir. 1990).

19. Nutrition 21 v. United States, 930 F.2d 867, 869 (Fed. Cir. 1991). *See* Hybritech, Inc. v. Abbot Lab., 849 F.2d 1446 (Fed. Cir. 1988); Critikon, Inc. v. Becton Dickinson Vascular Access, Inc., 28 U.S.P.Q.2d 1362, 1364 (D. Del. 1993).

20. *See A & E Prods.*, 28 U.S.P.Q.2d at 1044; Black & Decker, Inc. v. Hoover Serv. Ctr., 765 F. Supp. 1129, 1137 (D. Conn. 1991) (concluding that the plaintiff had failed to demonstrate a reasonable likelihood that the defendant's inequitable conduct defense would fail).

so without all evidence that may come out at trial."[21] The misuse defense may involve many disputed facts;[22] by introducing a number of distinct factual issues that bear on the misuse issue and hence on the enforceability of the patent, the defendant may render it difficult for a plaintiff to show a reasonable likelihood that the defendant's attack on the enforceability of the patent will fail.[23] It is equally clear, however, that a defendant cannot rest on the mere allegation of misuse, but must come forward with some facts to support the defense.[24] Even if a defendant is unable to make a particularly strong showing on the merits of the misuse defense, the additional uncertainty raised by the defense, coupled with uncertainties created by other defenses relating to invalidity, noninfringement, and inequitable conduct, may help to tip the balance against granting the preliminary injunction.

The misuse defense also comes into play in the last element of the preliminary injunction test, which is that the preliminary injunction

---

21. New England Braiding Co. v. A.W. Chesterton Co., 970 F.2d 878, 882-83 (Fed. Cir. 1992) (footnote omitted).

22. *See, e.g.*, Mallinckrodt, Inc. v. Medipart, Inc., 976 F.2d 700, 706 (Fed. Cir. 1992) (noting that where the licensing arrangement has not been held to be per se anticompetitive, the court must make a factual determination that the "effect of the license tends to restrain competition unlawfully in an appropriately defined relevant market").

23. *See* DSC Communications Corp. v. DGI Techs., Inc., 81 F.3d 597, 601 (5th Cir. 1996), *injunction granted*, No. 3 94-CV-1047-X, 1997 U.S. Dist. LEXIS 19068 (N.D. Tex. Nov. 17, 1997), *aff'd in part and rev'd in part, vacated in part, remanded in part sub nom.* Alcatel USA, Inc. v. DGI Techs., Inc., 166 F.3d 772 (5th Cir. 1999) (denying preliminary injunction in copyright case based on misuse defense); *Nutrition 21*, 930 F.2d at 872 (vacating a preliminary injunction in part because it was not clear from the record that the defendant's inequitable conduct defense was "entirely lacking substance"); *Black & Decker*, 765 F. Supp. at 1137.

24. *See* Norwich Pharmacal Co. v. International Brokers, Inc., 159 U.S.P.Q. 417, 422 (N.D. Ga. 1968) (noting that misuse is a grounds for denial of the injunction, but concluding that the plaintiff had made a strong prima facie case of validity and infringement).

would be in the public's best interest.[25] A defendant may be able to bolster its argument that the plaintiff's motion for a preliminary injunction should be denied by focusing on the equitable nature of injunctive relief, which is unavailable to a party with unclean hands.[26]

C. Discovery and Misuse

A misuse defense that is not disposed of at an early stage can have important implications for discovery and trial. In discovery, information about the reasons for and effects of the intellectual property owner's business practices may become relevant (at least in circumstances when proof of misuse entails a showing akin to that required of an antitrust violation).[27] While conducting this discovery is a considerable burden to the defendant, it also presents an opportunity to develop facts that may not only lead to a defense but may possibly expose the existence of potential antitrust violations. If the violation affects the defendant, it may emerge from discovery with a valuable antitrust counterclaim. Even if the conduct involves other parties but not the defendant, the risk of antitrust exposure may strengthen the defendant's settlement position. A defendant may also be able to derail the plaintiff's infringement case

---

25. *See* Multi-Tech Systems v. Hayes Microcomputer Prods., 800 F. Supp. 825, 843 (D. Minn. 1992) (concluding that the "public has an interest in ensuring that competition is not stifled by invalid patents").

26. In *United States Jaycees v. Cedar Rapids Jaycees*, 794 F.2d 379, 383 (8th Cir. 1986), the court denied the plaintiff a preliminary injunction on the ground that a trademark licensor "has no just title to the aid of a court of equity punishing" a licensee which had disagreed with it on subsequently resolved issues of policy).

27. *See* Diamond Crystal Salt Co. v. Package Masters, Inc., 319 F. Supp. 911, 913 (D. Del. 1970) (defendant's interrogatories inquiring of any request made to plaintiff to grant a license under the patent and any negotiations with respect to a license were relevant to the affirmative defense of patent misuse). For questions often relevant to a patent misuse defense, see Robert J. Hoerner, *Patent Misuse: Portents for the 1990s*, 59 ANTITRUST L.J. 687, 712-16 (1987).

entirely by asserting a misuse defense and moving for a stay of discovery in the infringement action until the misuse question has been decided.[28]

On the other hand, if the defendant files an antitrust counterclaim, the plaintiff may successfully argue that the antitrust claims should be severed from trial on infringement and validity and tried later under Federal Rule of Civil Procedure 42(b). Although the decision is committed to the discretion of the court, typically a court will allow the infringement suit to proceed first and stay the antitrust suit.[29] It may also try the misuse claim at the same time as the antitrust claim if it deems them closely related.[30]

---

28. *See* Western Elec. Co. v. Milgo Elec. Corp., 190 U.S.P.Q. 546, 550 (S.D. Fla. 1976) (granting defendant's motion to sever validity and infringement from misuse and to limit discovery to the misuse issue).

29. *See In re* Innotron Diagnostics, 800 F.2d 1077, 1084 (Fed. Cir. 1986) (noting that the district court and the movant cited in excess of twenty-three cases from at least eight regional circuits that show the "now-standard practice" of permitting the infringement and validity issues to be tried prior to the antitrust issues); Hunter Douglas, Inc. v. Comforter Corp., 44 F. Supp. 2d 145 (N.D.N.Y. 1999) (trifurcating trial with first phase limited to infringement, validity, and all nonmisuse defenses; second phase consisting of damages; and third phase consisting of antitrust and state law counterclaims and patent misuse defense); Carlisle Corp. v. Hayes, 635 F. Supp. 962, 967-68 (S.D. Cal. 1986). *See also* ABA SECTION OF ANTITRUST LAW, THE ANTITRUST COUNTERATTACK IN PATENT INFRINGEMENT LITIGATION (1994) [hereinafter ANTITRUST COUNTERATTACK] at 147-54. *But see* Ecrix Corp. v. Exabyte Corp., 191 F.R.D. 611 (D. Col. 2000) (bifurcating issues for trial but not staying antitrust discovery).

30. *Compare* Metal Film Co. v. Melton Corp., 272 F. Supp. 64, 65 (S.D.N.Y. 1967) (concluding that "a joint trial of the patent issues with the antitrust and misuse issues would be inconvenient and probably prejudicial to the presentation and determination of the patent issues"), *with* General Tel. & Elec. Lab., Inc. v. National Video Corp., 297 F. Supp. 981, 983 (N.D. Ill. 1968) (concluding that the antitrust "matters in the counterclaims do not seem so closely related to the patent claim that they would be determined by its validity nor so distantly related that they should not be tried at the same time" and that all claims should be tried at the same time). For various approaches taken toward trying the misuse issue at the same time

Whatever the posture of the case, the courts will be reluctant to permit mere fishing expeditions. Again, the importance of asserting the misuse defense as soon as possible cannot be overemphasized.[31] A defendant with a basis for a misuse defense would be well advised to devise a cogent discovery plan calculated to get at the pertinent contract, marketing, and sales files in a targeted way as early as possible. Valuable opportunities may be lost if the court regards the defense as nothing more than an afterthought.

The increase in complexity and volume of discovery involved in pursuing a misuse defense invariably translates into delay, which may be at least a subsidiary near-term goal of the defendant. In addition to delay, the plaintiff will also have to contend with the fact that discovery on the issue of misuse may involve examination of the plaintiff's relationship with third parties. Third-party discovery and the suggestion that the plaintiff's licensing agreement may be unlawful may disrupt the plaintiff's relationships with its licensees. Even if the third party was satisfied with the licensing agreement when it was consummated, it may seize the opportunity to extract a better deal if it finds a chance to do so. On the other hand, involvement of third parties can be a two-edged sword for the defendant if the witnesses are the infringer's potential customers or suppliers. They may resent being injected into the dispute and forced to answer awkward questions at a deposition.

To the intellectual property owner, the discovery on misuse can represent nothing but burden and risk. Its strategy would be to confine discovery as much as possible. A well-prepared plaintiff anticipating a misuse defense would investigate and document the burden of the discovery likely to be sought by the defendant and then use that showing

---

as or separately from the patent issues, see authorities cited at notes 95 to 100, *infra*.

31. *See, e.g.*, Lee v. Elec. Prods. Co., 37 F.R.D. 42 (N.D. Ohio 1963) (sustaining plaintiff's objections to defendant's interrogatories concerning information that might provide facts to support defense of misuse, where misuse had not yet been pleaded); General Indus. Co. v. Birmingham Sound Reproducers, Ltd., 194 F. Supp. 693 (E.D.N.Y. 1961) (defendant in patent infringement action not entitled to submit interrogatories as to alleged patent misuse where it had not pleaded misuse defense).

to demonstrate that discovery should be limited in an appropriate manner or perhaps deferred until development of the infringement case has taken place.

In some circumstances, however, the intellectual property owner might itself seek early determination of the misuse question by urging early scheduling of a motion or trial on the misuse issue in scheduling orders. This strategy might limit the time available for discovery on the misuse issue and perhaps require that much of it be conducted while the defendant is preoccupied with other matters. The plaintiff adopting this strategy would need to be sure, however, that it left itself adequate time to prepare a sound, well-supported motion. Otherwise, the motion could all too easily be denied, perhaps in a way likely to prejudice later assertion, and encouraging, rather than eliminating, further discovery on this issue. It is even possible that the defendant could successfully cross-move to dismiss the case on misuse grounds if a plaintiff's motion were hurriedly made and poorly supported.

D. Summary Judgment

1. Summary Judgment for the Defendant Dismissing Claims on Misuse Grounds

All of which brings us to the possibility of a summary judgment motion. The misuse doctrine actually owes its origin to a decision involving a summary judgment, *Morton Salt Co. v. G.S. Suppiger Co.*[32] In that case, the defendant moved for summary judgment shortly after the filing of a patent infringement action, relying on the existence of a standard contract by which the patentee tied purchase of salt to lease of patented salt machines.[33] The defendant was not party to such a contract, but a competitor of the patent owner that manufactured allegedly infringing salt machines.[34] Because the Supreme Court ruled that the existence of the tie was enough to constitute patent misuse,[35] it

---

32.   314 U.S. 488 (1942).
33.   *See id.* at 491.
34.   *See id.*
35.   *See id.* at 493.

granted summary judgment based solely on proof of the contract.[36] Similar results were reached in cases involving other possible forms of misuse, such as price-fixing agreements or postsale restrictions considered per se illegal under the antitrust laws.[37] In all these circumstances, a prompt summary judgment motion was an attractive option for the defendant because little, if anything, needed to be proved beyond the existence of the agreement itself.

Under the summary judgment standards of Federal Rule of Civil Procedure 56, *Matsushita*,[38] *Liberty Lobby*,[39] and *Celotex*,[40] the moving party must show that there is no genuine issue as to any material fact and that the moving party is entitled to judgment as a matter of law. Once the moving party has met the requirements of Rule 56(c), the adverse party "may not rest upon the mere allegations or denials of the adverse party's pleading, but . . . must set forth specific facts showing that there is a genuine issue for trial."[41]

Unfortunately for infringement defendants, much has changed since the days of *Morton Salt*.[42] Particularly in patent cases, the burden of making a summary judgment motion, even under the summary judgment standards of *Matsushita*, *Liberty Lobby*, and *Celotex*, has been substantially increased because of changes in the Patent Act and antitrust jurisprudence.

---

36. *See id.* at 494. At the time, prior to the recent amendments to 35 U.S.C. § 271(d), proof of market power or injury to the defendant comparable to that in an antitrust case was unnecessary.

37. *See, e.g.*, Robintech, Inc. v. Chemdus Wavin, Ltd., 450 F. Supp. 817, 822 (D.D.C. 1978) (patentee's summary judgment motion to strike patent misuse defense denied where patent license restricted export of product created by licensed process), *aff'd*, 628 F.2d 142 (D.C. Cir. 1980); American Indus. Fastener Corp. v. Flushing Enter., Inc., 362 F. Supp. 32, 39 (N.D. Ohio 1973) (summary judgment of unenforceability through misuse granted for infringer where patentee imposed territorial restraints in patent licenses).

38. Matsushita Elec. Indus. Co. v. Zenith Radio Corp., 475 U.S. 574 (1986).

39. Anderson v. Liberty Lobby, 477 U.S. 242 (1986).

40. Celotex Corp. v. Catrett, 477 U.S. 317 (1986).

41. FED. R. CIV. P. 56(e).

42. 314 U.S. 488.

a.   Patent Misuse and Tie-Ins

The treatment of tie-ins as misuse in patent cases has been affected by the legislation of 1952 and 1988. First, the 1952 amendments to the Patent Act added Section 271(d) to Title 35. Subsections (1) through (3) of Section 271(d) state that nonstaples forming a material part of an invention can be tied to a license to practice the invention without constituting misuse.[43] This statute has complicated proof of misuse arising from tying in patent cases in many circumstances. A defendant making a summary judgment motion based on misuse may now have to establish that there is no genuine factual issue that an item is a staple with substantial, noninfringing uses or that it is not a material part of an invention. In addition to the changes created by statute, case law developed thereafter requires a party asserting misuse to establish coercion,[44] a requirement again involving a showing beyond the simple existence of a contract.

Despite these complications, summary judgment has been granted to defendants in cases involving Section 271, most notably in the Federal Circuit's *Senza-Gel* decision.[45] In that decision, the Court of Appeals for the Federal Circuit sustained a summary judgment of misuse based on deposition testimony submitted after trial that a product had several uses and had never been licensed apart from the tie.[46]

A defendant's burdens in establishing misuse through tying in a patent case, regardless of whether staples or nonstaples are involved, have been compounded since *Senza-Gel* by the addition of subsections (4) and (5) to Section 271(d) in 1988. These subsections require proof, before misuse from tying can be found, that a patent or patented product actually confers market power "in view of the circumstances." While the precise degree of market power required is uncertain, the manifest

---

43.   *See* Dawson Chem. Co. v. Rohm & Haas Co., 448 U.S. 176 (1980).
44.   *See* Zenith Radio Corp. v. Hazeltine Research, Inc., 395 U.S. 100 (1969).
45.   Senza-Gel Corp. v. Seiffhart, 803 F.2d 661 (Fed. Cir. 1986).
46.   *See id.* at 668-69. At the same time, the Federal Circuit, applying Ninth Circuit law, agreed that summary judgment should be denied on antitrust tying claims. According to the court, questions existed whether the issues of separate market demand existed for the alleged tying and tied products and whether the patent holder had market power over the tying product. *Id.* at 669.

intent of the section is to prevent tying from being found without some proof of market power in a relevant market similar to that in an antitrust case. Thus, even where the staple/nonstaple dichotomy of the first three subsections of Section 271(d) does not apply, a defendant wishing to prevail on its misuse defense now must demonstrate the absence of a genuine issue of fact on the market power question as well.[47]

b. Patent Misuse and Nonprice, Postsale Restrictions

Forms of patent misuse other than tying are not directly covered by Section 271(d). The change in antitrust jurisprudence regarding non-price postsale restrictions and the attitude of the Federal Circuit toward patent misuse and postsale restrictions have, however, substantially affected summary judgment practice involving this type of conduct.

At one time, price and nonprice postsale restrictions were considered per se illegal as an antitrust matter under *United States v. Arnold, Schwinn & Co.*[48] Misuse based on the existence of such restrictions in a patent license could therefore be found, whether condemned because they constituted or closely resembled conduct in violation of the antitrust laws or because they were thought to be improper attempts to extend the scope of patent protection after the exhaustion of patent rights.[49]

---

47. *See In re* Recombinant DNA Tech. Patent & Contract Litig., 850 F. Supp. 769, 777 (S.D. Ind. 1994). Some legislation indicates that in the minds of some legislators the "in view of the circumstances" language has a broader significance and might permit economically sound business reasons to defeat a misuse defense. *House and Senate Action on Patent Misuse in PTO Authorization Bill (HR 4972), reprinted in* 36 Pat. Trademark & Copyright J. (BNA) 774, 776 (1988). *See also* Texas Instruments Inc. v. Hyundai Elecs. Indus. Co., 49 F. Supp. 2d 893, 907-13 (E.D. Tex. 1999). If this view is adopted, the defendant's burden on a summary judgment motion would be heightened still further. The defendant might have to submit evidence showing not only the existence of market power in a relevant market but also that the patentee had no plausible, procompetitive business justifications for the tie.
48. United States v. Arnold, Schwinn & Co., 388 U.S. 365 (1967).
49. *See* American Indus. Fastener Corp. v. Flushing Enterprises, Inc., 362 F. Supp. 32 (N.D. Ohio 1973); Ansul Co. v. Uniroyal, Inc., 306 F. Supp. 541 (S.D.N.Y. 1969), *rev'd in part on other grounds*, 448 F.2d 872 (2d Cir. 1971).

The Supreme Court's decision in *Continental T.V. v. GTE Sylvania*[50] reversed *Schwinn* and established that nonprice vertical restraints are generally evaluated under the rule of reason for antitrust purposes. The possible limiting effect of such restraints on *intrabrand* competition is considered of importance only if *interbrand* competition is not effective in maintaining competitive pressure on prices. Thus, under the antitrust laws, market power and business reasons for territorial or customer restrictions must be explored before they can be condemned as illegal.

To the extent patent misuse law embodies only competitive considerations, antitrust standards become extremely relevant to, if not dispositive of, the showing that a defendant asserting a misuse defense must make.[51] Unless conduct constituting a per se violation of the antitrust laws is involved, summary judgment becomes an extremely difficult hurdle for a defendant to surmount because of the need to establish market power and lack of justification.

If, on the other hand, patent misuse law is thought to be derived primarily from a concern that a patentee may attempt to extend through licenses the patent protection it could not claim directly from the scope of the patent, a stricter misuse rule would be possible. Under such a rule, market power might be largely irrelevant. Summary judgment would be correspondingly much easier for a defendant, requiring proof of little, if anything, beyond an agreement containing the restrictions. This type of misuse rule would be consistent with the original patent misuse case, *Morton Salt*.

In practice, the patent misuse rules on postsale restrictions have been heavily influenced by trends in antitrust jurisprudence, although misuse may exist in circumstances where an antitrust violation would not be found to exist.[52] Some courts, including the Seventh Circuit, speaking

---

50.   Continental T.V., Inc. v. GTE Sylvania, Inc., 433 U.S. 36 (1977).
51.   *See* USM Corp. v. SPS Techs., Inc., 694 F.2d 505, 512 (7th Cir. 1982) (Posner, J.).
52.   *Compare* Robintech, Inc. v. Chemidus Wavin, Ltd., 628 F.2d 142 (D.C. Cir. 1980), *with* United States v. Studiengesellschaft Kohle, m.b.H., 670 F.2d 1122 (D.C. Cir. 1981). *See* C.R. Bard, Inc. v. M3 Systems, Inc., 157 F.3d 1340, 1372 (Fed. Cir. 1998) (citing Zenith Radio Corp. v. Hazeltine

through the influential Judge Posner, and the Federal Circuit, have suggested that the standards of misuse should be conflated with antitrust standards, so that proof of market power, if not per se conduct, would often be a critical element.[53] This tendency has been accelerated by the Federal Circuit's decision in *Mallinckrodt, Inc. v. Medipart, Inc.* in which the Federal Circuit held that a sale of a patented item may be conditioned on postsale restrictions, and that such restrictions will not be deemed misuse unless beyond the scope of the patent and unreasonable in their competitive impact.[54]

The Federal Circuit has reiterated these standards in three later decisions.[55] The Federal Circuit view is particularly significant because the Federal Circuit has exclusive jurisdiction over appeals of all patent infringement actions—including suits for violations of the postsale restrictions now made actionable as infringements. Thus, a defendant challenging a postsale, nonprice restriction as patent misuse should be prepared to demonstrate the absence of a genuine issue of material fact on issues of anticompetitive impact and lack of justification, a showing broadly similar to, if less exacting than, that in an antitrust case. Summary judgment has, nonetheless, been granted to at least one defendant under these standards in a case involving extension of patent rights after the first sale of the patented article.[56]

c. Other Forms of Patent Misuse

The showing required for every form of patent misuse is not necessarily affected directly by 35 U.S.C. § 271(d), changes in the

---

Research, Inc., 395 U.S. 100 (1969)); PSC Inc. v. Symbol Techs. Inc., 26 F. Supp. 2d 505, 511 (W.D.N.Y. 1998).
53. *See* AKZO N.V. v. International Trade Comm., 808 F.2d 1471 (Fed. Cir. 1986); Windsurfing Int'l, Inc. v. AMF Inc., 782 F.2d 995 (Fed. Cir. 1986); *USM Corp.*, 694 F.2d 505.
54. *See* Mallinckrodt, Inc. v. Medipart, Inc., 976 F.2d 700 (Fed. Cir. 1992).
55. *See* C.R. Bard, Inc. v. M3 Sys., Inc., 157 F.3d 1340 (Fed. Cir. 1998); Virginia Panel Corp. v. MAC Panel Co., 133 F.3d 860 (Fed. Cir. 1997); B. Braun Med., Inc. v. Abbott Lab., 124 F.3d 1419, 1426-27 (Fed. Cir. 1997).
56. *See PSC Inc.*, 26 F. Supp. 2d 505.

antitrust laws, or *Mallinckrodt*. For example, it is likely that minimum postsale price restrictions—per se illegal under the antitrust laws—will continue to be a species of per se misuse.[57] Proof of an agreement fixing resale price should be all that is necessary for a defendant to obtain summary judgment on misuse grounds.

Postexpiration royalties similarly may continue to constitute a species of per se misuse not requiring proof of market power or other circumstances and therefore an attractive candidate for summary judgment.[58] Not all courts hold that these provisions are misuse, however. Many simply refuse to enforce the contractual provision but not the patent.[59]

Total sales royalties fall in something of a middle ground. While package licensing of patents is treated as tying by Section 271(d)(5) (because the conditioning of one patent on the licensing of another is specifically addressed in the statute), demanding a total sales royalty regardless of which patents, if any, are actually used is not. A defendant

---

57. *See Mallinckrodt*, 976 F.2d at 704.
58. *See Virginia Panel Corp.*, 133 F.3d 860; Sanford Redmond, Inc. v. Mid-Am. Dairymen, Inc., 29 U.S.P.Q.2d 1222 (S.D.N.Y. 1992), *aff'd without op.*, 993 F.2d 1534 (2d Cir. 1993).
59. *See* Brulotte v. Thys Co. 379 U.S. 29 (1964). *Brulotte* arose after the patent had expired and simply refused to enforce the postexpiration payment provisions. It did not necessarily hold that a misuse rendering the patent unenforceable was involved, though this seems at least one logical corollary from the logic of unjustified extension of the patent. *See also* Meehan v. PPG Indus., Inc., 802 F.2d 881 (7th Cir. 1986), *cert. denied*, 479 U.S. 1091 (1987) (refusing to enforce postexpiration royalties; no misuse issue raised). As discussed in Chapter II dealing with specific practices, courts have split on whether this conduct is a misuse rendering the patent unenforceable. Similarly, several cases have held no contest clauses to be unenforceable but not to constitute misuse rendering the patent unenforceable. *See* Panther Pumps & Equip. Co., Inc. v. Hydrocraft, Inc., 468 F.2d 225, 232 (7th Cir. 1972) (fact that patent holder granted license which included no-contest clause did not constitute misuse of patent which foreclosed recovery of damages from unlicensed infringer); Robintech, Inc. v. Chemidus Wavin, Ltd., 450 F. Supp. 817, 821 (D.D.C. 1978); Congoleum Indus., Inc. v. Armstrong Com. Co., 366 F. Supp. 220, 233 (E.D. Pa. 1973).

could not, however, simply submit evidence of the existence of such an arrangement; under *Zenith Radio Corp. v. Hazeltine*,[60] it must prove coercion and, therefore, on a summary judgment motion, establish the absence of any genuine issue that coercion occurred.

Finally, in some courts, introducing proof of a tie-out—an agreement not to deal in goods or services competitive with those of the licensor— might suffice to establish misuse without any necessity of proving market power.[61] Ultimately, however, justification evidence, as well as some proof of market power, may be considered relevant, if not indispensable, by the Federal Circuit. Already two district courts have held that a tie-out is sufficiently analogous to a tie-in to require the same market power showing mandated by Section 271(d),[62] even though the wording of the statute does not literally embrace this conduct.

d. Copyright Misuse

In most circuits, misuse has now been acknowledged as a possible defense to a copyright infringement suit, though in relatively few has it been successful on a motion for summary judgment. Courts may insist on proof similar to that of antitrust proof,[63] and a showing of market power may, if anything, be even more difficult when a copyright is involved than when a patent is at issue, since a copyright protects only substantial similarity in expression, not a class of products or processes

---

60. Zenith Radio Corp. v. Hazeltine Research, Inc., 395 U.S. 100 (1969). *See also* Engel Indus., Inc. v. Lockformer Co., 96 F.3d 1398 (Fed. Cir. 1996); A.C. Aukerman Co. v. R.L. Chaides Constr. Co., 29 U.S.P.Q.2d 1054, 1059-60 (N.D. Cal. 1993).
61. *See, e.g.*, Compton v. Metal Prods., Inc., 453 F.2d 38 (4th Cir. 1971); Berlenbach v. Anderson & Thompson Ski Co., 329 F.2d 782 (9th Cir. 1964); Stewart v. Motrim, Inc., 192 U.S.P.Q. 410 (S.D. Ohio 1975).
62. *See* Texas Instruments Inc. v. Hyundai Elecs. Indus. Co., 49 F. Supp. 2d 893 (E.D. Tex. 1999); *In re* Recombinant DNA Tech. Patent & Contract Litig., 30 U.S.P.Q.2d 1881, 1898 (S.D. Ind. 1993).
63. *See* Saturday Evening Post Co. v. Rumbleseat Press, Inc., 816 F.2d 1191 (7th Cir. 1987); Nihon Keizai Shimbon, Inc. v. Comline Business Data, Inc., 98 Civ. 641 DLC, 1998 U.S. Dist. LEXIS 6806 (S.D.N.Y. Apr. 14, 1998).

as a patent does.[64] One court has applied the staple/nonstaple dichotomy of Section 271(d) by analogy to deny a summary judgment motion.[65] Under the approach in the Fourth Circuit's *Lasercomb* case,[66] however, copyright misuse may be found from the mere existence of any agreement deemed to control "idea" rather than "expression." The Fourth Circuit determined that an offending clause constituted misuse based solely on its finding that the clause was an attempt to suppress the creation of lawful independent computer programs, without considering any showing of market power, coercion, or actual anticompetitive effect.[67] Although *Lasercomb* did not involve a summary judgment motion, introduction of the offending contract, together with a demonstration of why and how it goes beyond protecting expression, should suffice to establish the copyright misuse defense as a matter of law.

In *LucasArts Entertainment Co. v. Humongous Entertainment Co.*,[68] the court denied the defendant's motion for summary judgment on a copyright misuse claim and instead granted the plaintiff's cross-motion for summary judgment dismissing the claim, finding no illegal extension of the copyright on undisputed facts. Two later cases from other circuits, however, have applied *Lasercomb* to dismiss copyright infringement claims at the pleading or summary judgment stage based on contracts containing broad noncompete provisions.[69]

---

64. *See Saturday Evening Post*, 816 F.2d 1191.
65. *See* Atari Games Corp. v. Nintendo of Am., Inc., 975 F. 2d 832 (Fed. Cir. 1992) (plaintiff who asserted misuse as a ground for a declaratory judgment that certain conduct was illegal and unenforceable sought, but was denied, partial summary judgment and preliminary injunctive relief on the misuse claim).
66. Lasercomb Am., Inc. v. Reynolds, 911 F.2d 970 (4th Cir. 1990).
67. *See id.* at 979. *See also* PRC Realty Sys., Inc. v. National Ass'n of Realtors, 1992 Copyright L. Dec. (CCH) ¶ 26,961, 1992 U.S. App. LEXIS 18017 (4th Cir. 1992) (finding misuse from best efforts clause deemed to have practical effect of a tie-out).
68. 815 F. Supp. 332 (N.D. Cal. 1993).
69. *See* Practice Management Info. Corp. v. AMA, 121 F.3d 516, 520-21 (9th Cir. 1997) (directing entry of summary judgment for defendant); Tamburo

2. Partial Summary Judgment for the Plaintiff Dismissing Misuse Defenses

Summary judgment, of course, is not solely the province of defendants. As *LucasArts* suggests, plaintiffs, too, could be expected to take advantage of the Supreme Court's trilogy of *Celotex, Liberty Lobby,* and *Matsushita* in seeking to dismiss misuse defenses at a relatively early stage of the proceedings.[70] They would have many incentives to do so, in terms of reduced discovery, simplification of issues, and reduction of risk at trial.

In patent cases involving tie-ins, at least, the 1988 amendments to Section 271(d) should make such motions by the plaintiff a possibility where market share is small, although the Supreme Court's *Kodak* case[71] may presage a fact-intensive approach to the market share question. In addition, even if market power exists, a patent owner in a tie-in case might be able to establish on a summary judgment motion that a tied item is a nonstaple.[72]

Summary judgment might also now be a possibility for the patent owner with an unequivocally small market share in some non-tie-in cases governed by *Mallinckrodt.*[73] Where the equivalent of proof of an antitrust violation is required, a plaintiff seeking to dismiss a misuse defense in an infringement suit would need to make a showing roughly comparable to that of a defendant seeking summary judgment in an

---

v. Calvin, No. 94 C5206, 1995 WL 121539, at *6-7 (N.D. Ill. Mar. 15, 1995) (granting motions to dismiss copyright claims).

70. For a case that recently granted summary judgment to a plaintiff dismissing a patent misuse claim, see *Zeneca Ltd. v. Pharmachemie B.V.,* 37 F. Supp. 2d 85 (D. Mass. 1999). Two other recent cases have denied trademark misuse defenses, one on a motion to dismiss, the other on a summary judgment motion. *See* Juno Online Servs., L.P. v. Juno Lighting, Inc., 979 F. Supp. 684 (N.D. Ill. 1997) (motion to dismiss); Northwestern Corp. v. Gabriel Mfg. Co., 48 U.S.P.Q.2d 1902 (N.D. Ill. 1998) (motion for summary judgment).

71. Eastman Kodak Co. v. Image Tech. Servs., Inc., 504 U.S. 451 (1992) (denying summary judgment to a defendant on tying antitrust claims).

72. *See* Hodosh v. Block Drug Co., Inc., 833 F.2d 1575 (Fed. Cir. 1987).

73. 976 F.2d 700 (Fed. Cir. 1992).

antitrust case.[74] If a practice has been long discontinued, a patent owner might also seek to obtain summary judgment on the theory that the misuse has been purged.[75]

In a copyright case such as *Lasercomb*, summary judgment might also be a possibility since the question whether a provision protects more than what is entitled to copyright protection would seem primarily a matter of contractual interpretation.[76] In courts that reject a per se approach to copyright misuse, proof of lack of market power comparable to that necessary to dismiss an antitrust case should also defeat a claim of misuse as a matter of law.[77]

Whether courts will be receptive to such motions by patent or copyright owners is not clear. Unlike a summary judgment dismissing an antitrust case, a motion for partial summary judgment dismissing a misuse claim does not dispose of an entire case but only a defense. Courts might therefore be somewhat more inclined to postpone decision until the verge of trial or perhaps until after the infringement case has come in at trial. Indeed, if the alleged patent misuse seems unrelated to the issues of patent validity and infringement and likely to add some

---

74.   *See* Lund Indus., Inc. v. Westin, Inc., 764 F. Supp. 1342, 1344-45 (D. Minn. 1990).

75.   See the discussion of purge in Chapter I.

76.   *See, e.g.,* LucasArts Entertainment Co. v. Humongous Entertainment Co., 815 F. Supp. 332 (N.D. Cal. 1993); Microsoft Corp. v. BEC Computer Co., 818 F. Supp. 1313, 1316-17 (C.D. Cal. 1992) (distinguishing contract at issue from the contract at issue in *Lasercomb*), *clarified*, No. CV 92-2427 KN 1992, U.S. Dist. LEXIS 20870 (C.D. Cal. Nov. 5, 1992); Budish v. Gordon, 784 F. Supp. 1320, 1336-37 (N.D. Ohio 1992) (contract "does not rise to the level of misuse that is contemplated by the cases which recognize the defense").

77.   *See* Bellsouth Adver. & Publ'g Corp. v. Donnelly Info. Publ'g, Inc., 933 F.2d 952, 960-61 (11th Cir. 1991), *vacated on reh'g, en banc*, 977 F.2d 1435 (11th Cir. 1992), *rev'd on other grounds*, 999 F.2d 1436 (11th Cir. 1993). *See also In re* Independent Serv. Orgs. Antitrust Litig., 964 F. Supp. 1479 (D. Kan. 1997); Northwestern Corp. v. Gabriel Mfg., Inc., No. 95 C 2004, 1996 WL 732519 (N.D. Ill. Dec. 18, 1996) (striking antitrust misuse defense in trademark case for failure to plead markets and other elements of antitrust claim).

degree of complication, the issue might even be bifurcated, to be decided only if a case of infringement has been established.[78]

E. Trial and Misuse

1. Evidentiary Issues

At trial itself, misuse is an affirmative defense on which the defendant has the burden of proof.[79] When misuse is tried at the same time as the infringement case, evidence with respect to the misuse defense normally would be presented by the defendant at the close of the plaintiff's affirmative case. Evidence of justification, lack of market power or illegal conduct, and purge would then be offered on rebuttal, although the patent owner might wish to anticipate some of these themes in its case-in-chief. The plaintiff would be wise to address the defense fully in its pretrial briefs and should probably say something about it, though perhaps only briefly, in the opening statement.

When the issues are tried together, a tension could develop between proof pertinent to the case-in-chief and proof pertinent to misuse. The tension exists because the plaintiff (the intellectual property owner) would ordinarily seek to adduce evidence of the commercial importance and breadth of the claims of a patent or copyright in order to enhance its damages, and also, in many cases, to overcome an obviousness

---

78. This result often, though not invariably, occurs when the misuse defense is accompanied by a substantial antitrust claim involving essentially the same conduct. *See* text and authorities cited at 30, *supra;* Virginia Panel Corp. v. MAC Panel Co., 133 F.3d 860 (Fed. Cir. 1997). *See also* Texas Instruments Inc. v. Hyundai Elecs. Indus. Co., 49 F. Supp. 2d 893 (E.D. Tex. 1999) (bifurcating issue when defense asserted six days before trial).

79. *See* Congoleum Indus., Inc. v. Armstrong Cork Co., 366 F. Supp. 220 (E.D. Pa. 1973) (burden of establishing misuse defense rests upon party asserting it), *aff'd*, 510 F.2d 334 (3d Cir. 1975); Ransburg Electro-Coating Corp. v. Nordson Corp., 293 F. Supp. 448 (N.D. Ill. 1968); Holley v. Outboard Marine Corp., 241 F. Supp. 657 (N.D. Ill. 1964), *aff'd*, 345 F.2d 351 (7th Cir. 1965).

defense.[80]   Witnesses testifying for the plaintiff on the scope and importance of the patent might be asked questions on cross-examination designed to make them appear either equivocal about their direct testimony or to lead them to emphasize that the patent confers substantial market power or allows the patent owner to insist on coercive terms.   In this way the defendant could seek to have the plaintiff's witnesses paint the plaintiff into something of a corner on the factual predicates of the misuse defense, which would then be echoed and elaborated by the defendant's own witnesses.[81]

2.   Who Should Decide—Judge or Jury?

Whether patent misuse is an issue for a jury to decide or for the court to decide is an open issue.[82]   In one recent case, the issues of patent

---

80.   Proof of commercial success and satisfaction of a long-felt need are highly relevant factors under the Supreme Court's *Graham v. John Deere & Co.* decision, 383 U.S. 1 (1966), and subsequent Federal Circuit decisions.

81.   In one case, a defendant attempted to amend its answer to include a claim that the manner in which the plaintiff calculated its infringement damages itself constituted misuse. Intra-Video, Inc. v. Hughes Electronics Corp., 51 U.S.P.Q.2d 1383 (S.D.N.Y. 1999). The court rejected this attempt, holding that only a business transaction can constitute misuse; a damages theory in litigation, by contrast, cannot constitute misuse. *Id.* at 1384.

82.   Cases in which the court decided the patent misuse issue include: Glaverbel Societe Anonyme v. Northlake Mktg. & Supply, Inc., 45 F.3d 1550 (Fed. Cir. 1995) (trial before magistrate); Senza-Gel Corp. v. Seiffhart, 803 F.2d 661 (Fed. Cir. 1986); DuBuit v. Harwell, 540 F.2d 690 (4th Cir. 1976); Glen Mfg. v. Perfect Fit Indus. Inc., 420 F.2d 319 (2d Cir. 1970); Inland Steel Products Co. v. MPH Mfg. Corp., 25 F.R.D. 238 (N.D. Ill. 1959); Texas Instruments Inc. v. Hyundai Elecs. Indus. Co., 49 F. Supp. 2d 893 (E.D. Tex. 1999); Duplan Corp. v. Deering Milliken, Inc., 444 F. Supp. 648 (D.S.C. 1977), *aff'd in part, rev'd in part*, 594 F.2d 979 (4th Cir. 1979). Cases in which a jury decided the issue of patent misuse include: C.R. Bard, Inc. v. M3 Sys., Inc., 157 F.3d 1340 (Fed. Cir. 1998); Virginia Panel Corp. v. MAC Panel Co., 133 F.3d 860 (Fed. Cir. 1997); B. Braun Med. Inc. v. Abbott Lab., 124 F.3d 1419 (Fed. Cir. 1997); Randomex, Inc. v. Scopus Corp., 849 F.2d 585 (Fed. Cir.

misuse and equitable estoppel were submitted to the jury over plaintiff's objection.[83] The trial court reasoned that, as both issues had been submitted to juries in cases reviewed by the Federal Circuit, and as the determination of both issues turned on resolution of factual disputes, the submission of the issues to the jury was an appropriate exercise of the court's discretion under Federal Rule of Civil Procedure 39(b).[84] The Federal Circuit reversed the finding of misuse on the merits but refrained from deciding whether submitting the issue to the jury had been correct.[85] A recent Fifth Circuit decision treated copyright misuse as a jury question.[86]

Treatment of misuse as a jury question is inconsistent with the equitable nature of patent misuse and may also conflict with the Supreme Court's recent determination that patent claim interpretation is an issue for the court alone to decide.[87] The patent misuse doctrine originated as a form of unclean hands defense to a patentee's efforts to extend the patent beyond the scope of the patent claims and has always been considered equitable in nature.[88] Because the doctrine is an

---

1988); Solvex v. Freedman, 459 F. Supp. 440 (W.D. Va. 1977). In the first three of these cases, however, the jury verdict of misuse was reversed by the Federal Circuit. In *Arcade, Inc. v. Minnesota Mining and Mfg. Co.*, 24 U.S.P.Q.2d 1578 (E.D. Tenn. 1991), *aff'd*, Nos. 91-1458, 91-1459, 1993 U.S. App. LEXIS 14976, the court employed an advisory jury before deciding the issue itself.

83. *See* B. Braun Med. Inc. v. Abbott Lab., 892 F. Supp. 112, 113 (E.D. Pa. 1995), *rev'd on other grounds*, 124 F.3d 1419 (Fed. Cir. 1997).

84. *See id.* at 114-15.

85. *See* B. Braun Med., Inc. v. Abbott Lab., 124 F.3d 1419, 1423 (Fed. Cir. 1997).

86. *See* Alcatel USA Inc. v. DGI Techs. Inc., 166 F.3d 772 (5th Cir. 1999).

87. *See* Markman v. Westview Instruments, Inc., 517 U.S. 370 (1996). In addition to holding that issues of patent misuse and equitable estoppel were properly submitted to the jury, the *B. Braun* district court had also held that patent claim interpretation was a proper issue for the jury to decide. *See* B. Braun Med. Inc. v. Abbott Lab., 892 F. Supp. 112, 113-14 (E.D. Pa. 1995). This holding is not good law after *Markman*.

88. *See* United States Gypsum Co. v. National Gypsum Co., 352 U.S. 457, 465 (1957); Morton Salt Co. v. G.S. Suppiger Co., 314 U.S. 488, 491-92

equitable one, there would seem to be no constitutional right to have a jury decide the misuse issue absent consent of the parties or overlap with other issues triable of right by the jury.

The Supreme Court has reaffirmed its use of a "historical test" for determining whether the Seventh Amendment preserves a right to a jury trial on a particular issue.[89] First, the Court asked

> whether we are dealing with a cause of action that either was tried at law at the time of the Founding or is at least analogous to one that was .... If the action in question belongs in the law category, we then ask whether the particular trial decision must fall to the jury in order to preserve the substance of the common-law right as it existed in 1791.[90]

If the historical test did not provide an answer, the Court would look to "existing precedent and consider the relative interpretive skills of judges and juries and the statutory policies that ought to be furthered by the allocation."[91]

An application of this test favors having judges, rather than juries, decide patent misuse issues. Patent misuse did not exist at the time of the Founding, and it is not analogous to any action that was tried at law at that time. It was created by the courts as a purely equitable defense, based on unclean hands. Judges are more likely to be adept at applying policies behind the misuse doctrine to particular facts than are juries, and the policy of misuse is furthered by the relative consistency of application by judges rather than juries.

Additional ground for believing that patent misuse should be tried to the court absent overlap with other issues is found in the treatment of the related issues of patent misuse purge and inequitable conduct. A district court has held that the issue of purge is an equitable issue separate from infringement that could be tried separately to the court and prior to the

---

(1942); C.R. Bard, Inc. v. M3 Sys. Inc., 157 F.3d 1340, 1372 (Fed. Cir. 1998); Atari Games Corp. v. Nintendo of Am. Inc., 975 F.2d 832 (Fed. Cir. 1992); James B. Kobak, Jr., *The New Patent Misuse Law*, 71 J. PAT. [& TRADEMARK] OFF. SOC'Y 859, 861 (Nov. 1989).

89.   *Markman*, 517 U.S. at 376.
90.   *Id.*
91.   *Id.* at 384.

jury trial on infringement.[92] The court determined that the factual issues were not so common that this procedure would frustrate the patent owner's jury trial right. The Federal Circuit and lower courts have also ruled in several cases that there is no right to a jury trial on inequitable conduct in proceedings before the Patent Office—another equitable defense rendering a patent unenforceable[93]—except in cases of factual overlap between the misuse issue and issues triable by the jury in the patent case.

Therefore, while the law is unclear, it seems likely that, absent consent or overlap with issues such as an antitrust counterclaim triable to a jury, misuse should be considered an issue for the court rather than the jury. Indeed, a Federal Circuit panel, although reviewing a jury determination in the case before it, recently spoke of misuse as "an equitable issue normally reserved for the court."[94]

3. Bifurcation of Infringement and Misuse Claims

Jury trial questions affect the dynamics of proof considerably. Basically, where no antitrust or similar issue is involved, there are now five procedural choices as to how and when the misuse issue should be tried:

1. try everything to the jury by consent under Federal Rule of Civil Procedure 39(c);
2. try misuse to the jury with the infringement case, but with the judge, not the jury, making the findings of fact on the misuse issues;[95]

---

92. *See In re* Yarn Processing Patent Validity Litig., 472 F. Supp. 180 (S.D. Fla. 1979).
93. *See* Paragon Podiatry Lab., Inc. v. KLM Lab., Inc., 984 F.2d 1182, 1190 (Fed. Cir. 1993); Gardco Mfg., Inc. v. Herst Lighting Co., 820 F.2d 1209, 1211-13 (Fed. Cir. 1987); Burroughs Wellcome Co. v. Barr Lab. Inc., 828 F. Supp. 1200 (E.D.N.C. 1993); Gentex Corp. v. Donnelly Corp., 26 U.S.P.Q.2d 1558 (W.D. Mich. 1993).
94. Virginia Panel Corp. v. MAC Panel Co., 133 F.3d 860 (Fed. Cir. 1997).
95. This was the procedure adopted by the district court in *Burroughs Wellcome*, 828 F. Supp. 1200.

3. try the issues to the jury together, using the jury as an advisory jury on the misuse issues;[96]

4. try the misuse issue to the court prior to the infringement jury trial on the theory that there is little, if any, factual overlap between issues that would implicate jury trial rights and the outcome may be dispositive;[97] or

5. try the misuse defense to the court after the jury trial, if necessary.[98]

The option that will be chosen depends on the type and complexity of the misuse claim and its relation to the factual issues in the infringement claim. If there should be substantial factual overlap, the intellectual property owner will argue that the jury trial must at least proceed first and determine the factual issues, lest its right to have the jury determine those issues be prejudiced.[99] A misuse claim based on the same facts as an antitrust claim on which a jury trial is sought may have to be tried to the jury simultaneously with the antitrust claim.[100]

---

96. This was the procedure adopted by the district courts in *Gentex Corp.*, 26 U.S.P.Q.2d 1558, and *Arcade, Inc. v. Minnesota Mining and Mfg. Co.*, 24 U.S.P.Q.2d 1578 (E.D. Pa. 1995).

97. *See In re* Yarn Processing Validity Litig., 472 F. Supp. 180 (trying the issue of purge before infringement).

98. This was the procedure adopted by the district court in *Texas Instruments* when the defense was asserted for the first time six days before trial. *See* Texas Instruments, Inc. v. Hyundai Elecs. Indus. Co., 49 F. Supp. 2d 893 (E.D. Tex. 1999)

99. *See* Cabinet Vision v. Cabnetware, 129 F.3d 595 (Fed. Cir. 1997).

100. This was the procedure adopted in *Virginia Panel Corp. v. MAC Panel Co.*, 133 F.3d 860 (Fed. Cir. 1997), where antitrust and misuse issues were bifurcated from infringement issues and tried separately after the patent case. All the patent, antitrust, and misuse issues were apparently tried together in *C.R. Bard, Inc. v. M3 Sys., Inc.*, 157 F.3d 1340 (Fed. Cir. 1998). In *Alcatel USA Inc. v. DGI Techs. Inc.*, 166 F.3d 772 (5th Cir. 1999), copyright and trade secret injunctive and damages claims as well as antitrust and misuse claims were also all apparently tried to the jury together. The Fifth Circuit regarded the jury's finding of misuse as binding as long as permissible under the evidence. In *Hunter Douglas,*

A relatively simple extension of monopoly-type of misuse issue, such as a total sales royalty or a tie-out, should stand a much better chance of being tried first than an antitrust-type violation or a misuse tying claim related to a substantial antitrust claim. In a suit on a license where the defendant tries to prove that it was coerced into agreeing to provisions claimed to be misuse, the misuse claim might have to be tried either at the same time or after the contract claim to ensure preservation of the jury trial right. Counsel must carefully weigh the opportunities in deciding what claims to plead and be alert not to waive inadvertently any procedural advantages that may be available.

F. Settlement

Settlement of a case with a substantial misuse issue may also require careful consideration and weighing of options. Ideally, from the defendant's standpoint, the intellectual property owner will drop the offending provision in the defendant's license (if that is the nature of the misuse) or, if the defendant is not directly affected by the provision, the intellectual property owner will dismiss the case with prejudice or execute a covenant not to sue and release.

Potential issues can arise in more complicated settlements. The defendant, for example, may drop its misuse attack in exchange for a license which allows it to practice the perhaps unenforceable patent or copyright while precluding other competitors, or the parties may wish to agree to license terms containing price, territorial, or customer restrictions.

Both parties should keep in mind, however, that depending on the circumstances, an exclusionary license might be characterized in subsequent litigation as a conspiracy jointly to enforce a patent known to be unenforceable or an attempt or conspiracy to monopolize if a large

---

Inc. v. Comfortex Corp., 44 F. Supp. 2d 145 (N.D.N.Y. 1999), the court noted that since a misuse claim does not have to be based on an antitrust violation, it would make theoretical sense to group the trial of the misuse issue with the patent issues. However, the court decided that the practical reality of misuse defenses is that they are often based on facts more likely to be adduced during the antitrust claim phase of the trial than the patent phase. The court accordingly held that the misuse defense would be tried with the antitrust counterclaims.

market share is involved.[101] This is not to say that all such settlements are illegal or will lead to liability but to caution that their terms may have to be carefully considered and drafted and their relative risks and benefits carefully evaluated. By embodying the settlement of the misuse issue in a consent decree as well as the settlement agreement, the parties to a patent case can bar relitigation of the misuse issue between themselves, although not by third parties.[102]

Settlements of infringement suits may also themselves be attacked as constituting misuse. In *Zeneca Limited v. Pharmachemie B.V.*,[103] the defendant claimed that the plaintiff's settlement with another infringer while the case was on appeal constituted misuse. Pharmachemie's theory was that Zeneca had no patent rights once the district court held that its patent was unenforceable. The settlement, however, was conditioned upon the Federal Circuit vacating the district court's judgment; vacating of such invalidity decisions had been done as a matter of course by the Federal Circuit prior to the Supreme Court's direction in the *Cardinal Chemical* case[104] not to do so. Pharmachemie claimed that Zeneca had extended the temporal scope of its patent by obtaining years of protection after the date a court had held the patent invalid. The district court held, however, that the practice of obtaining vacaturs of lower court opinions as part of settlement was permissible (and frequently employed) at the time, and could not constitute misuse.

---

101. *See* ANTITRUST COUNTERATTACK, *supra* note 29, at 87-88, 191-93. Indeed, Biovail Corporation International is facing a number of lawsuits alleging that its settlement of a patent infringement suit against Andrx Pharmaceuticals, Inc. violated the antitrust laws. Specifically, the plaintiffs claim that Biovail agreed to a settlement in which it paid Andrx $10 million a quarter in order to postpone the triggering of a generic pharmaceutical company's six-month exclusivity period under the Patent Term Restoration Act. According to the plaintiffs, this delayed any generic version of Biovail's drug from reaching the market. *See, e.g.*, Biovail Corp. Int'l v. Hoechst Aktiengesellschaft, 49 F. Supp. 2d 750 (D.N.J. 1999).

102. *See* Foster v. Hallco Mfg. Co., 947 F.2d 469 (Fed. Cir. 1991).

103. 37 F. Supp. 2d 85 (D. Mass. 1999).

104. Cardinal Chemical Co. v. Morton Int'l, Inc., 506 U.S. 813 (1992).

Attempting to achieve the same result today, after *Cardinal Chemical,* might be dealt with more harshly.

G. Appeals

All appeals in patent infringement cases—but not necessarily cases to enforce an intellectual property license—now go to the Federal Circuit.[105] The Federal Circuit applies its own law to patent-related issues such as misuse.[106] In several cases, the circuit has indicated that it will be reluctant to find misuse from any conduct not held to be per se unlawful by Supreme Court precedent unless the conduct can be shown to be both outside the scope of the patent grant and unreasonably restrictive of competition.[107] In another case, the circuit (hearing a copyright issue related to a patent case) held that a copyright misuse defense could not be raised by a defendant deemed to have unclean hands because it had lied to the Copyright Office to obtain a copy of the software it wished to copy.[108]

---

105. 28 U.S.C. § 1295(a)(1) (1993). *See* ANTITRUST COUNTERATTACK, *supra* note 29, at 201-07 (1994). Under the *Mallinckrodt* decision, a patentee may treat as an infringement, not simply a breach of contract, breaches of the conditions on which a patented item is sold, so that these claims, as well as misuse defenses related to them, would now fall within the jurisdiction of the Federal Circuit. *See* Malinckrodt, Inc. v. Medipart, Inc., 976 F.2d 700 (Fed. Cir. 1992).

106. On purely procedural, nonpatent-related issues that may arise in connection with the misuse issue, the Federal Circuit applies the law of the regional federal circuit from which the case originates. *See* Bio-Rad Lab. Inc. v. Nicolet Instrument Corp., 739 F.2d 604 (Fed. Cir. 1984). Appeals in copyright and trademark cases go to the appropriate regional circuits.

107. *See C.R. Bard, Inc.,* 157 F.3d 1340 (Fed. Cir. 1998); Virginia Panel Corp. v. MAC Panel Co., 133 F.3d 860 (Fed. Cir. 1997); B. Braun Med., Inc. v. Abbott Lab., 124 F.3d 1419, 1425-27 (Fed. Cir. 1997); *Mallinckrodt,* 976 F.2d at 706, 708; Windsurfing Int'l, Inc. v. AMF Corp., 782 F.2d 995, 1001-02 (Fed. Cir. 1986); *see also* Hodosh v. Block Drug Co., 833 F.2d 1575 (Fed. Cir. 1987).

108. *See* Atari Games Corp. v. Nintendo of Am. Inc., 975 F.2d 832 (Fed. Cir. 1992).

CHAPTER V

THE MISUSE DOCTRINE:
AN ECONOMIC REASSESSMENT

by *Edward F. Sherry and David J. Teece*[*]

This chapter provides an economic framework within which to assess certain conduct under the misuse doctrine. This framework is then applied to several stylized examples to illustrate the general points. Section V.A identifies the main outlines of the misuse doctrine and its relationship to the antitrust and intellectual property laws. Section V.B introduces general economic principles that are applied to the core features of the misuse doctrine in Section V.C.

A. What Is Misuse?

1. Conduct Constituting Misuse

Misuse is a catch-all term which comprises a number of conceptually distinct types of substantive conduct. Chapter II identifies a number of suspect activities that could be considered misuse: tying (or "tie-ins"), covenants not to deal in competing goods (or "tie-outs"), field of use and customer limitations, territorial limitations, price limitations (including resale price maintenance), package licensing, royalties based on total sales, refusals to license, discriminatory royalties, excessive royalties, postexpiration royalty payments, grantback clauses, bad faith enforcement of intellectual property rights, and the use of a patent as an "ingredient" in an antitrust violation. (An additional possibility, fraud on the Patent Office, will be discussed below.)

---

[*] *Authors' Note:* We wish to thank Professors Thomas Jorde and Mark Lemley, and Joseph L. McEntee, Esq., for helpful comments and suggestions. For further discussion, see Mark Lemley, *The Economic Irrationality of the Patent Misuse Doctrine*, 78 CAL. L. REV. 1599-1632 (1990).

These activities conceptually fall into four categories: (1) conduct that also would constitute an antitrust violation if practiced by firms with substantial market power, (2) conduct that does not rise to the level of an antitrust violation but nevertheless violates competition policy, (3) conduct that violates policies inherent in intellectual property law generally, and (4) conduct that constitutes "unclean hands."[1]

2. Procedural Aspects

Procedurally, the misuse doctrine is in many ways sui generis. The idea that misuse is a shield, not a sword, is widely recognized: misuse essentially is invoked only as a defense to a claim of intellectual property infringement and not as an independent ground for liability. Another unusual feature of misuse is that a party invoking the misuse defense (the infringement defendant) need not show that it has been harmed by the misuse.[2] In fact, in a number of cases, the infringement defendant has successfully interposed a misuse defense by referring to practices by the patent holder (the infringement plaintiff) that have not been applied to the infringement defendant.[3] That is, not only does the infringement defendant not have to show harm, the defendant does not even have to show that it has been subject to the proscribed practice. Finally, an intellectual property holder, if found to have committed misuse, will be unable to collect damages for infringement, even from those unaffected by the misuse, until that misuse has been "purged."

3. The Misuse Doctrine and Its Relationship to Other Policies

a. Antitrust

Many actions that constitute misuse also are antitrust violations, suggesting that the misuse doctrine is intended to protect against many

---

1.   As the unclean hands doctrine is not based on economics, we do not discuss it.
2.   See Morton Salt Co. v. G.S. Suppiger Co., 314 U.S. 488 (1942).
3.   See id.; Noll v. O.M. Scott & Sons Co., 467 F.2d 295 (6th Cir. 1972); Blohm & Voss AG v. Prudential Grace Lines, Inc., 346 F. Supp. 1116 (D. Md. 1972), rev'd on other grounds, 489 F.2d 231 (4th Cir. 1973).

of the same harms to society that the antitrust laws were designed to address. However, although the misuse doctrine is moving in the direction of closer conformance with antitrust law, three major differences remain.

First, while an essential prerequisite for a finding of antitrust liability for all but the few per se offenses is that the defendant have market power, monopoly power in the relevant market, or a "dangerous probability" of obtaining such monopoly power, there has historically been no need to show that the patent holder has market power in misuse cases. This result has been changed with respect to one category of patent misuse by the Patent Misuse Reform Act of 1988,[4] which not only makes it clear that a patent holder can refuse to license its patent but allows tying of the patented product or process to another patent or product unless the patent holder has sufficient market power in the relevant market for the patent or the patented product to coerce the licensee into the tying arrangement. This statutory market power requirement, however, does not apply to other forms of patent misuse or to misuse with respect to other forms of intellectual property.

Second, an antitrust plaintiff needs standing to bring suit; the plaintiff must show that he or she has suffered harm arising out of the antitrust defendant's unlawful acts. This showing of individual harm is not required under the *Morton Salt* doctrine.[5]

Third, the remedies are significantly different. Under antitrust law, a successful plaintiff is entitled to treble damages and attorneys' fees. An intellectual property holder who has committed misuse is barred from collecting damages from infringers but is not otherwise liable to the infringement defendant for damages.

b. Intellectual Property Law Policy

The second major justification for the misuse doctrine is to protect the integrity of the intellectual property system. Grants of intellectual property protection create monopolies, at least over a product or technology, if not over an economically relevant "market." Monopoly

---

4.   35 U.S.C. § 271(d)(5) (1988).
5.   314 U.S. 488.

power creates a temptation to manipulate the intellectual property system to ends that it was never intended to serve. The misuse doctrine is intended, in part, to check this temptation.

However, the misuse doctrine is very selective in the types of conduct it seeks to deter. Three far more obvious forms of manipulation of the intellectual property system are not addressed by the misuse doctrine as it currently stands, yet these forms of abuse are much more problematic than the typical sort of misuse reflected in the modern cases. The first is fraud on the Patent Office, in the form of overbroad claims or failure to disclose information which would have caused the application to be rejected. The second is overreaching litigation claims made by an intellectual property rights holder who claims in bad faith that the defendant has infringed.[6] The third is licensing terms that make it risky for licensees to challenge what may well be dubious or invalid intellectual property grants.

B. General Economic Principles

The general framework for an economic analysis of the misuse doctrine is well known within the economics fraternity. It consists of four basic principles: the economic theory of monopoly, the economics of information and innovation, the theory of deterrence, and issues of transaction costs and incomplete information. Attorneys and courts typically evaluate the intellectual property/competition interaction in developing and applying the misuse doctrine. In so doing, they often focus on the first two principles, failing to take into account the latter two principles.

---

6.   As noted in Chapter II, a few courts have recently assumed without discussion that this misconduct might constitute misuse. However, they have required that the suit be both objectively baseless and maintained in subjective bad faith and on this basis have rejected the application of the defense in the cases before them. *See* Glaverbal Societe Anonyme v. Northlake Mktg. & Supply, Inc., 45 F.3d 1550, 1558-59 (Fed. Cir. 1996); *In re* Independent Serv. Orgs. Antitrust Litig., 964 F. Supp. 1479, 1482 (D. Kan. 1997); Raines v. Switch Mfg. Co., 44 U.S.P.Q.2d 1195 (N.D. Cal. 1997); Religious Tech. Center v. Lerma, 40 U.S.P.Q.2d 1569 (E.D. Va. 1996).

1. Monopoly and Its Effects

Monopoly has one fundamental symptom and two principal effects. The symptom is that the monopolist restricts output to raise price. The first and most obvious effect is that the monopolist earns higher-than-normal (supracompetitive) profits (often referred to as "monopoly rents"). The second, somewhat less obvious, effect is that this causes a "deadweight loss" to society in the form of disappointed customers who are willing to buy the good or service supplied by the monopolist at a price that exceeds the cost of supplying that good or service, but who refrain from purchasing at the monopoly price.[7]

Foregone consumption is the principal reason why economists object to monopoly. Surprisingly to many noneconomists, the "rents" are much less objectionable; customers pay a higher price, but the monopolist receives a higher revenue, so the impact of the rent on the economy is purely redistributional (money flows from consumers to the monopolist), rather than a reduction in output and consumption.

The extent of both the monopoly profits/rents and the deadweight loss depends primarily on the elasticity of demand for the good or service, which in turn depends on availability of substitutes for such good or service. In particular, a firm can be the sole supplier of a particular good or service but face significant competition from suppliers of substitute goods or services. This is often quite important in the patent field; a firm may have a "patent monopoly" on a particular product or process but have no market power because it faces competition from competing products or processes.

2. The Economics of Innovation

Another assumption of economic theory is that the development of new information, or innovation, and the dissemination of such information together are necessary for productivity enhancement and economic growth. The "static" and "dynamic" aspects of information

---

7.   *See* DENNIS CARLETON & JEFFREY PERLOFF, MODERN INDUSTRIAL ORGANIZATION ch. 5 (2d ed. 1994).

described below inform a legal system that attempts to balance the competing aspects of such innovation and dissemination.

Use of a tangible economic good, like a croissant, by one individual precludes others from using that same good. If one person eats the croissant, another person cannot eat the same croissant. Goods like croissants are "rival" goods; there is an inherent rivalry between potential consumers, each of whom wishes to use or consume the good, with each aware that, if he or she consumes the good, others cannot. Pricing the good at a certain level in effect "rations" the good in favor of those who value the good the most.

Knowledge does not share this feature of rivalry. Once a particular piece of knowledge has been learned, that information can be used by others. The fact that one person knows how to bake bread—that one person possesses and uses that particular bit of know-how—does not preclude a second person from knowing and using that same bit of know-how. The dissemination of this know-how would not impair any single consumer's ability to use it. Thus, if know-how were a fixed quantity, there would be no reason to ration it by setting a price on it. Under this theory—the "static theory" of information economics—the know-how should be made available to all consumers at no cost (beyond the relatively low cost involved in conveying the information to consumers).

Know-how, of course, is not a fixed quantity, given the constant development of new ideas. Such new idea development often requires expending considerable time and effort in research and development costs. Without prospect of a return on investment, innovation will suffer. The "dynamic" theory of information economics recognizes the need to provide the innovator with a return on its investment to encourage future innovation.[8]

---

8.   *See* Kenneth Arrow, *Economic Welfare and the Allocation of Resources for Invention, in* THE RATE AND DIRECTION OF INVENTIVE ACTIVITY: ECONOMIC AND SOCIAL FACTORS (National Bureau of Economic Research 1962). *See also* the material collected in pt. II of THE ECONOMICS OF TECHNICAL CHANGE (Edwin Mansfield & Elizabeth Mansfield eds., 1993).

The static and dynamic theories of information economics, then, create a fundamental paradox: society benefits from the wide dissemination of an innovation; at the same time, wide dissemination at little or no cost to the consumer provides little incentive to innovate. While in theory the law could (1) allow free use of all innovations while (2) encouraging innovation by compensating inventors by some other means (such as a centralized reward system), in practice the legal system has adopted a different approach to reconciling these two objectives.

The intellectual property law, in particular, seeks to strike this balance by giving the innovator a limited right to exclude others from using the innovation, thereby empowering the innovator to attempt to recoup its investment. Essentially, patent and copyright laws provide the developer of know-how or original expression with a "monopoly" (which may or may not involve market power in an economic sense). The innovator earns profits from this monopoly, and the private returns compensate the innovator for the effort associated with the innovation. This recoupment may involve licensing the innovation to others for a fee, using the innovation (and preventing competitors from using it) to give the inventor a competitive advantage in the marketplace, or some combination of these. The return on successful innovations is also supposed to allow for enough margin to compensate for the costs of unsuccessful efforts to innovate ("dry holes").

Of course, the monopoly period during which innovation is protected is limited by statute: twenty years from application for patents, and a much longer period for copyrights. While intellectual property law thus avoids the administrative burden of striking a balance between innovation and dissemination on a case-by-case basis, it may well undercompensate the innovator for some innovations and over-compensate the innovator for others. The rents earned by the innovator from the new technology depend on the market for that technology and on the commercialization strategy the innovator chooses to use.

By allowing the intellectual property holder to sell or license the technology to others (rather than merely preventing others from using the technology), the intellectual property laws encourage the holder to maximize the value of the innovation by selling or licensing the innovation to those who are willing to pay the most for the privilege. To the extent the innovation falls into the hands of those who can best commercialize and exploit it, the social returns on the new technology are increased.[9]

The concept of innovation carries the implicit premise that one can examine particular intellectual property and its licensing in isolation. However, innovations are often cumulative. For example, different firms may have patents on different pieces of the puzzle, and firms frequently have broad portfolios of related patents. To attain the maximum benefits from innovations and disseminate them to the public, it is often necessary to use patented technology belonging to many different firms in order to produce a commercially viable product. As a result, firms often license their entire portfolios of patents, or engage in broad portfolio cross-licensing. Similarly, firms often engage in "licensing programs" in which they seek to license their patents as a group to a number of potential licensees.[10] These features of real-world licensing pose special problems for the patent misuse doctrine, as discussed further below.

On balance, the rewards to innovation are often too low—and therefore tend to discourage innovation—because the dynamic nature of information undercuts its static nature: a monopoly (and the corresponding deadweight loss) is not likely to persist over time in the face of new innovation. Thus, the legal system should focus on rules that encourage the innovation and product enhancement that lead to dynamic economic growth rather than rules designed solely to eliminate inefficiencies in static markets.

3. The Economics of Deterrence

The economic theory of deterrence provides a useful framework for understanding the pros and cons of the per se and rule of reason

---

9.   Laws that hinder such transfers reduce both the private and social gains from innovation. To the extent that the misuse doctrine penalizes beneficial, neutral, or possibly even only marginally harmful provisions in such licenses, it discourages licensing and therefore reduces both private and social gains.

10.   *See* Peter Grindley & David Teece, *Managing Intellectual Capital: Licensing and Cross-Licensing in Semiconductors and Electronics*, 39 CAL. MGMT. REV. 1-34 (1997).

approaches to determine whether conduct is objectionable as misuse. The premise of the economic theory of deterrence is that people respond to incentives and deterrents, such as penalties imposed by the legal system. Increasing penalties reduces the penalized activity. "Optimal deterrence" is finding the level of penalties that deters all and only conduct that is deemed undesirable.[11]

A per se approach to analyzing conduct such as misuse is based on the assumption that if particular conduct is thought to be undesirable, the solution is to impose very high penalties on those found to be engaging in such conduct. In theory, the deterrent would be so extreme that no one would ever engage in the undesirable conduct, and the penalty would never have to be imposed.

The reasons this assumption is incorrect are fivefold. First, there are usually costs to society involved in imposing penalties (including the costs of operating the legal system). Second, courts make mistakes in applying these penalties. They may penalize people engaged in perfectly acceptable conduct ("Type I error" or a "false positive" error), or they may fail to penalize those engaging in unacceptable conduct ("Type II error" or a "false negative" error). While it is desirable to reduce both types of error, it may be prohibitively expensive to reduce the likelihood of making one type of error without increasing the likelihood of making the other type. Determining the optimal trade-off between Type I and Type II errors, between risking punishing the innocent and letting the guilty go free, is no easy matter.

Third, the prospect of error raises equity concerns. This generally rules out imposing very large penalties since imposing such penalties on those mistakenly found to have engaged in proscribed conduct strikes most people as wrong. Fourth, because people or situations differ, a penalty sufficient to deter most people may be insufficient to deter all.

Finally, there are few types of conduct that one would wish to deter unreservedly. The intellectual property system may be well served by deterring abuses of legal protection of the intellectual property. On the other hand, too much deterrence would be inimical to basic objectives of the intellectual property system: encouraging licensing of innovations

---

11. *See generally* STEVEN SHAVELL, ECONOMIC ANALYSIS OF ACCIDENT LAW (1987).

and allowing innovators to extract enough surplus to encourage future innovators.

The line between acceptable and unacceptable behavior is often a fine one. Because of differences among people or situations, the "correct" line may shift on a case-by-case basis in a way that may be very difficult to implement, and trying to draw fine distinctions in each case increases the likelihood of error. Moreover, uncertainty about where the line will be drawn will deter people from approaching that line, which may discourage otherwise desirable behavior.

If the rewards and penalties match the harm caused, optimal deterrence is achieved: all undesirable conduct—but only undesirable conduct—is deterred. A situation in which the penalty exceeds the harm leads to overdeterrence; conversely, if the penalty is less than the harm, it is likely to lead to underdeterrence. This argues for a fairly strong "coupling" of the penalty and the harm.

In the context of determining whether certain conduct is misuse, an economic analysis suggests that while a misuse doctrine should deter the intellectual property holder from misconduct, it should also deter others from infringing valid intellectual property grants. In addition, the doctrine should encourage people to negotiate a mutually acceptable license rather than act unilaterally.

4. *Transaction Cost Economics*

Transaction cost economics (TCE) is a recently developed theory focusing on the interplay of four elements of economic behavior.[12] These elements are:

1. *Bounded rationality.* People cannot foresee or evaluate all of the possible situations in which they might find themselves.
2. *Information impactedness.* Different people have different relevant information, and acquiring additional information is often very costly and sometimes impossible.

---

12.   *See* OLIVER WILLIAMSON, THE ECONOMIC INSTITUTIONS OF CAPITALISM (1985); OLIVER WILLIAMSON, MARKETS AND HIERARCHIES: ANTITRUST AND ECONOMIC IMPLICATIONS (1975).

3. *Opportunism.* People will generally act in their own self-interest, often in ways which may involve guile.
4. *The "small numbers" problem.* Once people or firms have entered into an economic relationship, they often make or have made investments that cannot readily be redeployed to alternative relationships, thereby lessening competitive conditions.

These four factors interact in important ways. For example, if it were not for bounded rationality, licensors and licensees could write complete contracts specifying what to do under every possible contingency, thereby alleviating the effects of information impactedness and opportunism. As a practical matter, this is virtually impossible and, at the least, excessively costly. Instead, licensors and licensees specify the basic parameters of their relationships and fill in the gaps as they go along, which invites opportunistic behavior, particularly when the information needed to fill in the gaps optimally is (because of information impactedness) in the control of only one of the parties.

Another example of the interrelation among the TCE factors is a relationship-specific investment, such as retooling by a patent licensee. Before the patent license is signed, the potential licensee has a wide range of options to retool its factory to build the patented product and can choose to walk away if the patent holder tries to impose unacceptable terms. However, once the licensee has committed itself (by retooling), the earlier options fade away; the licensee is now open to opportunistic behavior by the patent holder. Conversely, once the innovator has disclosed the innovation (to the licensee and others) when the patent is published, the innovator's strongest hold on the potential licensee is dissolved;[13] now the licensee can act opportunistically by, for example, using the patent without paying royalties.

---

13. This is especially true in situations where patents and trade secrets are complementary, in the sense that, for the licensee to fully exploit the patent, the innovator must also disclose trade secret know-how to the potential licensee. Once the license is signed and the know-how has been disclosed, the licensee has an incentive to renege on the license obligations.

Opportunism is the operative TCE element in "rent-seeking behavior."[14] Parties enter into economic relationships because they believe that those relationships will generate gains or rents from cooperation, yet each has an incentive to try to appropriate a larger share of those rents for itself by acting opportunistically. There is a tension between opportunistic rent-seeking, which both dissipates the overall rents and undermines the stability of the relationship, and the benefits from continuing the relationship, which are often large because of relationship-specific investments.

From a TCE standpoint, there are two fundamental concerns regarding an innovator who seeks to extend or overreach with its intellectual property rights:

1. the innovator may be overcompensated by extracting higher rents than would be possible if "proper" methods were used;
2. the innovator may expend real resources in seeking to affect the amount of rents it receives, rather than on productive behavior, making society as a whole worse off.

C. Economic Analysis of the Misuse Doctrine

The foregoing economic considerations disfavor the misuse doctrine, at least as courts have historically defined and applied it. First, many practices currently condemned as patent misuse serve procompetitive ends. Second, in the absence of market power, misuse is likely to harm no one but the intellectual property holder. Third, even when these considerations are not controlling, application of the misuse doctrine and the antitrust laws to the same conduct raises concerns that infringement will be underdeterred and hence that incentives to innovate or to disseminate innovation may be reduced. Fourth, even if this duplication were eliminated, the misuse doctrine, by "decoupling" the magnitude of the remedy from the amount of the harm, leads to an inappropriate amount of deterrence. Fifth, and finally, errors in characterizing certain

---

14.   *See* Richard Posner, *The Social Costs of Monopoly and Regulation*, 83 J. POL. ECON. 807-27 (1975).

conduct as misuse may result in deterring socially desirable conduct, including experimentation with alternative ways of disseminating innovations.

1. Some Patent Misuse Is Economically Neutral or Procompetitive

a. Postexpiration Royalties

A common type of conduct that courts have sometimes held to be unenforceable is the effort by the patent holder to extract payment from the licensee after the patent has expired.[15] Unfortunately, this conduct is least harmful to society from an economic perspective.

Suppose that a patent has ten more years to run, and that the right to use a patent is worth no more than $100 per year to a prospective licensee. Without considering the time-value of money, the licensee should be indifferent as to whether it pays a lump-sum fee of $1,000, ten equal yearly payments of $100, or $50 per year for twenty years. The last alternative, however, would involve extracting payment from the licensee after the patent has expired.

Even if the time-value of money is factored into the analysis, changing the numerical results, the underlying principle remains the same. At an interest rate of 10 percent per year, for example, a licensee would be indifferent as to whether it pays $100 at the beginning of the year or $110 at the end of the year. From an economic perspective, a licensee should have no preference among various payment schemes that have the same net present value. Some of these schemes may involve all payments occurring before the expiration of the patents; others may involve some of the payments (and possibly even the bulk of them) made after the patents expire.

The patent holder gives the licensee the right to use the technology today (and for all or part of the remaining life of the patent) in exchange

---

15.   A similar analysis could be given for several of the other categories of misuse described in Section V.B and in Chapter II. However, many categories, such as field of use limitations, require a case-by-case investigation of the circumstances under which such limitations are pro- or anticompetitive.

for payments, whether now or in the future.   Like any other intertemporal transaction, such as a loan, there may be mutually beneficial ways of structuring the overall payment that make both the licensor and the licensee better off.

The above example assumes that the value that the licensee places on the right to use the patent is known from the beginning.   With many new products and processes, neither the licensor nor the licensee knows how commercially valuable the product (or process) will turn out to be. This is one of the main reasons why many licenses provide for royalties to be paid out over a period of time rather than a single lump-sum payment: if the product turns out to be a success, both parties will share in the proceeds, but if it turns out to be a failure, the licensee's cost is limited.   Running royalties also are favored as a way of monitoring the extent to which the licensee uses the patent.

A licensor and licensee who agree to payment over time can always choose to have the payments stop when the patent expires, just as they could always choose to license the patent for a single lump-sum payment.   Allowing the parties the flexibility to stretch out payments over a longer period simply gives them another option, one that may be economically preferable to both parties.   A rule like the misuse rule, which encourages all payments to be made during the life of the patent, can prevent some of these mutually beneficial deals.

b.   Total Sales Royalties

Another type of conduct typically held to constitute patent misuse is requiring royalties to be based on total sales of products containing the patented component or using a patented process, rather than only on sales of the individual components.   Under a misuse analysis, it is unfair or inappropriate to calculate royalties on the larger total sales base rather than the narrower patented product/component/process base, and such calculation allows the licensor to extend the patent monopoly beyond its appropriate scope.

Again, economic analysis suggests that concerns underlying the misuse doctrine are overstated.   With a "fixed proportions" technology, the relationship between the value placed on the patented component or right to use the process and the value placed on total sales of the product containing such component or susceptible to use of a patented process is not disproportionate. For example, a patent may cover a particular component of an unpatented final product, and each final product may require exactly one such component. If the final product sells for $100, the component accounts for 10 percent of the value of the final product (or $10) and the licensor and licensee agree on a 25 percent royalty based on the value of the component (or $2.50/component), then both parties should be equally willing to specify a 2.5 percent royalty on the total sales (i.e., the final product selling at $100). In this hypothetical, basing royalties on total sales, rather than on the patented component alone, is economically neutral.[16]

Indeed, there may be sound reasons to base royalties on the value of the (unpatented) final product rather than the value of the (patented) component. In particular, the value of the component may itself be difficult to measure if there is no independent external market for the component. Even when the component is sold externally, such sales are often only for replacement parts at a significantly higher price than the value of the component as a part of the entire product. (For example, automobile manufacturers charge far more to buy all of the various parts of a car than they charge for the assembled car.) It may be in both parties' interests to agree to base royalties on the selling price of the finished product, which is determined by the objective forces of market competition, rather than to try to establish a separate measure of the value of the component.

Total sales-based royalties may make economic sense also because of the transactions cost to the licensor of monitoring the licensee's compliance with the terms of the license. If the patent involves a new process for making an otherwise unpatented product, for example, it may be extremely difficult for the licensor to monitor whether the licensee is

---

16. This neutrality is easy to see in the example in the text because of the fact that the ratio of components to final products is fixed (at one) and the ratio of the value of the component to the value of the final product is also fixed (at 10%). However, even in a "variable proportions" case, in which these ratios vary and make negotiations more complicated, the essential point, that calculating royalties based on total sales will be economically neutral, remains the same.

using the patented process or some competing process to make the product, unless the licensor engages in costly and intrusive behavior (e.g., unannounced spot-checks of the licensee's manufacturing process). Basing royalties on the licensee's total sales of the product eliminates the need to monitor.

This is not, of course, to suggest that total sales-based royalties are always innocuous. In fact, they raise more concerns than do postexpiration royalties, principally because there may be legitimate disputes as to the true scope of the patent. However, if the scope of the patent is not at issue, the concerns underlying the misuse doctrine as applied in this context are unfounded. The parties can always choose to have royalties based only on "infringing" sales rather than "total" sales; allowing royalties to be based on total sales merely gives them another option, one that may be economically preferable to both parties.[17]

c.   Portfolio Licensing

The existing patent misuse doctrine implicitly involves an evaluation of the license or sale of single patents or patented products, which is based on the single-patent, single-product paradigm. However, many contemporary licensing arrangements are far more complex, and their evaluation under traditional misuse principles is not only impractical, but contrary to economic objectives.

A given patent may apply to a wide range of products, or (more significantly) the design or manufacture of a given commercial product may involve many different patents, often belonging to many different inventors. In many high-technology industries, determining which patents apply to particular products is often an expensive and time-consuming activity. In industries in which new products are being

---

17.   Courts often make the erroneous assumption that the intellectual property holder imposed a payment schedule or a royalty base on the licensee. Many licenses are negotiated. Others may be offered at what are characterized as take-it-or-leave-it royalty terms, but in the absence of market power, this is fundamentally no different from saying that a grocery store imposed a price of apples on the consumer by posting a shelf price that the checkout clerk refused to negotiate.

developed and introduced frequently, and new patents are being issued (and older patents expiring) on a daily basis, the effort continually to redetermine which patents apply to which products would be prohibitively expensive. In these contexts, patent holders commonly use broad portfolio licenses (or cross-licenses). Such licensing obviates the need to determine, on a product-by-product, patent-by-patent basis, precisely which products are covered by which patents.

However, many of the standard categories of conduct typically held to be patent misuse do not readily fit modern licensing practices. For example, the concepts of postexpiration royalties or royalties based only on infringing sales do not apply in the context of broad portfolio licensing because they are based on the premise that the parties to the license have determined which patents apply to particular products. Because a primary purpose of portfolio licensing is to avoid the need to make such a determination, these patent misuse concepts seem misplaced, given the justifiable economic rationale for using a portfolio license in the first place.

d. Other Conduct

Other forms of conduct historically held to be patent misuse also may have legitimate economic purposes. In fact, the *Intellectual Property Guidelines* issued jointly by the Department of Justice and the Federal Trade Commission explicitly state that certain other types of conduct which have formerly been identified as misuse—notably field of use and territorial restrictions—can actually be procompetitive:

> Field-of-use, territorial, and other limitations on intellectual property licenses may serve procompetitive ends by allowing the licensor to exploit its property as efficiently and effectively as possible. . . . They may also increase the licensor's incentive to license, for example, by protecting the licensor from competition in the licensor's own technology in a market niche that it prefers to keep to itself.[18]

---

18. U.S. Dep't of Justice & Federal Trade Comm'n, Antitrust Guidelines for the Licensing of Intellectual Property § 4.1 (1995), *reprinted in* 4 Trade Reg. Rep. (CCH) ¶ 13,132.

2. Misuse without Market Power Is Not a Significant Policy Concern

A misuse determination does not necessarily require a finding that the licensor has market power in the market in which the licensed product competes. Even in the absence of market power, the misuse doctrine embodies a concern that the intellectual property holder will extort undeserved rents from its licensees. However, TCE considerations may be significant enough to prevent misconduct by the licensor without requiring a legal remedy such as the misuse doctrine.

a. Prelicense Misuse Is Harmful to the Misuser

If a licensor has a patent or copyright on one of ten competing products (or processes) that are all roughly comparable, an effort by the licensor to abuse its monopoly power in its product or process is almost certain to lead potential licensees to deal with one of the competitors instead. As analyzed under TCE, before a license has been issued, the prospective licensees have made no relation-specific investments; they can respond to efforts to exploit them by going elsewhere. Thus, in the absence of market power in an economic market of competing goods, any effort at misuse is only likely to hurt the one engaging in the abusive conduct.

b. Negotiations Preclude Postlicense Misuse

The licensing contract, not the misuse doctrine, should be the device for addressing any change in the parties' relative bargaining power after a license has been granted and the licensee has tooled up to manufacture the protected product, often precluding the manufacture of one of the competing alternatives. Without contract language specifying the parties' respective rights, the licensor might engage in ex post, opportunistic behavior. This situation is fundamentally no different from long-term relationships in any industry, even those not involving intellectual property; for example, the same sort of incentives for opportunism arise in long-term supply contracts in a wide variety of industries. There seems to be little need for additional misuse principles in the specific context of intellectual property.

One reason courts may misinterpret the underlying economic nature of the licensing transaction is that they examine the situation only after the parties have agreed to a licensing arrangement and after the relation-specific investments have been made. This perspective ignores the parties' initial relative bargaining positions, at which time the licensee should have negotiated protection against possible future opportunistic behavior by the licensor. The correct framework within which to analyze these cases, then, is from an ex ante perspective.[19]

c.   The Effect of the Misuse Doctrine on Transaction Costs

A legal rule developed to reduce the transaction costs imposed by a licensor's rent-seeking behavior is worthwhile if it is likely to eliminate these costs. However, the misuse doctrine fails to accomplish this goal.

The principal difficulties in imposing legal constraints on such conduct are threefold. First, changes in the substantive law (in this case, the intellectual property system) tend to shift the relative bargaining position of the parties. Thus, the parties' negotiations will, in part,

---

19.   A TCE analysis further suggests that one form of conduct not generally thought of as misuse is especially problematic from an economic perspective. The so-called "submarine patent" involves a patent application that is substantially and deliberately delayed in the Patent Office, often by the applicant filing large numbers of amendments, while technological progress proceeds apace. The technology covered by the patent application is widely (and unwittingly) adopted in the industry. The patent then issues, and large numbers of firms find that they have made substantial investments using the (now newly patented) innovation. This is a perfect opportunity for the patent holder to take advantage of the sunk investments to act opportunistically by extracting a sizable fraction of the economic rents. While the inventor might have had little market power if the innovation had been disclosed earlier (so that the firms could have chosen to invest in alternative technologies), once those investments have been made, the inventor has a substantial degree of market power over the (now captive) customers. The misuse doctrine fails to address this undesirable conduct.

offset these changes, minimizing their impact. A rule, for example, that makes it easier to challenge intellectual property protection strengthens the potential infringer's position and weakens the intellectual property holder's position, which affects where the bargain is likely to be struck. While the resulting bargain is likely to be more favorable to potential infringers than the bargain that would have been struck under the old rule, it is difficult to predict exactly how or to what extent.

Second, it is often hard to predict the effect of changes in substantive law on transaction costs. Not only does the strategic behavior (such as bluffing or commitment) adopted by the parties make it difficult to predict how outcomes change as the underlying rules change, but the parties' attempts to compensate for these changes during negotiations renders uncertain the way in which total transaction costs vary as the substantive rules change.

For example, preventing the patent holder from collecting payments after expiration of a patent will, at first blush, benefit licensees at the expense of the patent holder because the patent holder's ability to collect royalties is reduced. However, this perception is misleading. Knowing that it may be impossible to collect payments after the patent expires, the patent holder will try to negotiate a payment scheme which falls within the patent period. It is not easy to predict in every case whether this results in higher or lower total transaction costs—including both negotiation costs and the costs of enforcing the agreement—but it is logical to believe that in some cases at least the costs will be higher. This is because, from a TCE standpoint, the parties would only have agreed to the longer payment period if they believed it involved lower transaction costs.

Third, and most significantly, transactions costs and costs imposed by the licensor's opportunism are likely to be "second order" effects, i.e., much less significant than they might appear. An economic theory known as the Coase Theorem[20] suggests that there are unlikely to be large social welfare gains from prohibiting substantively inefficient practices because parties "contract around" the worst of the effects of those practices. Thus, a change in intellectual property law, such as

---

20.   Ronald Coase, *The Problem of Social Cost*, 3 J.L. & ECON. 1-44 (1960).

imposing the misuse doctrine, may go much farther than necessary to address such effects.

3. Cumulative Effects of Patent Misuse and Antitrust Remedies

An infringement defendant who also files an antitrust counterclaim can potentially obtain remedies under both legal doctrines: the misuse "shield" (not having to pay royalties for infringement), and the antitrust "sword" (treble damages for antitrust injuries). The flip side of this coin is that an intellectual property holder who engages in misuse may not only lose royalties but also have to pay antitrust damages for what is fundamentally the same conduct. Thus, the net effect of the cumulative nature of the two remedies is to underdeter infringement and over-deter the economically desirable behavior of innovation and licensing.

4. Decoupling Sanctions from Harm

Under the misuse doctrine, the private cost of infringing is decoupled from the social harm. If the intellectual property holder engages in misuse, the infringer pays nothing, regardless of how substantial or how blatant the infringement, at least until intellectual property holder purges the misuse.[21] Similarly, the intellectual property holder can recover nothing, regardless of how significant or how trivial the misuse was, how large the royalties would otherwise have been, or whether the infringer was harmed.

The problem of decoupling sanctions from harm is well known in the economic literature on liability rules. The standard solution involves

---

21. In those cases where the intellectual property holder is able to purge the misuse, the ability to do so will ameliorate the decoupling concern on a going-forward basis, although the intellectual property holder's inability to collect damages for past infringement because of the misuse may nevertheless be significant. However, in some cases, it may not be feasible to purge the misuse. Moreover, as discussed in Chapters I and III, the standards for what must be done in order to purge misuse, or to determine when such a purge has been accomplished, are not particularly well defined in the case law. Therefore, relying on a purge may not sufficiently mitigate the decoupling issue.

reinstating the coupling between one's own conduct and the costs (or benefits) one incurs, by making the obligations of each party independent. In the context of intellectual property law, the infringer would pay for infringement; the intellectual property holder would be separately penalized in some way for misuse. The problem with the misuse doctrine as it is currently formulated is that it merges together, on an all-or-nothing basis, what should be two essentially separate considerations.

5. Categorization Errors

Also relevant to an economic analysis is the fact that courts sometimes make mistakes.[22] It is well recognized that certain conduct formerly seen by the courts as having no procompetitive rationale and as therefore worthy of condemnation as per se illegal can, in the appropriate circumstances, serve procompetitive ends.[23] However, even when the court's analysis proceeds on a rule of reason basis, courts not infrequently mischaracterize as anticompetitive conduct that actually has a procompetitive impact, whether in hindsight, or in light of additional information, or when seen as part of a larger pattern of conduct. These Type I or false positive errors can have a chilling effect, preventing licensors from experimenting with innovative or unusual methods of licensing their technology. While it may seem likely to a licensor that a given practice will be upheld, the potential downside losses to the licensor if he or she predicts incorrectly may outweigh any possible upside gains from the practice. Such uncertainty hinders potentially procompetitive licensing arrangements.[24]

---

22.   "Mistakes" means mistakes from an economic perspective. While courts often do not fully appreciate the economic issues involved, courts also seek to serve legitimate ends beyond those of theoretical economics.

23.   *See* State Oil Co. v. Kahn, 522 U.S. 3 (1997); Continental T.V., Inc. v. GTE Sylvania Inc., 433 U.S. 36 (1977).

24.   Courts also may make Type II or false negative errors, in which they fail to condemn conduct that is in fact anticompetitive. Because the intellectual property system generally provides too little incentive to innovate, in our view, the likelihood of these sorts of errors is generally of less concern.

A false positive error can be particularly problematic if the conduct at issue is a tie-out, i.e., a license that conditions the grant of the license on an agreement not to use a competing product or technology. To be sure, such a provision may interfere with the normal economic presumption that people should be able to choose how to mix and match goods or technologies so as to best achieve their own ends. A tie-out limits this flexibility by imposing an either/or constraint: "if you use our product or process, you agree not to use our competitors' product or process." Such conduct impedes one of the wellsprings of innovation, the ability to combine information from diverse sources to yield novel combinations.

On the other hand, there can also be procompetitive business reasons for tie-out provisions. The most obvious of these occurs in situations where the licensor seeks to collect royalties and the licensee resists on the grounds that it was using not the licensor's innovation but a competing innovation instead. A tie-out provision would limit these sorts of disputes by precluding a licensee's claim of legitimate use of the competing innovation, thereby promoting economic efficiencies.[25] If a court erroneously holds that a tie-out in all circumstances is misuse and therefore illegal under per se analysis, this procompetitive advantage would be lost in the cases where it is applicable.

D. Conclusion

1. Summary

From a purely economic perspective, the current misuse doctrine seems flawed. Certain classes of conduct typically analyzed under the misuse doctrine, such as collecting royalties after the expiration of a patent, are at worst likely to be economically neutral and at best may be economically desirable and therefore should be permitted. Moreover, absent some market power, any attempted abuse of the intellectual property system is likely to harm only the intellectual property holder prior to entering into a licensing agreement; the license itself is the licensee's protection against ex post opportunism by the intellectual

---

25. See the discussion of monitoring in connection with royalties based on total output in Section V.C.1 *supra*.

property holder. There is little reason for a misuse doctrine to intervene in such cases and some loss of efficiency may result from possible categorization errors that may be made by the courts.

Even in cases where (1) the conduct itself is not economically neutral and (2) the intellectual property holder has some market power in a relevant market, we believe that the misuse doctrine in its present form is flawed because:

1. it fails to deter infringement when the intellectual property holder has engaged in "unrelated" misuse, since the penalty imposed by the misuse doctrine—an inability to collect damages for infringement until the misuse has been purged—bears little or no relationship to the harm caused by the misuse; and
2. misuse remedies and antitrust liability are sometimes cumulative, which can result in excessive deterrence of economically favorable conduct by the intellectual property holder.

2. Proposals

Despite the doctrine's deficiencies, we do not believe that the entire law of misuse should necessarily be abandoned. A "private attorney general" role may exist for those sorts of misuse, such as unjustified tie-outs, that do not necessarily rise to the level of antitrust liability. However, in such cases, the law should compel the infringer to pay royalties while allowing an offset for the harm directly caused by the misuse. This offset might take the form of case-specific damages or might be in the form of some statutory offset for various classes of misuse (possibly with an additional fine to be collected by the government). Moreover, only a party affected by the misuse should have standing to raise the misuse defense in an infringement lawsuit. The misuse doctrine would not then undermine the deterrent effect of lawsuits on infringement by nonaffected parties.

Even limited in this fashion, the misuse doctrine may serve to deter innovative means of structuring licensing deals, thereby reducing the incentive to license and retarding the diffusion of innovation in a socially undesirable fashion. Thus, even if the intellectual property holder has some degree of market power in the relevant market, the presumption should be in favor of finding such conduct permissible. One possible (although imperfect) solution is to require the party challenging the conduct as misuse to bear the burden of proof, perhaps under a clear and convincing standard.

CHAPTER VI

PATENT MISUSE IN THE UNITED KINGDOM

by Christopher P. Tootal and James B. Kobak, Jr.

From 1907 to 1998 the United Kingdom, the Republic of Ireland, and certain Commonwealth countries had a statutory misuse rule for certain classes of agreements concerning patents. This rule, most recently embodied in Section 44 of the U.K. Patents Act of 1977, was limited to what U.S. lawyers would call tie-ins and tie-outs. The U.K. statute provided, in effect, that a patent subject to an offending agreement (defined with considerable specificity by the act) was unenforceable as long as the agreement was in force.[1] This aspect of the rule was analogous to the U.S. patent misuse doctrine announced in *Morton Salt*[2] and applied more recently in copyright cases such as *Lasercomb*[3] and *Practice Management Information Corp. v. American Medical Association.*[4] Section 44 was repealed in 1998 as part of Britain's effort to conform its jurisprudence to the antitrust laws of the European Union, which does not have a separate patent misuse doctrine.

The British experience in enacting, applying, and repealing this statute is relevant to an assessment of the U.S. misuse doctrine. The U.S. Supreme Court cited the forerunner of the U.K. statute (Section 38 of the U.K. Patents Act of 1907) in a footnote to its 1931 *Carbice* decision in support of the proposition that a patent owner "may not exact as the condition of a license that unpatented materials used in connection with the invention shall be purchased only from the licensor, and if it does so, relief against one who supplies such unpatented materials will be denied."[5] *Carbice* was a case denying relief against a contributory

---

1.   *See* Patents Act 1977 § 44(3) (Eng.).
2.   Morton Salt Co. v. G.S. Suppinger Co., 314 U.S. 488 (1942).
3.   Lasercomb Am., Inc. v. Reynolds, 911 F.2d 970 (4th Cir. 1990).
4.   121 F.3d 516 (9th Cir. 1997).
5.   Carbice Corp. of Am. v. American Patents Dev. Corp., 283 U.S. 27, 31, at n.1 (1931).

infringer, but it and the *Motion Pictures Patents*[6] case established a policy against permitting patent owners to use patent licenses assert rights to control use of unpatented items. This policy was the basis for the rule established in *Morton Salt* that including patent-extending restrictions in a license would constitute a misuse, rendering the patent unenforceable even in direct infringement actions. Thus, the British experience was part of the historical basis for the U.S. misuse doctrine. Interestingly, however, the British statute was confined to a narrow class of tie-ins and never expanded in the way the misuse doctrine did in the United States. The fact that the statute was repealed to bring British law more in line with European Union (E.U.) competition law may also have implications for the future of the patent misuse doctrine in the United States.

A.   Section 38 of the U.K. Patents Act of 1907

Section 38 of the U.K. Patents Act of 1907 applied to the sale or lease of any patented article or process or a license to use or work any patented article or process. It made unlawful the insertion of a condition in a license that (1) prohibited a purchaser, lessee, or licensee from using articles or processes owned by another (a negative tie or tie-out); or (2) required the purchaser, lessee, or licensee to acquire from the patent owner "any article or class of articles not protected by the patent" (a positive tie or tie-in).[7] Such a condition was declared null and void as in

---

6.   Motion Picture Patents Co. v. Universal Film Mfg. Co., 243 U.S. 502 (1917). The *Motion Picture Patents* case overruled *Henry v. A.B. Dick*, 224 U.S. 1 (1912). It is interesting to note that some of the turn-of-the-century British tying and use restriction cases cited by the majority in the *A.B. Dick* case in support of the inherent rights of patent owners to impose tying conditions, *id.* at 39-43, may actually have been overruled legislatively by the 1907 U.K. Act, which the Supreme Court did not cite in *A.B. Dick*.

7.   *See* Patents and Designs Act 1907, 7 Edw. 7 c29 § 38(1) (Eng.):
      It shall not be lawful in any contract made after the passing of this Act in relation to the sale or lease of, or license to use or work, any article or process protected by a patent to insert a condition the effect of which will be—

restraint of trade and against public policy.[8] In addition, the existence of such a condition at the time of infringement was specifically made a defense to an action for patent infringement not only against a contributory infringer, as U.S. case law had held prior to *Morton Salt*,[9] but also against a direct infringer.[10]

Although the broad intentions of the statute seem clear, the Irish and British courts have respectively remarked that it is "infamously obscure" and "not easy to interpret" in practice.[11] The category of conduct that established what U.S. law would consider a misuse defense was strictly and narrowly defined. Because of its "penal" nature, the British House of Lords construed the statute to apply only to royalty provisions that would directly give the licensee a financial advantage by using the licensor's goods, i.e., not to all royalty or payment provisions that might induce the licensee to accept a tie.[12] Similarly, the statute applied only to royalty provisions that specifically prohibited "use" of third-party goods and required "acquisition" of the patent owner's goods. It did not specifically cover a provision, for example, requiring a licensee to *manufacture* and *sell* a patented product using only articles purchased

---

<ol>
<li type="a">to prohibit or restrict the purchaser, lessee, or license from using any article or class of articles, whether patented or not, or any patented process, supplied or owned by any person other than the seller, lessor, or licensor or his nominees; or</li>
<li type="b">to require the purchaser, lessee, or licensee to acquire from the seller, lessor, or licensor, or his nominees, any article or class of articles not protected by the patent;</li>
</ol>

and any such condition shall be null and void, as being in restraint of trade and contrary to public policy.

8.   *See id.*
9.   *See Motion Picture Patents*, 243 U.S. 502; *Carbice Corp.*, 283 U.S. 27; Leitch Mfg. Co. v. Barber Co., 302 U.S. 458 (1938).
10. *See* Patents and Designs Act 1907, 7 Edw. 7 c29 § 38(4) (Eng.); Sarason v. Frénay, 31 R.P.C. 352 (1914).
11. *See* Thomas Hunter Limited's Patent, [1965] R.P.C. 416 (Ir. H. Ct. 1964); Tool Metal Mfg. Co. v. Tungsten Elec. Co., [1955] 72 R.P.C. 209 (House of Lords 1955).
12. *See Tool Metal Mfg. Co.*, [1955] 72 R.P.C. at 220, 221.

from the patent owner[13] (although the language of the later Section 44 did clearly cover such a provision). The statute applied only to the defined tie-in and tie-out situations, not to the myriad other practices that have sometimes been considered misuse under U.S. law.

The 1907 statute specifically exempted a contract from its coverage if each of two requirements was satisfied: (1) the patent owner could prove that the purchaser, lessee, or licensee had been presented with a reasonable alternative arrangement; and (2) the contract contained a provision allowing the licensee to terminate the condition on three months' notice, with alternative compensation to be determined by an arbitrator appointed by the Board of Trade.[14]   The statute also specifically permitted a patent owner to require that articles used to repair a patented item be purchased from it.[15]

The British statute originally was enacted against a backdrop of widespread and abusive license conditions similar to those which the Supreme Court noted in the *Motion Pictures Patents* case.[16] In a report of a committee appointed "to inquire into the working of the Patents Acts" published on January 10, 1901, reference was made to the "clause of defeasance" that appeared in all U.K. letters patent. Apparently, since before the Statute of Monopolies of 1623, a proviso in the following terms always appeared:

---

13.   *See* Huntoon Co. v. Kolynos Inc., [1930] 47 R.P.C. 403 (Chancery Div. 1930).

14.   *See* Patents and Designs Act 1907, 7 Edw. 7 c29 § 38(1)(i)-(ii) (Eng.).

15.   *See id.* at § 38(5)(d). In the United States, repair, as opposed to reconstruction of an item sold or licensed by the patent owner, is not considered patent infringement.   Thus, supplying means to repair a lawfully produced item cannot be enjoined by the patent owner as contributory infringement.   *See* Aro Mfg. Co. v. Convertible Top Replacement Co., 365 U.S. 336 (1961).   Under 35 U.S.C. § 271(d) of the United States Patent Act, a patent owner may nevertheless tie items used for repair if the patent owner does not have market power.

16.   Motion Picture Patents Co. v. Universal Film Mfg. Co., 243 U.S. 502, 513 (1917).   *See* H. FLETCHER MOULTON, THE PRESENT LAW AND PRACTICE RELATING TO LETTERS PATENT FOR INVENTION 248 (1913).

provided that these our letters patent are on this condition, that if at any time during the said term it be made to appear to us, our heirs or successors, or any six or more of our Privy Council, that this our grant is contrary to law, or prejudicial or inconvenient to our subjects in general, . . . these our letters patent shall forthwith . . . be void to all intents and purposes.

When Parliament subsequently debated a draft patents and designs bill, the driving force to penalize restrictive conditions was provided by the British shoe industry. The British industry had found itself in need to mechanize. The major source of machinery was the eastern United States, and the American machinery manufacturers seem to have been in a position to exact somewhat onerous terms. Undoubtedly some of the machinery was patented, but the agreements entered into appear to have

1. been leases for a term of twenty years (when the term of a U.K. patent was, at that time, only fourteen years);
2. required continued payment of the royalty if any improvement, whether patented or not, was made to the machinery;
3. entitled the American manufacturer to attach such improvements to the machinery; and
4. required that no other machinery should be used alongside the machinery which was the subject of the agreement.[17]

Under the circumstances, coupled with a touch of xenophobia, it is not entirely surprising to find in the bill, as published on June 4, 1907, that the section dealing with such contracts provided that

[t]he insertion by the patentee in a contract made after the passing of this Act of any condition which by virtue of this section is null and void shall be a ground on which the patent may be revoked.

---

17. These conditions appear to have been similar to those which accompanied the lease-only policy of the dominant machine manufacturer, which was eventually held illegal under U.S. antitrust law in *United States v. United Shoe Machinery Corp.*, 110 F. Supp. 295 (D. Mass. 1953), *aff'd*, 347 U.S. 521 (1954).

This provision was presumably considered too draconian, and it was amended simply to provide a defense available to anyone sued for infringement of the patent. A successful defense resulted in the remedy of nonenforceability of the patent until the offending contractual condition was removed. As explained by Lloyd-George in Parliament:

> The hon. and learned Gentleman knew how difficult it was to provide a perfectly watertight clause which would prevent operations by trusts for the evasion of the law. It had been attempted many times, but the trusts had been able to walk round the law. There was only one way of doing it, and that was by making them feel that if they endeavored to evade the law or the principle of the law in this respect they would endanger the patent for the time being. If a man abused the special privilege which was granted to him when he obtained a patent by using it to the detriment of the trade of this country, he must know that he could not bring an action for infringement of the patent as long as he was abusing the privilege. He did not think that man should be allowed to go into Court and sue for damages in respect of the infringement of the patent. That was the principle on which he had proceeded, and he thought it was the only way to prevent people in future from operations of the kind complained of. That would make it worth their while not to repeat these operations.[18]

This speech makes clear why the U.K. legislature adopted a *Morton Salt* rule thirty-five years before *Morton Salt*.[19]

---

18. Lloyd-George, Hansard, Aug. 13, 1097, column 1174.

19. The same statutory regime was adopted in Ireland where the language of what qualifies as a restrictive condition tended to be read less narrowly than in England. *See* Thomas Hunter Limited's Patent, [1965] R.P.C. 416 (1964) (interpreting Industrial and Commercial Property (Protection) Act, No. 16 (1927) § 54, which mirrored § 38 of the U.K.'s 1907 act). Again, the Irish statute specifically made the existence of a restrictive condition a defense to any infringement action. Industrial and Commercial Property (Protection) Act, No. 16 (1927) § 54(4). A somewhat similar substantive rule exists in Canada, but there the existence of a restrictive condition or other abuse of exclusive rights does not provide a defense to an unlicensed infringer; instead, the remedy is a petition to the Commissioner of Patents to require compulsory licensing or revocation of the patent on

B. Section 44 of the Patents Act of 1977

The British law as set out in Section 44 of the Patents Act of 1977, quoted as an appendix to this chapter, was similar in most material respects to Section 38. Under Section 44(3), a patent holder will not prevail in an infringement action if, at the time of the infringement, there was in force a contract relating to the patent made by or with the consent of the plaintiff or a licensee under the patent granted by him or with his consent, and containing in either case a condition or term void by virtue of the section.

However, it was not until almost twenty years after Section 44's enactment that a defense under Section 44(3) was successful. In *Chiron Corporation v. Murex Diagnostics Limited,*[20] Chiron had identified the Hepatitis C virus (HCV) and sequenced extensive portions of the HCV genome. The patent claimed, inter alia, DNA sequences having antigenic properties. The market of immediate commercial importance to Chiron and its exclusive licensee, Ortho Diagnostic Systems, Inc., was testing kits to identify blood donors who had become infected with HCV or Human Immunodeficiency Virus (HIV). The kits contained the patented HCV antigens, which would provide a signal if the blood of a donor contained antibodies to HCV (the presence of such antibodies being evidence of the body's reaction to an infection by HCV).

Chiron and Ortho entered into a written agreement under which Chiron granted to Ortho an exclusive worldwide license, without the

---

the ground of abuse of exclusive rights. Canadian Patents Act §§ 67(2)(d-f), 68. HAROLD FOX, CANADIAN PATENT LAW 290-92, 297-300, 353-61 (1969). As under U.S. antitrust law, such a provision might in some circumstances violate the Canadian Competition Act; under Section 32 of that act, the Federal Court of Canada may also make an order restraining the licensor's conduct, declaring an agreement void or expunging or canceling a patent on application of the Attorney General. An abuse might also in some circumstances provide a defense to a suit under a license agreement as a covenant in unreasonable restraint of trade. An attempt to use tied selling as a defense to a patent infringement claim was rejected on the facts in the case of *Zelon v. Bonar & Bessus*, (1978) 39 C.P.R. (2d) 5.

20. [1996] 18 R.P.C. 535 (Ct. App. 1995).

right to sublicense, except to principal affiliates, "to the Chiron know-how and any existing Chiron patents . . ." that "relate to or are used directly or indirectly in connection with the development, manufacture, or use of antigens, antibodies or products" related to HCV (the 1989 Agreement). Ortho also agreed to purchase all HIV, as well as HCV, antigens and antibodies required for use in the testing kits from Chiron.

The defendant, Murex Diagnostics Limited, submitted that these provisions contravened Section 44 and gave it a defense to the patent infringement action Chiron had filed against it. Murex submitted that the 1989 Agreement was both a patent license and a contract for the supply of a patented product. Clause 6.1 of the Agreement required Ortho, the licensee, to acquire from Chiron, the licensor—and also prohibited Ortho from acquiring from anybody except Chiron—antigens for HIV, which were not the patented product (HCV products).

Chiron argued that, as of the date of the Agreement's execution, it had not yet obtained a U.K. patent; therefore, Section 44 did not apply. Because Section 130 of the U.K. Patents Act of 1977 defined a patented product as "any product which is a patented invention, or, in relation to a patented process, a product obtained directly by means of the process or to which the process has been applied" and the word "patent" in Section 44 was defined as "a patent under this Act," the plaintiff argued that Section 44 could only apply where the relevant patent was granted before the Agreement was consummated.

Neither the trial judge nor the court of appeal accepted this argument. According to the courts, the 1989 Agreement contemplated that upon grant of a patent on the then-pending U.K. patent application, Ortho would become exclusive licensee under the patent:

> there is not difficulty about agreeing what should happen if a particular event occurs.   Here what was expressly provided for was the contingency of an invention being patented.   That occurrence renders the contract void.   If it were not so, such a contract would be made immediately before the grant of a patent in order to escape avoidance.[21]

---

21.   *Id.* at 630.

Chiron, by a letter dated October 20, 1992, modified the 1989 Agreement by executing a waiver permitting Ortho to purchase from other sources antigens "required for the manufacture of Units of Product made, used, imported or sold in the United Kingdom," except to the extent the manufacture, use, sale, or importation would infringe any Chiron patent in the United Kingdom. Murex alleged that, although the waiver effectively modified the Agreement, it was not sufficient to avoid Section 44 because it did not permit Ortho to manufacture HIV antigen in the United Kingdom and export it to another country for kit manufacture; instead, the parties' arrangement still required Ortho to purchase that antigen from Chiron. The trial judge (Aldous, J.) agreed with the defendants, holding that such an obligation violated Section 44(1)(b).

On appeal, Chiron argued that Section 44 was concerned only with unwarranted extensions of the patentee's U.K. monopoly, and that export was not part of the monopoly conferred by a U.K. patent because export was not an act of infringement under Section 60 of the Patents Act of 1977. The court of appeal again rejected the plaintiff's argument:

> That submission assumes a territorial restriction on the operation of section 44, for which there is no warrant. The section is aimed at the patentee who abuses his bargaining position by seeking to make the grant of a license under the patent conditional upon acceptance by the licensee of a tie in relation to other goods. The restriction therefore was relevant, and this argument fails.[22]

Chiron and Ortho Inc. further amended their Agreement after the lower court's decision to avoid infringement of Section 44(1)(b). However, Chiron and Ortho Inc. were not able to recover damages from third-party infringement of Chiron's patent for the period of some two years that preceded the latter amendment because the court held that the patent was invalid during the effective period of the offending contractual provisions.

Chiron, Ortho Inc., and an Ortho subsidiary, Ortho Limited, had also entered into a separate deed on the day the U.K. patent was granted (the

---

22.   *Id.* at 631.

1992 Agreement), whereby Chiron granted to Ortho Limited an exclusive license under that patent to offer for sale, sell, and supply microtiter format tests in the United Kingdom. Ortho Inc. retained its exclusive license under the U.K. patent in all other respects. The deed did not contain any restriction that would be void under Section 44, nor did any clause of the deed make the license to Ortho Limited subject to the terms of the 1989 Agreement. On the same date, the three companies filed suit against Organon Teknika, an alleged third-party infringer of the U.K. patent.

Judge Aldous held that Section 44(3) precluded Ortho Limited, as licensee of the patent, from enforcing the patent against a third-party infringer on the same basis as Chiron was so precluded. However, the court of appeal disagreed, holding that Section 44(3) only precluded Ortho Limited if Ortho Limited *consented* to the tying clause:

> Ortho Limited was not a party to any form of tie under the 1989 Ortho agreement, nor did it consent to any such tie either at the time when the Ortho Agreement was made or by entering into the 1992 Agreement. The defense under section 44 is therefore not available against Ortho Limited. . . .[23]

C. Article 2(5) of Commission Regulation (EC) No. 240/96

Although the British statute was originally phrased in terms of restraint of trade, it was never intended to be a strict antitrust rule: some contractual provisions not reached by the statute might violate British or E.U. competition law, while other provisions to which the statute applied would not necessarily run afoul of those laws. Consistent with this approach, Article 2(5) of Commission Regulation (EC) No. 240/96 (the "technology transfer block exemption") provides an exception to the competition laws for certain conduct that would have violated the British statute. A tie-in of unpatented products is permitted in cases where it is necessary for a "technically proper exploitation of the licensed technology" or to ensure that the licensee's product "conforms to the

---

23.   *Id.* at 633.

minimum quality specifications that are applicable to the licensor and other licensees."

D. Comparison with U.S. Patent Misuse Doctrine

In comparing the scope and nature of the former British statute with U.S. patent misuse doctrine, a few points are worthy of note:

1. The British statute was first passed shortly after the turn of the century as a reaction to unreasonable or abusive licensing practices improperly extending the scope of a patent grant; the same pattern of conduct compelled the U.S. Supreme Court's decision in the *Motion Picture Patents*[24] case. Concern developed on both sides of the Atlantic that, without some severe limitations on a patentee's conduct, patent owners were apt to go farther than necessary to secure a reward for their actual invention.

2. The British statute did adopt a *Morton Salt*[25]-type rule of unenforceability, indicating the depth of the concern and the need for deterrence. By its terms, however, the statute rendered an unlawful provision a defense to an infringement suit only while the contract containing the condition was in force. Unlike the situation in the United States under *Morton Salt,*[26] misuse could clearly be purged immediately (but for the future only) by revoking the contractual provision.

3. The British statute did not contain a market power standard, nor was one read into the statute by the courts. The statute also did not adopt a staple/nonstaple distinction such as that contained in the original 35 U.S.C. § 271(d) in the United States.

4. While the British statute did not have any market power requirements, it did share the U.S. statute's requirement that the restrictive provision have been "conditioned" in the sense that

---

24. Motion Picture Patents Co. v. Universal Film Mfg. Co., 243 U.S. 502 (1917).
25. Morton Salt Co. v. G.S. Suppinger Co., 314 U.S. 488 (1942).
26. *Id.*; B.B. Chem. Co. v. Ellis, 314 U.S. 495 (1942).

the licensee was offered no reasonable alternative. Under Section 44, the patent owner had the burden of proving a lack of conditioning. In the first *Chiron* case, the court of appeal held that allegedly willing acceptance of the tie did not alter its unlawfulness if no alternative was, in fact, offered.[27]

5. The British misuse rule was solely a creature of statute and was narrowly defined. It condemned some ties but permitted others, such as the tying of materials for the repair of patented articles. The narrowness of the condition and specificity of the definitions did not, however, remove all ambiguity, and under a narrow construction, the statute's prohibitions could be avoided through differential royalty rates or other changes in form, such as that in the *Ortho Limited* case.

6. The British misuse rule has now been repealed in favor of a unified body of competition law rules more consistent with the competition rules of the European Union. This development does not appear to have been motivated by a considered decision to abandon the misuse rule in favor of antitrust rules so much as a desire to achieve harmonization with the European Community and perhaps to avoid disadvantaging British intellectual property owners in comparison to their continental European counterparts. Nevertheless, it may be a further example of the tendency of patent misuse to yield or at least accommodate itself to antitrust principles.

---

27.   Chiron Corp. v. Murex Diagnostics Ltd., [1996] R.P.C. 535.

Appendix: Text of Relevant Sections of Former Section 44 of the British Patents Act of 1977

"(1) Subject to the provisions of this section, any condition or term of a contract for the supply of a patented product or of a license to work a patented invention, or of a contract relating to any such supply or license, shall be void insofar as it purports:

(a) in the case of a contract for supply, to require the person supplied to acquire from the supplier, or his nominee, or prohibit him from acquiring from any specified person, or from acquiring except from the supplier or his nominee, anything other than the patented product;

(b) in the case of a licence to work a patented invention, to require the licensee to acquire from the licensor or his nominee, or prohibit him from acquiring from any specified person, or from acquiring except from the licensor or his nominee, anything other than the product which is the patented invention or (if it is a process) other than any product obtained directly by means of the process or to which the process has been applied;

(c) in either case, to prohibit the person supplied or licensee from using articles (whether patented products or not) which are not supplied by, or any patented process which does not belong to, the supplier or licensor, or his nominee, or to restrict the right of the person supplied or licensee to use any such articles or process.

* * *

(3) In proceedings against any person for infringement of a patent it shall be a defence to prove that at the time of the infringement there was in force a contract relating to the patent made by or with the consent of the plaintiff or pursuer or a licence under the patent granted by him or with his consent and containing in either case a condition or term void by virtue of this section.

(4) A condition or term of a contract or licence shall not be void by virtue of this section if—

(a) at the time of the making of the contract or granting of the licence the supplier or licensor was willing to supply the product, or grant a licence to work the invention, as the case may be, to the person supplied or licensee, on reasonable terms specified in the contract or licence and without any such condition or term as is mentioned in subsection (1) above; and

(b) the person supplied or licensee is entitled under the contract or license to relieve himself of his liability to observe the condition or term on giving to the other party three months' notice in writing and subject to payment to that other party of such compensation (being, in the case of a contract to supply, a lump sum or rent for the residue of the term of the contract and, in the case of a licence, a royalty for the residue of the term of the licence) as may be determined by an arbitrator or arbiter appointed by the Secretary of State.

(5) If in any proceeding it is alleged that any condition or term of a contract or licence is void by virtue of this section it shall lie on the supplier or licensor to prove the matters set out in paragraph (a) of subsection (4) above.

(6) A condition or term of a contract or licence shall not be void by virtue of this section by reason only that it prohibits any person from selling goods other than those supplied by a specific person or, in the case of a contract for the hiring of or licence to use a patented product, that it reserves to the bailor (or, in Scotland, hirer) or licensor, or his nominee, the right to supply such new parts of the patented product as may be required to put or keep it in repair."

CHAPTER VII

COPYRIGHT AND TRADEMARK MISUSE

by Ralph Jonas, Michele E. Beuerlein,
George G. Gordon, and Charles W. Cohen

Alleged infringers of copyrights and trademarks have asserted misuse defenses through the years. Courts addressing these defenses have often looked to the patent misuse doctrine for guidance. However, many courts have noted that the different features of copyrights and trademarks, including the different extent to which they offer their owners exclusivity and the different methods they provide for obtaining enforceable rights, may make the analogy to patent misuse a flawed one.

While there is still disagreement among courts and commentators as to whether copyright misuse should exist at all, the current trend is in favor of finding that at least some conduct can constitute copyright misuse. Currently the Fourth, Fifth, and Ninth Circuits and lower courts from several other circuits appear to accept the doctrine of copyright misuse, while some other district courts reject it or are uncertain of its status in their circuits. Moreover, only in recent years have courts actually held that conduct in the cases before them sufficed to establish a copyright misuse. Notwithstanding the relative infancy of the copyright misuse doctrine, the rise of software and information-based businesses to prominence in today's economy may result in the copyright misuse doctrine eclipsing the patent misuse doctrine in importance. The extent to which trademark misuse is accepted is murkier, and its future is also uncertain.

Section VII.A, the copyright misuse section of this chapter, describes the history of the copyright misuse defense and examines the current state of the law. It then discusses some of the issues that the case law has addressed: (1) whether an alleged infringer must prove the existence of an antitrust violation or market power to establish copyright misuse, (2) whether a party not directly affected by the misuse can assert a copyright misuse defense, (3) whether copyright misuse should be an affirmative claim for relief, and (4) whether the copyright owner should be permitted to "purge" misuse. It concludes with a discussion of the need for the copyright misuse defense, particularly in light of the differences between patents and copyrights.

Section VII.B, the trademark misuse section of this chapter, sets forth the historical background in which a few courts have applied—and others have rejected—a misuse doctrine based on either unclean hands from conduct such as misrepresentation or antitrust violations. The section then discusses the few recent cases comparing the justification for a trademark misuse doctrine with the justifications for the patent and copyright misuse doctrines. It concludes by addressing whether a misuse doctrine can be harmonized with the policies underlying trademark protection.

A. Copyright Misuse

Copyright misuse, like patent misuse, is an equitable doctrine that permits courts to "withhold their aid where the plaintiff is using the right asserted contrary to the public interest."[1] In fact, the copyright misuse doctrine has evolved out of a long line of patent misuse cases dating back to 1942, when the Supreme Court first applied patent misuse as a defense to an infringement action.[2] The type of conduct that might constitute copyright misuse has been described, in language similar to that used to describe patent misuse, as "an attempt to extend the exclusionary power granted by copyright beyond the protected work itself."[3]

1. History of Copyright Misuse from 1948 to 1990

Historically, few courts have refused to enforce a copyright on the ground that the copyright owner misused its copyright. The first court to do so was the District Court of Minnesota in *M. Witmark & Sons v.*

---

1.   Morton Salt Co. v. G.S. Suppiger Co., 314 U.S. 488, 492 (1942).

2.   *See id.* at 494. Chapter I describes the evolution of the patent misuse doctrine.

3.   BellSouth Adver. & Publ'g Corp. v. Donnelly Info. Publ'g, Inc., 719 F. Supp. 1551, 1562 (S.D. Fla. 1988), *aff'd*, 933 F.2d 952 (11th Cir. 1991), *vacated on reh'g, en banc,* 977 F.2d 1435 (11th Cir. 1992), *rev'd on other grounds*, 999 F.2d 1436 (11th Cir. 1993).

Jensen.[4] The conduct at issue in *Witmark* involved the licensing practices of the American Society of Composers, Authors and Publishers (ASCAP), which obtained exclusive rights from its thousands of members and required motion picture theater owners to obtain blanket licenses covering every song in the ASCAP repertoire instead of only the songs in the films.[5] The theater owners' failure to purchase such licenses prompted ASCAP to sue for copyright infringement, and the theater owners asserted the copyright misuse defense. The court found that ASCAP's blanket licensing practices constituted an impermissible use of the copyright grant because such practices created a monopoly over the music in films. In refusing to enforce ASCAP's copyrights against the theater owners, the court stated:

> Public interest transcends plaintiffs' rights under their copyrights, and where the relief sought would serve to continue the unlawful practices here condemned, it should be withheld. One who unlawfully exceeds his copyright monopoly and violates the anti-trust laws is not outside the pale of the law, but where the Court's aid is requested, . . . and the granting thereof would tend to serve the plaintiffs in their plan . . . to extend their copyrights in a monopolistic control beyond their proper scope, it should be denied.[6]

No subsequent holding until the Fourth Circuit's decision in *Lasercomb America, Inc. v. Reynolds,*[7] forty-two years later, clearly applied the copyright misuse doctrine to bar an infringement action.[8]

---

4. 80 F. Supp. 843 (D. Minn. 1948), *appeal dismissed sub nom.* M. Witmark & Sons v. Berger Amusement Co., 177 F.2d 515 (8th Cir. 1949).

5. *See Witmark*, 80 F. Supp at 844-45.

6. *Id.* at 850.

7. 911 F.2d 970 (4th Cir. 1990).

8. *See* Phillip Abromats, *Copyright Misuse and Anticompetitive Software Licensing Restrictions: Lasercomb America, Inc. v. Reynolds*, 52 U. PITT. L. REV. 629, 630-31 (1991); David J. Grais, *Copyright Misuse and Fraud on the Copyright Office*, PRACTICING LAW INSTITUTE: INTELLECTUAL PROPERTY/ANTITRUST, 351, 363 (1994); Leslie Wharton, *Misuse and Copyright: A Legal Mismatch*, 8:3 COMPUTER LAW. 1 (1991); Stephen A. Stack, Jr., *Recent and Impending Developments in Copyright and*

The U.S. Supreme Court has never explicitly addressed the issue of copyright misuse. The Court may tacitly have recognized the copyright misuse doctrine in *United States v. Paramount Pictures, Inc.*,[9] where it stated:

> Block-booking [of feature films] prevents competitors from bidding for single features on their individual merits. The District Court felt it illegal for that reason and for the reason that it "adds to the monopoly of a single copyrighted picture that of another copyrighted picture which must be taken and exhibited in order to secure the first." That enlargement of the monopoly of the copyright was condemned below in reliance on the principle which forbids the owner of a patent to condition its use on the purchase or use of patented or unpatented materials. The court enjoined defendants from performing or entering into any license in which the right to exhibit one feature is conditioned upon the licensee's taking one or more other features.
> We approve that restriction.[10]

Subsequently, in *United States v. Loew's, Inc.*[11] the Supreme Court stated that "[t]he principles underlying our Paramount Pictures decision have general application to tying arrangements involving copyrighted products." In *Sony Corp. of America v. Universal City Studios, Inc.*,[12] the court denied a copyright contributory infringement claim upon the determination that the allegedly infringing product was a product having substantial noninfringing use. Its analysis was based on the patent contributory infringement statute, 35 U.S.C. § 271(c), which it applied by analogy because of the close relationship between patents and

---

Antitrust, 61 ANTITRUST L.J. 331 (1993); Note, *Clarifying the Copyright Misuse Defense: The Role of Antitrust Standards and First Amendment Values*, 104 HARV. L. REV. 1289 (1991); Jere M. Webb & Lawrence A. Locke, *Intellectual Property Misuse: Developments in the Misuse Doctrine*, 4 HARV. J.L. & TECH. 257 (Spring 1991).

9.   334 U.S. 131 (1948).
10.   *Id.* at 156-58 (citations omitted).
11.   371 U.S. 38, 50 (1962).
12.   464 U.S. 417, 439-42 (1984).

copyrights.[13] The court noted, however, that applying patent principles to copyrights had to be done with caution because of important substantive differences between the two forms of intellectual property.[14]

Both *Paramount Pictures* and *Loew's* are antitrust cases, not infringement cases, and the language of those decisions is entirely consistent with traditional tying claim analysis.[15] Nothing in either *Paramount Pictures* or *Loew's*, however, implies that if presented with conduct by the plaintiff constituting copyright misuse in an infringement action, the Supreme Court would necessarily bar the infringement claim. At least one lower court has noted that, in *Loew's*, "the Court did not use the opportunity to create a copyright misuse doctrine."[16] On the other hand, the Federal Circuit has stated that "the United States Supreme Court has given at least tacit approval of the defense."[17]

Care is therefore required in drawing inferences from the Supreme Court's references to patent misuse cases in *Paramount Pictures* and *Loew's*. Although *Paramount Pictures* and *Loew's* are clear in their condemnation of block-booking practices, neither case would suggest that a blatant copier of *Gone with the Wind* could escape liability simply by asserting copyright misuse based on the fact that the copyright holder had previously tied one or more films to *Gone with the Wind* in a licensing agreement with a third party. In both *Paramount Pictures* and *Loew's*, the remedy selected by the Court was enjoining the offending practice rather than holding the copyright unenforceable or requiring mandatory licensing.

The Supreme Court's decision in *Broadcast Music, Inc. v. Columbia Broadcasting System, Inc.*[18] is also of interest with respect to the

---

13.   The patent contributory infringement doctrine and its relationship to misuse are described in Chapter I.

14.   *See* 464 U.S. at 439 n.19.

15.   *See* Troy Paredes, *Copyright Misuse and Tying: Will Courts Stop Misusing Misuse?* 9:2 HIGH TECH. L.J. 271, 324-25 (1994).

16.   Broadcast Music, Inc. v. Hearst/ABC Viacom Entertainment Servs., 746 F. Supp. 320, 328 (S.D.N.Y. 1990).

17.   Atari Games Corp. v. Nintendo of America Inc., 975 F.2d 832, 846 (Fed. Cir. 1992) (citing United States v. Loew's Inc., 371 U.S. 38 (1962)).

18.   441 U.S. 1 (1979).

copyright misuse defense. In that case, the plaintiff raised the copyright misuse doctrine, as an adjunct to a private antitrust action, seeking a declaratory judgment that the defendants misused their copyrights through blanket licensing practices.[19] The Second Circuit Court of Appeals, reversing a lower court decision, held that the defendants' blanket licensing practices constituted per se price fixing and copyright misuse.[20] Without separately addressing the copyright misuse question, the Supreme Court reversed and remanded the Second Circuit's holding that the defendants' blanket licensing practice was per se price fixing, thereby also reversing the holding of the court of appeals on copyright misuse.[21] Some commentators take the position that the Supreme Court implicitly recognized the misuse claim by remanding that issue, as well as the antitrust issue, rather than dismissing it.[22]

2. *Current Case Law Adopting the Copyright Misuse Doctrine*

The seminal recent opinion adopting and defining the copyright misuse doctrine is the Fourth Circuit's 1990 opinion in *Lasercomb America, Inc. v. Reynolds*.[23] In *Lasercomb*, a developer of computer-assisted die-making software filed a copyright infringement action against an alleged infringer, but the court refused to enforce the copyright in the software because of noncompetition provisions in the

---

19. *See id.* at 6.
20. *See* Columbia Broadcasting Sys., Inc. v. American Soc'y of Composers, Authors & Publishers, 562 F.2d 130, 140-41 (2d Cir. 1977), *rev'd sub nom.* Broadcast Music, Inc. v. Columbia Broadcasting Systems, Inc., 441 U.S. 1 (1979).
21. *See Broadcast Music*, 441 U.S. at 25.
22. *See, e.g.*, Godin, *Broadcast Music, Inc. v. Columbia Broadcasting System, Inc.: The Copyright Misuse Doctrine*, 15:3 NEW ENG. L. REV. 683, 684, 693 (1980); John Baker McClanahan, *Copyright Misuse as a Defense to an Infringement Action: Lasercomb America, Inc. v. Reynolds*, 49 WASH. & LEE L. REV. 213, 233 (1992); Thomas M. Susman, *Tying, Refusals to License, and Copyright Misuse: The Patent Misuse Model*, 36 J. COPYRIGHT SOC'Y USA 300, 305-06 (1989); Paredes, *supra* note 15, at 288-89 (1994).
23. 911 F.2d 970 (4th Cir. 1990).

developer's standard software license agreement.[24] The offending provisions prohibited any licensee and its directors and employees from directly or indirectly writing, developing, producing, or selling competing computer-assisted die-making software for ninety-nine years.[25]

The court determined that the defendant intentionally and fraudulently infringed the copyright. The infringer had refused to sign a license agreement, so it was not bound by the challenged provision. Thus, *Lasercomb* squarely presented the issue whether the infringer's copyright misuse defense would bar an infringement action, notwithstanding the defendant's intentional infringement and the fact that the defendant itself was not affected by the conduct alleged to be copyright misuse.

In its opinion, the Fourth Circuit reviewed the origins of patent and copyright law in English law, the similar treatment of these two aspects of intellectual property by the framers of the Constitution, and later statutory and judicial developments. Based on this review, the court concluded that parallel public policies underlie the protection of both types of intellectual property rights.[26] The court then determined, in summary fashion, that these parallel policies called for application of the misuse defense in copyright law as well as patent law.[27]

The court further held that conduct need not necessarily rise to the level of an antitrust violation to constitute copyright misuse.[28] Instead, the court considered whether the plaintiff was using its copyright in a manner violative of the public policy underlying the grant of a copyright.[29] It found that the plaintiff's broad covenant against licensing or creating other computer-assisted die-making software actually stifled new, independent expression; this broad suppression of new expression contravened the fundamental goal of copyright law and therefore constituted copyright misuse. Analogizing to patent law cases such as

---

24. *See id.*
25. *See id.* at 973.
26. *See id.* at 974.
27. *See id.*
28. *See id.* at 978.
29. *See id.*

Morton Salt,[30] the court held that the defense of copyright misuse was available to the defendant despite the fact that it had not been injured by the misuse.[31]

In *PRC Realty Systems v. National Association of Realtors,*[32] the Fourth Circuit went even further, holding that a clause requiring a licensee to use its best efforts to promote the publication of the plaintiff's copyrighted multiple real estate listing service constituted copyright misuse. The court determined that it would be inconsistent with the "best efforts" clause for the licensee to develop a competing software product; therefore the license violated public policy by suppressing independent development of an online publishing service for multiple listings. The court held that although the plaintiff had the right to ensure that its software was not exploited without compensation, it was not permitted to use its copyright to prevent all future development of an independent expression of the idea underlying the licensed software by the defendant or any other licensee.[33]

The Fifth Circuit has also applied the misuse doctrine, refusing to grant relief for infringement to a copyright holder in *Alcatel USA, Inc. v. DGI Technologies.*[34] In that case, the defendant, DGI Technologies, was attempting to develop a microprocessor card for use on telephone switches manufactured by the plaintiff, DSC Communications. In order to ensure that its microprocessor card was compatible with DSC's switches, DGI had to test the card on a DSC switch, which necessarily involved copying DSC's copyrighted operating system. However, the license agreements between DSC and its switch customers prohibited customers from copying the software and only allowed customers to use the software for their own use in conjunction with a telephone switch purchased from DSC.

After a trial on the merits, the jury determined that DSC's license agreements constituted copyright misuse. The Fifth Circuit sustained

---

30.   Morton Salt Co. v. G.S. Suppiger Co., 314 U.S. 488 (1942).
31.   *See Lasercomb,* 911 F.2d at 979.
32.   1992 Copyright L. Dec. (CCH) ¶ 26,961, 1992 U.S. App. LEXIS 18017 (4th Cir. 1992).
33.   *See id.*
34.   166 F.3d 772 (5th Cir. 1999).

this finding, holding that a reasonable juror could conclude that "DSC has used its copyrights to indirectly gain commercial advantage over products DSC does not have copyrighted, namely, its microprocessor cards."[35] According to the court, "without the freedom to test its cards in conjunction with DSC's software, DGI was effectively prevented from developing its product, thereby securing for DSC a limited monopoly over its uncopyrighted microprocessor cards."[36] The misuse defense was sustained even though an antitrust claim based on the same conduct was rejected as a matter of law because of lack of market power in the market for switches.[37]

In *Practice Management Information Corp. v. The American Medical Association*,[38] the Ninth Circuit also expressly adopted a copyright misuse defense, refusing to enforce the copyright on a medical procedure coding system known as the Physician's Current Procedure Terminology (CPT), owned by the American Medical Association (AMA). In that case, Practice Management Information Corporation, a publisher, purchased copies of the CPT for resale but objected to the price charged; it filed a declaratory judgment action claiming that, inter alia, the AMA misused its copyright by entering into an agreement with the Health Care Financing Administration (HCFA) in which the HCFA agreed to use only the CPT and not any other "system of procedure

---

35.   *Id.* at 793.
36.   *Id.* at 794. Most courts that have considered the issue have concluded that such a unilateral refusal to license does not constitute misuse. *See, e.g., In re* Independent Serv. Orgs., Antitrust Litig., 203 F.3d 1322 (Fed. Cir. 2000); Triad Sys. Corp. v. Southeastern Express Co., 64 F.3d 1330, 1337 (9th Cir. 1995); Service & Training, Inc. v. Data Gen. Corp., 963 F.2d 680, 690 (4th Cir. 1992); *In re* Independent Serv. Orgs. Antitrust Litig., 85 F. Supp. 2d 1130 (D. Kan. 2000); Advanced Computer Servs. v. MAI Sys. Corp., 845 F. Supp. 356, 368-69 (E.D. Va. 1994); Warner/Chappel Music, Inc. v. Pilz Compact Disc, Inc., 52 U.S.P.Q.2d 1942 (E.D. Pa. 1999).
37.   *Alcatel*, 166 F.3d at 781-84.
38.   121 F.3d 516, 519-21 (9th Cir. 1997), *amended by* 133 F.3d 1140 (9th Cir. 1998).

nomenclature . . . for reporting physicians' services" eligible for federal reimbursement.[39]

The Ninth Circuit held that such an agreement constituted copyright misuse:

> What offends the copyright misuse doctrine is not HCFA's decision to use the AMA's coding system exclusively, but the limitation imposed by the AMA licensing agreement on HCFA's rights to decide whether or not to use other forms as well.[40]

The court further stated that the terms under which the AMA licensed the use of the CPT to the HCFA gave the AMA "a substantial and unfair advantage over competitors" and that the AMA had used its copyright in a manner violative of the public policy embodied in the grant of a copyright.[41] Significantly, although the AMA's agreement with the HCFA was, in effect, an exclusive dealing arrangement—which is not per se unlawful under the antitrust laws—the court did not engage in a rule of reason analysis. To the contrary, the court agreed with the Fourth Circuit that "a defendant in a copyright infringement suit need not prove an antitrust violation to prevail on a copyright misuse defense."[42]

Relying in part on *Lasercomb* and patent law principles, a district court in *qad. Inc. v. ALN Associates, Inc.*[43] refused to enforce a copyright where the plaintiff had misrepresented the extent of its entitlement to copyright protection with respect to the copyright it was seeking to enforce. In support of its copyright misuse defense, the defendant asserted that (1) despite the significant incorporation of components of another firm's software into the plaintiff's software, the plaintiff failed to identify its software as a derivative work in its copyright registrations;

---

39. *Id.* at 517.
40. *Id.* at 521. *Accord* Veeck v. Southern Bldg. Code Congress Int'l, Inc., 49 F. Supp. 2d 885 (E.D. Tex. 1999) (no misuse where municipalities adopted building code but were under no contractual restriction not to adopt competing codes).
41. *Practice Management*, 121 F.3d. at 521.
42. *Id.*
43. 770 F. Supp. 1261, 1265-70 (N.D. Ill. 1991), *aff'd in part, reversed in part*, 974 F.2d 834 (7th Cir. 1992).

and (2) for nearly three years, the plaintiff had prosecuted its infringement claim against the defendant falsely asserting that the plaintiff's software was a completely original work.[44] The defendant argued that this "improper extension and overstatement of [the plaintiff's] copyrights is a misuse which [the court] should remedy by declaring [the plaintiff's] copyrights unenforceable against [the defendant]."[45]

The court held that the prosecution of an invalid copyright constituted misuse of both the judicial process and the copyright laws. It further held that when a copyright holder attempts to use legal proceedings to protect an improper extension of a copyright, the court may refuse to enforce the copyright on the ground of copyright misuse.[46]

In *Tamburo v. Calvin*,[47] a district court dismissed copyright infringement claims on the ground that the plaintiff committed copyright misuse. The misuse in *Tamburo* was a clause in a software license and resale agreement prohibiting the reseller from developing any product, whether or not computer-based, that competed with the software it was reselling under license.[48] While the noncompete clause recited a ten-year limit, its terms also prevented the reseller from developing a competing product for as long as the reseller was involved with the software.[49] The court held that the noncompete clause purported to extend the licensor's copyright beyond the copyrighted software to cover any product developed for the same purpose, regardless of whether those

---

44. *See id.* at 1265-66.
45. *Id.* at 1266.
46. *See id.* The court did not reach the issue whether the copyright holder's failure to state on its copyright registrations the fact of the work's derivation from a competitor's work also constituted copyright misuse. *Id.* at 1267. In subsequent proceedings between the parties, the court held that its earlier copyright misuse holding precluded the plaintiff from prevailing on its assertion that the defendant infringed the plaintiff's related software manuals. qad. Inc v. ALN Assoc., Inc., No. 88 C 2246, 1992 WL142650, *5-6 (N.D. Ill. June 11, 1992).
47. No. 94 C 5206, 1995 WL 121539 (N.D. Ill. Mar. 15, 1995).
48. *See id.* at *2-3.
49. *See id.* at *3.

products were even computer-based.[50] The court found these restrictions "more egregious than [the clauses] struck down in *Lasercomb*."[51]

In addition to the decisions that have refused to enforce a copyright on misuse grounds, several decisions have recognized the validity of the copyright misuse defense (at least in dicta), even though they did not apply it in cases where the particular facts did not warrant a finding of misuse.[52] In addition to tying clauses, courts have indicated that the following types of conduct might constitute misuse:

1. the attempted enforcement of a software license agreement provision which grants the licensor "sole ownership" of all

---

50. *See id.* at *18.
51. *Id.*
52. *See, e.g.*, Service & Training, Inc. v. Data Gen. Corp., 963 F.2d 680, 690 (4th Cir. 1992) (rejecting defense because the appellants offered no evidence that the copyright holder did anything beyond limiting the use of software to the repair and maintenance of specific hardware); Religious Tech. Ctr. v. Lerma, 40 U.S.P.Q.2d 1569 (E.D. Va. 1996) (rejecting misuse defense based on claimed use of infringement litigation to harass alleged infringer and gain access to personal files); *In re* Independent Servs. Orgs. Antitrust Litig., 989 F. Supp. 1131, 1143 (D. Kan. 1997) (copyright misuse is a viable defense, but a copyright holder's unilateral refusal to license does not constitute misuse) *aff'd* 203 F.3d 1322, 1328 n.2 (Fed. Cir. 2000); Advanced Computer Serv. v. MAI Sys. Corp., 845 F. Supp. 356, 368-69 (E.D. Va. 1994). *See also* Triad Sys. Corp. v. Southeastern Express Co., 64 F.3d 1330, 1337 (9th Cir. 1995); Mitchell Bros. Film Group v. Cinema Adult Theater, 604 F.2d 852 (5th Cir. 1979); Mastercraft Fabrics Corp. v. Dickson Elberton Mills, Inc., 821 F. Supp. 1503, 1511 n. 7 (M.D. Ga. 1993); LucasArts Entertainment Co. v. Humongous Entertainment Co., 870 F. Supp. 285, 290 (N.D. Cal. 1993); F.E.L. Publications, Ltd. v. Catholic Bishop of Chicago, 214 U.S.P.Q. 409, 413 n.9 (7th Cir. 1982) ("Dismissal of a copyright claim for misuse is an equitable defense which requires a balancing of the equities. We think that in this case, the scales are tipped in [the copyright holder's] favor.").

software programs developed by the licensee in the same field as the licensed software,[53]

2. "us[ing] . . . monopoly power to force cable program services to purchase [a] blanket license at exorbitant prices,"[54] and

3. applying in one's own name for copyright registrations for works that were copied from others.[55]

One commentator has also suggested that copy protection devices in computer software may constitute copyright misuse because they prevent copying of copyrighted works even after the copyright expires.[56]

---

53. *See, e.g.*, Reliability Research, Inc. v. Computer Assocs, Int'l., Inc., 793 F. Supp. 68 (E.D.N.Y. 1992).

54. Broadcast Music, Inc. v. Hearst/ABC Viacom Entertainment Serv., 746 F. Supp. 320, 328 (S.D.N.Y. 1990) (recognizing the existence of copyright misuse, but stating that "recovery appears remote" and rejecting the cable program services' assertion of copyright misuse as a vehicle for affirmative relief). *See also* Coleman v. ESPN, Inc., 764 F. Supp. 290, 295 (S.D.N.Y. 1991) (concluding that copyright misuse is a cognizable defense and that there were issues of fact as to the availability of alternatives to the blanket license offered by the licensor which precluded summary judgment on the licensor's copyright infringement claim).

55. *See* Michael Anthony Jewelers, Inc. v. Peacock Jewelry, Inc., 795 F. Supp. 639 (S.D.N.Y. 1992) (court refused to dismiss counterclaims alleging copyright misuse and antitrust violations based on plaintiff's alleged practice of applying in its own name for copyright registrations for jewelry designs that were copied from its competitors and willfully omitting all references to any work from which the designs were copies). *See also* Willsea v. Theis, No. 98 Civ. 6773 (BSJ), 1999 WL 595629 (S.D.N.Y. Aug. 6, 1999) (fraud on copyright alleged as misuse; court noted interesting questions raised, including whether copyright misuse should be recognized in Second Circuit, but denied defense based on prior release and settlement).

56. *See* McClanahan, *supra* note 22, at 233 (1992). *See also* Marshall Leaffer, *Engineering Competitive Policy and Copyright Misuse*, 19:3 U. DAYTON L. REV. 1087 (1994) (exploring the copy protection device issue).

3. Current Case Law Rejecting the Copyright Misuse Doctrine

Although many courts have accepted, or at least commented favorably on, the copyright misuse doctrine, some courts have expressly rejected the doctrine or its substantive equivalents, such as the "antitrust defense" to infringement.[57] At least one court has found, for example, that given the uncertainty regarding the acceptability of the copyright misuse doctrine, an allegation of copyright misuse would not prohibit the grant of at least temporary relief to a copyright holder in an infringement action.[58]

Other courts have expressed an unwillingness to extend patent misuse principles to copyright cases without explicit instructions to do so from the Supreme Court. In *Rural Telephone Service Co., Inc. v. Feist Publications, Inc.*,[59] for example, a public utility providing telephone service brought a copyright infringement action against a telephone directory publisher based upon alleged copying of white pages. In response, the publisher alleged various antitrust violations as an affirmative defense. The district court rejected the affirmative defense,

---

57. *See* Harms, Inc. v. Sansom House Enterprises, Inc., 162 F. Supp. 129, 135 (E.D. Pa. 1958), *aff'd on other grounds sub nom.* Leo Feist, Inc. v. Lew Tendler Tavern, Inc., 267 F.2d 494 (3d Cir. 1959); Orth-O-Vision, Inc. v. Home Box Office, 474 F. Supp. 672, 686 (S.D.N.Y. 1979); Rural Tel. Serv. Co., Inc. v. Feist Publications, Inc., 663 F. Supp. 214, 219-20 (D. Kan. 1987), *aff'd*, 916 F.2d 718 (10th Cir. 1990), *rev'd on other grounds*, 499 U.S. 340 (1991). *See also* Peter Pan Fabrics, Inc. v. Candy Frocks, Inc., 187 F. Supp. 334, 336 (S.D.N.Y. 1960); Foreign Car Parts, Inc. v. Auto World, Inc., 366 F. Supp. 977, 979 (M.D. Pa. 1973).

58. *See, e.g.,* Data Gen. Corp. v. Grumman Sys. Support Corp., 1989 Copyright L. Dec. (CCH) ¶ 26,399, 1988 U.S. Dist. LEXIS 16427 (D. Mass. Dec. 29, 1988). Eventually, the First Circuit rejected the copyright misuse claim. *See* Data Gen. Corp. v. Grumman Sys. Support Corp., 36 F.3d 1147, 1169-70 (1st Cir. 1994).

59. 663 F. Supp. 214 (D. Kan. 1987), *aff'd*, 916 F.2d 718 (10th Cir. 1990), *rev'd on other grounds*, 499 U.S. 340 (1991).

noting the absence of express direction from the Supreme Court concerning extension of the misuse doctrine to copyright law.[60]

Similarly, in *Orth-O-Vision v. Home Box Office*,[61] the plaintiff, an affiliate of a transmitter of pay television subscription programs, sued the transmitter and others alleging violation of federal antitrust laws and breach of contract when the transmitter terminated its agreement with the affiliate. The transmitter and its parent corporation counterclaimed for violations of, inter alia, the Copyright Act and common-law unfair competition. In rejecting the plaintiff's affirmative defenses to the counterclaims based on the alleged antitrust law violations, the court stated that, "[a]s a general rule, it is no defense to a copyright infringement claim that the copyright owner is violating antitrust laws," and noted that the Supreme Court has never expressly held that a court of equity should decline to enjoin infringement if the copyright owner is engaged in anticompetitive activity.[62]

4. Issues Raised by the Case Law Recognizing a Copyright Misuse Doctrine

a. The Roles of Antitrust Violations and Market Power

In *Lasercomb*,[63] the court held that conduct need not necessarily rise to the level of an antitrust violation to constitute copyright misuse.[64] Instead, the *Lasercomb* court identified the central issue as whether the copyright is being used in a manner violative of the public policy embodied in the grant of a copyright.[65] In *Practice Management*, the

---

60. See *Rural Telephone*, 663 F. Supp. at 220, *citing Orth-O-Vision*, 474 F. Supp. at 686; *Peter Pan*, 187 F. Supp. at 336; *Harms*, 162 F. Supp. at 135. Ultimately, in *Rural Telephone*, the Supreme Court held that white pages were not copyrightable, thereby dismissing the infringement action and making the assertion of the copyright misuse defense moot. See 499 U.S. at 361-63.

61. 474 F. Supp. 672 (S.D.N.Y. 1979).

62. *Id.* at 686.

63. Lasercomb Am., Inc. v. Reynolds, 911 F.2d 970 (4th Cir. 1990).

64. *See id.* at 978.

65. *See id.*

Ninth Circuit agreed, stating that "a defendant in a copyright infringement suit need not prove an antitrust violation to prevail on a copyright misuse defense."[66] Other courts have similarly stated, directly or indirectly, that a copyright misuse defense may be based on either an antitrust violation or another violation of public policy.[67]

For example, citing *Lasercomb*, the Fourth Circuit reached this conclusion in *Service & Training, Inc. v. Data General Corp.*[68] On the facts of that case, however, the court rejected the alleged infringer's misuse argument, finding "no evidence that Data General did anything beyond limiting the use of the software to repair and maintenance of specific computer hardware, activity that is protected as an exclusive right of a copyright owner."[69] Thus, while an antitrust violation is not a prerequisite to establishing copyright misuse, the absence of an antitrust violation requires the party asserting misuse to show that the copyright holder somehow illegally extended its monopoly or otherwise violated the public policy underlying the copyright law.[70]

---

66. Practice Mgmt. Info. Corp. v. AMA, 121 F.3d 516, 521 (9th Cir. 1997).
67. *See* Atari Games Corp. v. Nintendo of Am., Inc., 975 F.2d 832, 846 (Fed. Cir. 1992); Advanced Computer Servs. v. MAI Sys. Corp., 845 F. Supp. 356, 366-67 (E.D. Va. 1994); Microsoft Corp. v. BEC Computer Co., 818 F. Supp. 1313, 1316 (C.D. Cal. 1992); National Cable Television Ass'n, Inc. v. Broadcast Music, Inc., 772 F. Supp. 614, 652 (D.D.C. 1991); Broadcast Music, Inc. v. Moor-Law, Inc., 527 F. Supp. 758, 772-73 (D. Del. 1981); Sega Enterprises v. Accolade, Inc., 785 F. Supp. 1392, 1399 (N.D. Cal. 1991); K-91, Inc. v. Gershwin Pub. Corp., 372 F.2d 1, 2 (9th Cir. 1967). Commentators supporting this view include Timothy H. Fine, *Misuse and Antitrust Defenses to Copyright Infringement Actions*, 17 HASTINGS L.J. 315 (1965); Richard Stitt, *Copyright Self-Help Protection as Copyright Misuse: Finally the Other Shoe Drops*, 57 UMKC L. REV. 899 (1989); David Scher, *The Viability of the Copyright Misuse Defense*, 20 FORDHAM URB. L.J. 89 (1992).
68. 963 F.2d 680 (4th Cir. 1992).
69. *Id.* at 690. *See also* Syncsort, Inc. v. Sequential Software, Inc., 50 F. Supp. 2d 318 (D.N.J. 1999) (restriction prevented licensees from using licensor's intellectual property in competing products but not from licensing or developing competing software).
70. *See also National Cable*, 772 F. Supp. at 652.

A number of courts, however, take a contrary view, determining that an antitrust violation is required to establish copyright misuse.[71] Indeed, courts have historically used antitrust concepts to define conduct constituting copyright misuse.[72] As the Seventh Circuit pointed out in *Saturday Evening Post Co. v. Rumbleseat Press, Inc.*,[73] the concepts of "monopolistic abuse" that lie at the heart of the patent misuse doctrine were developed in antitrust law:

> If misuse claims are not tested by conventional antitrust principles, by what principles shall they be tested? Our law is not rich in alternative concepts of monopolistic abuse; and it is rather late in the day to try to develop one without in the process subjecting the rights of patent holders to debilitating uncertainty.[74]

According to the court, the point that misuse should be based on antitrust principles applies with even greater force to copyright misuse, where the likelihood that a copyright confers substantial market power is

---

71. *See* Bellsouth Advertising & Publishing Corp. v. Donnelley Info. Publishing, Inc., 933 F.2d 952, 960-61 (11th Cir. 1991); United Tel. Co. of Mo. v. Johnson Publishing Co., 855 F.2d 604, 612 (8th Cir. 1988); Saturday Evening Post Co. v. Rumbleseat Press, Inc., 816 F.2d 1191, 1200 (7th Cir. 1987); Edward B. Marks Music Corp. v. Colorado Magnetics, Inc., 497 F.2d 285, 290-91 (10th Cir. 1973); Electronic Data Sys. Corp. v. Computer Assoc. Int'l, Inc., 802 F. Supp. 1463, 1466 (N.D. Tex. 1992); Basic Books, Inc. v. Kinko's Graphics Corp., 758 F. Supp. 1522, 1538-39 (S.D.N.Y. 1991). Commentators supporting this view include Byron A. Bilicki, *Standard Antitrust Analysis and the Doctrine of Patent Misuse: A Unification Under the Rule of Reason*, 46 U. PITT. L. REV. 209 (1984); J. Diane Brinson, *Patent Misuse: Time for a Change*, 16 RUTGERS COMPUTER & TECH. L.J. 357 (1990); Scott A. Miskimon, *Divorcing Public Policy From Economic Reality*, 69 N.C. L. REV. 1672 (1991); Abromats, *supra* note 8.
72. *See* Paredes, *supra* note 15, at 291.
73. 816 F.2d 1191 (7th Cir. 1987).
74. *Id.* at 1200.

likely to be less than in the case with respect to a patent.[75] Moreover, even those courts, such as the *Lasercomb* court, which ultimately held that no antitrust violation is required to establish copyright misuse, have discussed copyright misuse in terms of antitrust policy.[76]

A related issue is whether or not proof of market power should be a required element in a misuse defense. In cases where the assertion of misuse is based on an antitrust violation, the answer seems easy—the antitrust violation itself may require proof of market power. Similarly, to the extent that courts in copyright misuse cases continue to rely on patent misuse principles, market power should be required in copyright misuse cases involving tying claims.[77] However, some commentators have argued that proof of market power should be a necessary element of all copyright misuse claims, regardless of whether they are based on an antitrust violation or some other violation of the public policy underlying the copyright laws. These commentators argue that in the absence of market power or other ability to coerce third parties, a copyright owner should be free to exploit the exclusionary rights granted under the copyright laws. Without market power, the copyright holder's conduct is less likely to cause any significant harm and more likely to be, in fact, mutually advantageous.[78]

In those misuse cases where proof of market power is required (e.g., misuse cases involving certain antitrust violations, such as tying), there is the additional issue of whether the copyright itself should give rise to a presumption of market power. In *Loew's*, the Supreme Court stated that in an antitrust tying case, the requisite market power in the tying product "is presumed when the tying product is patented or

---

75. *See id., quoting* USM Corp. v. SPS Technologies, Inc., 694 F.2d 505, 512 (7th Cir. 1982). *See also* McClanahan, *supra* note 22, at 231; Paredes, *supra* note 15, at 291, 295-96.

76. *See* Lasercomb Am., Inc. v. Reynolds, 911 F.2d 970, 978-79 (4th Cir. 1990).

77. *See* 35 U.S.C. § 271(d).

78. *See* James Kobak, Jr., *A Sensible Doctrine of Misuse for Intellectual Property Cases*, 2 ALB. L.J. SCI. & TECH. 1, 34-35, 45 (1992) (arguing that market power serves as a useful tool for differentiating coercion in misuse cases from consensual agreement to the allegedly offending provision); Paredes, *supra* note 15, at 303-09.

copyrighted."[79] The Court agreed with the district court's conclusion that "each defendant, by reason of its copyright, had a 'monopolistic' position as to each tying product" and, thus, possessed "sufficient economic power" for purposes of showing a tying violation.[80] The Court repeated its conclusion that copyrights confer sufficient uniqueness to give rise to a presumption of market power in *United States Steel Corp. v. Fortner Enterprises, Inc.*[81] In *Jefferson Parish Hospital District No. 2 v. Hyde*, Justice Stevens stated in dictum that if a product is protected by a patent, "it is fair to presume that the inability to buy the product elsewhere gives the seller market power."[82]

Although the presumption of market power established by the Supreme Court in *Loew's* has never been expressly abandoned, the better reasoned cases on patent misuse support a trend away from the presumption.[83] In fact, the critics of the presumption as applied to patents include several Supreme Court justices. In her concurring opinion in *Jefferson Parish*, Justice O'Connor criticized the presumption as a "common misconception," noting that "a patent holder has no market power in any relevant sense if there are close substitutes for the

---

79. United States v. Loew's, Inc., 371 U.S. 38, 45 (1962).
80. *Id.* at 48.
81. 429 U.S. 610, 619-20 (1977); *see also* Digidyne Corp. v. Data Gen. Corp., 734 F.2d 1336, 1341 (9th Cir. 1984), *cert. denied sub nom* Data Gen. Corp. v. Digidyne Corp., 473 U.S. 908 (1985).
82. 466 U.S. 2, 16 (1984).
83. *See* Abbot Lab. v. Brennan, 952 F.2d 1346, 1354-55 (Fed. Cir. 1991) (no presumption of market power from intellectual property right); Xeta, Inc. v Atex, Inc., 852 F.2d 1280 (Fed. Cir. 1988); Mozart Co. v. Mercedes Benz of N. Am., Inc., 833 F.2d 1342 (9th Cir. 1987) (dictum that market power should not be presumed merely from a copyright); A.I. Root Co. v. Computer/Dynamics, Inc., 806 F.2d 673, 676 (holding that the presumption as set forth in *Loew's* is overbroad); Ralph C. Wilson Indus., Inc. v. Chronicle Broadcasting Co., 794 F.2d 1359 (9th Cir. 1986); SCM Corp. v. Xerox Corp., 645 F.2d 1195 (2d Cir. 1981); Broadcast Music, Inc. v. Hearst/ABC Viacom Entertainment Servs., 746 F. Supp. 320, 328 (S.D.N.Y. 1990). *But see* MCA Television, Ltd. v. Public Interest Corp., 171 F.3d 1265 (11th Cir. 1999) (following *Loew's* presumption in an antitrust case).

patented product."[84]   Moreover, the Supreme Court has refused to presume market power for patented products in the context of certain monopolization claims.[85] In addition, in their opinion dissenting from denial of certiorari in *Data General Corp. v. Digidyne Corp.*, Justices White and Blackmun stated that "this case raises several substantial questions of antitrust law and policy, including . . . what effect should be given to the exercise of a copyright or other legal monopoly in determining market power."[86]

Congress also departed from the presumption of market power in patent misuse cases by enacting the 1988 Patent Reform Act. As discussed in Chapter I, the act provides, in relevant part, that a patent owner shall not be deemed to have misused its patent based on allegations that it tied the license or sale of a patent or patented product to the license or sale of a separate product, "unless, in view of the circumstances, the patent owner has market power in the relevant market for the patent or patented product on which the license or sale is conditioned."[87] If Congress intended market power to be presumed from the existence of a patent, the language in the 1988 Patent Reform Act requiring inquiry into market power would be superfluous.[88]

If, as Justice O'Connor and Congress have suggested, a presumption of market power in the patent context is improper then, a fortiori, a presumption of market power in the copyright context is improper as well. Copyrights have many "product substitutes" due to the fact that the scope of the copyright grant extends only to the expression of an idea and not to the idea itself.[89] Therefore, copyright holders may, in general,

---

84.   466 U.S. at 37 n.7.
85.   *See* Walker Process Equip., Inc. v. Food Mach. & Chem. Corp., 382 U.S. 172, 178 (1965).
86.   473 U.S. 908 (1985).
87.   35 U.S.C. § 271(d)(5) (1988).
88.   *But see* Grid Systems Corp. v. Texas Instruments Inc., 771 F. Supp. 1033 (N.D. Cal. 1991), *amended by* 91 Daily Journal D.A.R. 9374 (N.D. Cal. 1991) (holding that the presumption of market power from the ownership of a patent may survive in the context of an antitrust, as opposed to a misuse, claim).
89.   Aylwald, *Copyright Law: The Fourth Circuit's Extension of the Misuse Doctrine to the Area of Copyright Misuse: A Misuse of the Misuse*

be less likely to possess market power by virtue of the scope of their intellectual property protection than patent holders.[90]

The Department of Justice and Federal Trade Commission have rejected the notion that any type of intellectual property right—patent, copyright, trade secret, or know-how—creates a presumption of market power. One of the three general principles reflected in the agencies' *Antitrust Guidelines for the Licensing of Intellectual Property* is that "the Agencies do not presume that intellectual property creates market power in the antitrust context."[91] The *Guidelines* recognize that although intellectual property confers the right to exclude with respect to a specific work, product, or process, "there will often be sufficient actual or potential close substitutes for such product, process, or work to prevent the exercise of market power."[92]

b. Parties with Standing to Assert Copyright Misuse

(1) The Relevance of Injury from the Alleged Misuse

The Supreme Court in *Morton Salt* explicitly stated that an alleged infringer asserting a patent misuse defense need not have been injured by the alleged conduct.[93] Relying on *Morton Salt*, the *Lasercomb* court came to the same conclusion, holding that the misuse defense was available to the defendants despite the fact that they had not signed a

---

Doctrine? 17:2 U. DAYTON L. REV. 661, 689 n.230 (1992); Stitt, *supra* note 67, at 904; Paredes, *supra* note 15, at 306-09.

90. *See* Kobak, *supra* note 78, at 32. Commentators have also suggested that copyright owners be given an opportunity to prove justification for their conduct rather than having misuse determined on a per se basis. *See id.* at 35; McLanahan, *supra* note 22, at 216. *See also* Melissa Hamilton, *Software Tying Arrangements Under the Antitrust Laws: A More Flexible Approach*, 71:3 DENV. U. L. REV. 607, 609 (1994) (identifying some of the virtues of tying arrangements).

91. U.S. DEP'T OF JUSTICE & FEDERAL TRADE COMM'N, ANTITRUST GUIDELINES FOR THE LICENSING OF INTELLECTUAL PROPERTY § 2.0 (1995), *reprinted in* 4 Trade Reg. Rep. (CCH) ¶ 13,132.

92. *Id.* at § 2.2.

93. Morton Salt Co. v. G.S. Suppiger Co., 314 U.S. 488 (1942).

license agreement containing the challenged provision.[94] According to the *Lasercomb* court, the relevant question was not whether the alleged infringers were parties to the challenged license agreements, but rather "whether Lasercomb [was] using its copyright in a manner contrary to public policy."[95] The primary argument in favor of permitting the collateral assertion of a misuse defense by a party not harmed by the challenged conduct is that the threat of such a defense may act as a deterrent for copyright holders contemplating actions that would constitute copyright misuse.

Some commentators argue that copyright misuse should only be asserted by parties seeking relief from the misuse. Otherwise, blatant infringers who are not bound by the offending provision could benefit unfairly.[96] Indeed, to permit the misuse defense to be asserted by a willful infringer not personally injured by the copyright holder's conduct may actually encourage willful infringement of copyrights and discourage the creation of new copyrightable works.[97] For example, if *Gone with the Wind* had been part of a block-booking package, a blatant infringer could copy the film and screen it publicly without the threat of successful prosecution of an infringement action. Similarly, a computer software developer could market an exact duplicate of a competitor's software, as long as the competitor's form of software license contained a tying provision or other provision constituting copyright misuse. Allowing such infringement seems contrary to the public policy of encouraging competitors to create new copyrightable works.[98]

(2) Alleged Infringers with Unclean Hands

A related question is whether an alleged infringer can assert the misuse defense despite its own "unclean hands." The misuse defense is

---

94. *See* Lasercomb Am., Inc. v. Reynolds, 911 F.2d 970, 979 (4th Cir. 1990).
95. *Id.*
96. *See, e.g.*, Kobak, *supra* note 78, at 35; Abromats, *supra* note 8, at 655-58.
97. *See, e.g.*, Abromats, *supra* note 8, at 631-32; Paredes, *supra* note 15, at 273-76, 329-30.
98. *See* Sony Corp. of Am. v. Universal City Studios, Inc., 464 U.S. 417, 432 (1984); United States v. Loew's, Inc., 371 U.S. 38, 46 (1962) (*quoting Paramount Pictures*, 334 U.S. 131, 158 (1948)); Mazer v. Stein, 347 U.S. 201, 219 (1954).

conceptually related to, if not rooted in, the doctrine of unclean hands.[99] Unclean hands is traditionally defined as an equitable defense asserted against a claimant whose conduct bars recovery or enforcement on public policy grounds. However, as an equitable defense, unclean hands can only be asserted if (1) the offending act of the other party has an immediate and necessary relation to the matter in controversy and (2) the party asserting unclean hands has been personally injured by the other party's conduct.[100] In addition, the equity of the unclean hands defense would be defeated if the party relying on such a defense were to come before the court with unclean hands itself.

In *Atari Games Corp. v. Nintendo of America, Inc.*, the Federal Circuit held that a party asserting copyright misuse must have clean hands or the defense will be barred.[101] The alleged infringer in *Atari* lied to the Copyright Office in order to obtain a copy of its competitor's copyrighted program.[102] Determining that copyright misuse is not a statutory defense but "solely an equitable doctrine," the court held that the alleged infringer could not assert a copyright misuse defense because of its own unclean hands. However, several courts, including *Lasercomb*, have held that even if both the copyright holder and the alleged infringer have unclean hands, the copyright holder is barred from enforcing its copyright if it has engaged in copyright misuse.[103]

---

99. *See* Morton Salt Co. v. G.S. Suppiger Co., 314 U.S. 488 (1942).

100. *See* Mitchell Bros. Film Group v. Cinema Adult Theater, 604 F.2d 852, 863 (5th Cir. 1979).

101. 975 F.2d 832, 846 (Fed. Cir. 1992).

102. *See id.* The district court for the Northern District of California subsequently granted the copyright owner's motion for summary judgment on its copyright infringement claim. 1993 U.S. Dist. LEXIS 6786 (N.D. Cal. May 18, 1993).

103. *See* Alcatel USA, Inc. v. DGI Techs., Inc., 166 F.3d 772, 794-95 (5th Cir. 1999); Lasercomb Am., Inc. v. Reynolds, Inc., 911 F.2d 970 (4th Cir. 1990); qad. Inc. v. ALN Assoc., Inc., 770 F. Supp. 1261, 1266 n.15 (N.D. Ill. 1991).

5. Copyright Misuse as an Affirmative Claim for Relief

Traditionally, courts have considered copyright misuse as an affirmative defense rather than an affirmative claim for relief. At least two courts have stated that although copyright misuse might be an affirmative defense to an infringement claim, it is not a vehicle for affirmative relief.[104]

Another court, however, suggested the contrary, at least with respect to declaratory relief. In *Electronic Data Systems Corp. v. Computer Assoc., Inc.*,[105] the licensee of certain software asserted copyright misuse as an affirmative claim, actionable under antitrust principles, and sought damages and a declaratory judgment that the licensor's misuse of its copyrights rendered them invalid and unenforceable.[106] The court did not reject the licensee's claims entirely on the ground that no cause of action for copyright misuse exists, as the licensor argued. Rather, the court permitted the affirmative misuse claim "[t]o the extent that [the licensee] seeks a declaration that it has not infringed [the licensor's] copyrights because of [the licensor's] alleged misuse of such copyrights . . . ."[107] The

---

104. *See* Broadcast Music, Inc. v. Hearst/ABC Viacom Entertainment Servs., 746 F. Supp. 320, 328 (S.D.N.Y. 1990); Warner/Chappel Music Inc. v. Pilz Compact Disc, Inc., 52 U.S.P.Q.2d 1942, 1947 n.3 (E.D. Pa. 1999); *see also* Juno Online Servs. L.P. v. Juno Lighting, Inc., 979 F. Supp. 684, 688-90 (N.D. Ill. 1997) (rejecting affirmative claim for trademark misuse); Susan G. Braden, *Copyright Misuse: If Not a Shield, a Sword, Practicing Law Institute, Patents, Copyrights, Trademarks, and Literary Property*, PRACTICING LAW INSTITUTE: INTELLECTUAL PROPERTY/ ANTITRUST (1993).

105. 802 F. Supp. 1463 (N.D. Tex. 1992).

106. The facts upon which the copyright misuse claim is based are unclear. The court stated only that the licensee alleged that the licensor misused its software copyrights by "restraining competition; imposing restrictions on the use of copyrighted software that extended beyond the exclusive rights granted by the copyright laws; and, tying the purchase of copyrighted software to other (licensor) products or services." *Id.* at 1465.

107. The court found that the licensee's copyright misuse claim, specifically the software tying allegation, stated a claim under Section 2 of the Sherman Act. *See id.* at 1466.

court further determined that, if the alleged copyright misuse is based on an antitrust violation, the antitrust violation would be separately actionable or may be asserted as a counterclaim. This result corresponds to the practice in patent misuse cases.[108]

6. Purging Copyright Misuse

As with patent misuse, once a copyright holder "purges" its misuse and all of the consequences of the misuse have dissipated, the copyright is enforceable again.[109] Under the doctrine of patent misuse, once the misuse has been purged, the patentee can recover for infringement from and after the date of the purge.[110] Presumably, the courts will apply a similar analysis to the copyright misuse doctrine. Because so few cases have applied the copyright misuse defense to bar an infringement action, there is little guidance on the requirements to purge copyright misuse. However, one would expect that, as with the doctrine of patent misuse, the abandonment of the offending practice and the dissipation of its effects will be required and will present questions of fact which are largely discretionary with the trial court.[111]

---

108. *See* B. Braun Med. Inc v. Abbot Lab., 124 F.3d 1419 (Fed. Cir. 1997); *see also* Chapter I, at 1-2 and nn. 2 & 3.

109. *See, e.g.*, Lasercomb Am., Inc. v. Reynolds, 911 F.2d 970, 979 n.22 (4th Cir. 1990); *see also* Budish v. Gordon, 784 F. Supp. 1320, 1337 n.12 (N.D. Ohio 1992). Although the court in *Budish* found it unnecessary to decide whether to recognize the copyright misuse defense, there is dicta in the opinion to the effect that a plaintiff will not be precluded from enforcing its copyright if any alleged misuse is purged.

110. *See, e.g.*, McCullough Tool Co. v. Well Surveys, Inc., 343 F.2d 381, 410 (10th Cir. 1965); Preformed Line Products Co. v. Fanner Mfg. Co., 328 F.2d 265, 278-79 (6th Cir. 1964).

111. *See* United States v. United States Gypsum Co., 340 U.S. 76, 89 (1950); International Salt Co., Inc. v. United States, 332 U.S. 392, 400-01 (1947); *Preformed Line*, 328 F.2d at 279.

7. Comparison of Copyright Misuse to Patent Misuse

The copyright misuse doctrine is rooted in concepts developed in patent infringement actions. A number of important distinctions between patents and copyrights, however, raise questions about the extent to which patent law misuse concepts should be applied in copyright actions. The Supreme Court has acknowledged that notwithstanding the "historic kinship" between patent law and copyright law, "[t]he two areas of law, naturally, are not identical twins" and that caution should be exercised "in applying doctrine formulated in one area to the other."[112]

A patent, for example, protects an inventor's idea as embodied in a process or device, but a copyright protects only an author's original expression of an idea in a particular work. Thus, a copyright does not preclude other independently created expressions of the same idea.[113] A good faith independent developer of an idea that already has been expressed in a copyrighted work may legally exploit the idea notwithstanding the copyrighted work.[114]

Because there are such fundamental differences in the exclusionary rights conveyed by patents and copyrights, the two forms of intellectual

---

112.   Sony Corp. of Am. v. Universal City Studios, Inc., 464 U.S. 417, 439 & n.19 (1984). Ultimately, the Court in *Sony* found that the contributory infringement doctrine in both the patent law and the copyright law was grounded in the same principle, thereby justifying the application of the patent law doctrine of contributory infringement (with its statutory limitations) to copyright law in that case. Other courts have also recognized that the patent misuse doctrine and the copyright misuse doctrine are not identical because neither the public policy considerations supporting them nor their respective goals are identical. *See, e.g.*, Mozart Co. v. Mercedes-Benz of North America, Inc., 833 F.2d 1342 (9th Cir. 1987); A.I. Root Co. v. Computer Dynamics, Inc., 806 F.2d 673 (6th Cir. 1986); Ralph C. Wilson Industries, Inc. v. Chronicle Broadcasting Co., 794 F.2d 1359 (9th Cir. 1986); Broadcast Music, Inc. v. Hearst/ABC Viacom Entertainment Services, 746 F. Supp. 320 (S.D.N.Y. 1990); *see also* WILLIAM C. HOLMES, INTELLECTUAL PROPERTY AND ANTITRUST LAW § 36.01 (1994).

113.   *See* 17 U.S.C. § 102(b) (1988); Mazer v. Stein, 347 U.S. 201, 217 (1954).

114.   *See Mazer,* 347 U.S. at 217-18.

property also may differ in their potential to cause anticompetitive effects. In *Saturday Evening Post*, Judge Posner of the Seventh Circuit stated:

> [A copyright] forbids copying the copyrighted work without the copyright holder's permission, but it does not forbid the making of close substitutes . . . . The danger of monopoly is more acutely posed by patent than by copyrights . . . . A patent empowers its owner to prevent anyone else from making or using his invention; a copyright just empowers its owner to prevent others from copying the particular verbal or pictorial or aural pattern in which he chooses to express himself. The economic power conferred is much smaller.[115]

In *Reed-Union Corp. v. Turtle Wax Inc.*,[116] the Seventh Circuit noted again that "copyrights do not exclude independent expression and therefore create less market power than patents."[117]

Patent and copyright protection differ in other ways as well. The system of patent prosecution, for example, differs significantly from the copyright registration process, both in the manner in which rights are obtained and the level of scrutiny to which the application is subject. These differences are significant because, as discussed in Chapters I and VIII, the policy arguments supporting the patent misuse doctrine include the preservation of the integrity and effectiveness of the patent examination system.[118] The integrity and effectiveness of the copyright registration system require less protection because the copyright registration system does not inquire in any significant degree into the merit of the application. The applicant must simply establish that the work submitted for copyright registration bears "at least some minimal degree of creativity."[119] More importantly, a copyright does not depend on registration for its existence, as a patent does.[120]

---

115. Saturday Evening Post Co. v. Rumbleseat Press, Inc., 816 F.2d 1191, 1198-1201 (7th Cir. 1987).

116. 77 F.3d 909 (7th Cir. 1996).

117. *Id.* at 913.

118. *See, e.g.,* Kobak, *supra* note 78, at 33-34; Chapter I.K; Chapter VIII.A.3.b.

119. Feist Publications v. Rural Tel. Serv. Co., 499 U.S. 340, 345 (1991).

120. *See* 35 U.S.C. § 154 (1988).

In *Lasercomb*, the court found that preventing alternate forms of expressing the ideas in the plaintiff's software was contrary to the specific public policy underlying copyright law regardless of whether such conduct violated the antitrust laws.[121] This expression-based policy rooted in copyright principles is similar to but somewhat different from the patent policies that originally animated the misuse doctrine. As noted above, the patent policy involved concern about undermining the system by which patent claims are closely examined and often limited before issuance by the Patent Office. Thus, whether viewed from a competitive or public policy perspective, differences between patents and copyrights suggest that the role a misuse defense should play in the intellectual property regimes, while broadly similar, need not be identical and that patent misuse principles should be applied cautiously to copyright cases. This issue is further addressed in Chapter VIII, which examines criticisms and justifications of the misuse doctrine.[122]

B. Trademark Misuse

The application of the misuse doctrine to trademarks has had a long history, but that history has not led to widespread acknowledgment of a trademark misuse defense. One reason for the relative obscurity of the trademark misuse doctrine is the fact that the cases addressing trademark misuse issues have relied on principles very different from those addressing patent or copyright misuse. The earliest cases relied on the equitable doctrine of unclean hands to deny enforcement of trademarks that misrepresent the products they signify. Other courts have looked to the Lanham Act of 1946, as subsequently amended,[123] and antitrust principles. Only recently have a few courts looked at the rationale underlying the patent and copyright misuse doctrines to determine what conduct, if any, should constitute trademark misuse.

---

121. 911 F.2d at 978.
122. *See* Chapter VIII.C.1.a.
123. 15 U.S.C. §§ 1051-1127 (1994).

1. Unclean Hands

As far back as 1883, well before the genesis of the patent misuse doctrine in *Morton Salt*, the Supreme Court denied relief to a trademark owner based on the trademark owner's conduct. In *Manhattan Medicine Co. v. Wood*,[124] the Court affirmed the dismissal of a bill in equity. The plaintiff, Manhattan Medicine Company, had obtained the recipe of a medicine called Atwood's Vegetable Physical Jaundice Bitters which was originally created and marketed by Moses Atwood of Georgetown, Massachusetts. Manhattan began to manufacture the medicine and packaged it in distinctive glass bottles labeled with the name of the product and a false notation that the product was "manufactured by Moses Atwood, Georgetown, Massachusetts, and sold by his agents throughout the United States." The defendants manufactured an imitation product and packaged it in packaging nearly identical to Manhattan's.

The Supreme Court held that Manhattan was not entitled to an injunction preventing the defendants from continuing to sell their imitation product because the statements that Manhattan's product was "manufactured by Moses Atwood" in "Georgetown, Massachusetts" were no longer true. The Court stated that the use of these statements constituted a misrepresentation to the public, and that a court of equity would not lend its aid to a plaintiff engaged in fraud.[125]

Twenty years later, the Supreme Court again denied relief to the owner of a trademark on the ground that the product name was misleading.[126] The plaintiff, the California Fig Syrup Company, manufactured a product called Syrup of Figs. It sued Clinton E. Worden & Company, alleging that Worden manufactured an imitation product. The Ninth Circuit granted relief. The Supreme Court reversed, noting that the California Fig Syrup Company had no right to the assistance of a

---

124. 108 U.S. 218 (1883).
125. *Id.* at 222.
126. *See* Clinton E. Worden & Co. v. California Fig Syrup Co., 187 U.S. 516 (1903).

court of equity because its Syrup of Figs contained few, if any, figs.[127] These cases did not use the term "trademark misuse," but the Supreme Court in *Morton Salt* referred to these cases as being misuse cases.[128]

A trademark misuse defense based on equitable principles was also successful in *United States Jaycees v. Cedar Rapids Jaycees*.[129] The national Jaycees organization revoked the ability of the local chapter of the Jaycees in Cedar Rapids to use the Jaycees trademark because the local chapter admitted women. The national organization then sued to enjoin the local chapter from using the trademark. By the time the case reached the Eighth Circuit, the national organization had begun admitting women. Yet the national organization still persisted with the lawsuit. The court held that it would be inequitable to enforce the trademark against the local chapter when the policy that had led to revocation of the chapter's rights had been changed.[130]

2. Trademark Misuse Cases Based on Antitrust Principles

a. Lanham Act or Equitable Defense

Section 1115(b)(7) of Title 15 of the U.S. Code, enacted in 1946, states that use of a mark to violate the antitrust laws is a defense to the statutory provision making a trademark registrant's exclusive right to a mark incontestable five years after registration, but it does not specifically state that an antitrust violation is a defense to an infringement suit. The statutory language reads, in pertinent part, as follows:

---

127. *See id.* at 538-40. The Lanham Act now specifically precludes registration of misdescriptive marks and provides for their cancellation. 15 U.S.C. §§ 1052(e)(1), (3), 1064(3), 1115(3) (1994). *See also* Renaud Sales Co. v. Davis, 22 F. Supp. 703 (D. Mass. 1938) (court denied relief to a trademark owner who had assigned its mark to another company which then used it on different goods); Independent Baking Powder Co. v. Boorman, 175 F. Supp. 448 (D.N.J. 1916) (changing principal ingredient of a product precluded enforcement of trademark).
128. Morton Salt Co. v. G.S. Suppiger Co., 314 U.S. 488, 494 (1942).
129. 794 F.2d 379 (8th Cir. 1986).
130. *See id.* at 383.

. . .

To the extent that the right to use the registered mark has become incontestable under section 1065 of this title, the registration shall be conclusive evidence of the validity of the registered mark and of the registration of the mark, of the registrant's ownership of the mark, and of the registrant's exclusive right to use the registered mark in commerce. . . . Such conclusive evidence of the right to use the registered mark shall be subject to proof of infringement as defined in section 1114 of this title, and shall be subject to the following defenses or defects:

. . .

(7) That the mark has been or is being used to violate the antitrust laws of the United States.

In 1966, a district court held that Section 1115(b)(7) may provide a complete defense to a trademark infringement action, and not simply a defense to incontestability, when the trademark is used in violation of the antitrust laws.[131] In *Phi Delta Theta Fraternity*, a jewelry manufacturer allegedly infringing the trademarks of various college fraternities and sororities claimed that the fraternities and sororities violated the antitrust laws by engaging in a scheme to grant one jewelry company the exclusive right to manufacture goods containing the logos of the fraternities and sororities. The court held that this conduct, if proved, could provide a defense to the infringement action.[132]

In *Carl Zeiss Stiftung v. V.E.B. Carl Zeiss, Jena*,[133] the court also held that using a trademark in violation of the antitrust laws could preclude infringement recovery, but did not follow the rationale of *Phi Delta Theta*. In *Zeiss*, the court initially held that 15 U.S.C. § 1115(b)(7) is not a defense to infringement, but merely a defense to incontestability of the

---

131. *See* Phi Delta Theta Fraternity v. J.A. Buchroeder & Co., 251 F. Supp. 968, 974 (W.D. Mo. 1966). The court found support for its holding in the statements of several senators in the legislative history of 15 U.S.C. § 1115(b)(7). *Phi Delta*, 251 F. Supp. at 978.

132. *See id.* at 974.

133. 298 F. Supp. 1309 (S.D.N.Y. 1969), *modified on other grounds,* 433 F.2d 686 (2d Cir. 1970).

trademark;[134] the court then acknowledged that apart from the statute, a court of equity may "deny enforcement of a trademark on the part of one who has used that trademark in violation of the antitrust laws."[135] Determining that "forces favoring exercise of such [equitable] power in a trademark suit are much weaker than those calling for its exercise in patent litigations," the court limited denial of trademark protection to those cases where the use of the trademark is "the basic and fundamental vehicle required and used to accomplish the [antitrust] violation."[136] In the case before it, the court did not find proof that the plaintiff had used or threatened to withhold the mark to coerce dealers to engage in anticompetitive conduct.

Even though the *Zeiss* court's holding is technically based on an equitable doctrine, the court specifically linked its power to deny relief to a violation of the antitrust laws dependent on use of the trademark itself. Other courts have followed this holding and recognized (but seldom applied) a misuse doctrine predicated on use of a trademark as a fundamental element of an antitrust violation.[137]

b. Tying

More recently, the trademark misuse doctrine as applied to anticompetitive activity has evolved into more than just a defense in infringement actions. Where the tie-in of a trademark to a nonprotected good or service constitutes the alleged trademark misuse, such conduct also has been the basis of affirmative antitrust claims.

---

134. *See id.* at 1311.
135. *Id.* at 1314.
136. *Id.* at 1314-15.
137. *See, e.g.,* Helene Curtis Indus., Inc. v. Church & Dwight Co., Inc., 560 F.2d 1325 (7th Cir. 1977); Union Carbide Corp. v. Ever-Ready Inc., 531 F.2d 366, 389 (7th Cir. 1976); Estee Lauder v. The Fragrance Counter, Inc., 189 F.R.D. 269 (S.D.N.Y. 1999); Electrical Info. Publications v. C-M Periodicals, 163 U.S.P.Q. 624, 633 (N.D. Ill. 1969) (use of fraudulently obtained generic name registrations to exclude competitors); The Coca-Cola Co. v. Howard Johnson Co., 386 F. Supp. 330, 335-38 (N.D. Ga. 1974) (requiring "immediate and necessary" relationship between use of mark and antitrust violation).

Franchisees, in particular, have raised tying claims not only as a misuse defense to franchisors' complaints seeking contractual damages or seeking to enjoin use of the trademark after termination of the franchise agreements, but also in declaratory judgment actions to forestall termination of the franchise agreements. The key issue in these cases is market definition. Defining the relevant market as the market for the franchisor's trademarked goods—i.e., a market in which the franchisor has complete control—favors the franchisees.[138] On the other hand, defining the relevant market as the market for franchises generally, or at least the market for franchises in the same general line of business, favors the franchisors.[139]

Since 1992, market definition in franchise cases has been governed by the Supreme Court's decision in *Eastman Kodak Co. v. Image Technical Servs.*[140] In *Kodak*, the Supreme Court approved certain single-brand markets and developed the "lock-in" theory of market power.[141] *Kodak* involved allegations that Kodak tied service to specialized parts available only from it by refusing to sell parts needed for many kinds of service to any third parties. Kodak had changed its policy, under which third-party providers had originally been given access to parts, so that purchasers with investments in machines found themselves "locked in" to relying solely on Kodak for parts and services in a way they could not have anticipated when they made their purchase decision. The Supreme Court held that Kodak could not be said as a matter of law to have no market power.

---

138. *See* Siegel v. Chicken Delight, Inc., 448 F.2d 43, 50 (9th Cir. 1971) (trademark conferred distinctive "goodwill and public acceptance unique to it and not enjoyed by other fast food chains").

139. *See* Mozart Co. v. Mercedes-Benz of North America, Inc., 833 F.2d 1342, 1346 (9th Cir. 1987) ("it is by no means clear" that prospective franchisees view franchise for even a distinctive product as different from other franchise opportunities).

140. 504 U.S. 451 (1992).

141. A thorough discussion of the competing arguments in the post-*Kodak* world may be found at Alan H. Silberman, *The Myths of Franchise "Market Power,"* 65 ANTITRUST L.J. 181 (1996).

In *Queen City Pizza, Inc. v. Domino's Pizza, Inc.*,[142] the Third Circuit interpreted *Kodak* to hold that an aftermarket is a valid market for antitrust purposes only when the aftermarket consists of unique goods; otherwise, the market must be defined as including all the franchises potentially available to a franchisee at the time of entering the franchise relationship.[143] Defining the relevant market as all franchises available to the franchisees originally, the Third Circuit held that Domino's Pizza could lawfully require its franchisees to purchase as much as 90 percent of their supplies from Domino's despite evidence that third parties could have supplied the franchisees more inexpensively.

The Sixth Circuit followed the *Queen City* rationale in *Valley Prods. Co. v. Landmark, Inc.*[144] Valley Products had been terminated as a supplier of soaps and other hotel products bearing the logo of one of Landmark's franchised hotels. It claimed that Landmark illegally subjected its franchisees to a tying arrangement through which the franchisees were forced to purchase logoed products only from Landmark as a condition of the franchise license. The court rejected Valley's claim that Landmark committed trademark abuse by refusing to use Valley as a supplier as inconsistent with the *Queen City Pizza, Inc. v. Domino's Pizza, Inc.* decision.[145]

However, the district court in *Collins v. International Dairy Queen, Inc.*[146] disagreed with the Third Circuit's *Queen City* decision. The *Collins* court did not interpret *Kodak* to apply only where the aftermarket consisted of unique products. The court distinguished *Queen City* by noting that Domino's expressly reserved the right to be the sole supplier of pizza ingredients to franchisees.[147] By contrast, the Dairy Queen franchise agreement provided that Dairy Queen was not the sole supplier of products and would be obligated to consider requests to use alternative suppliers. The Dairy Queen franchisees produced evidence that, in fact, Dairy Queen

---

142.   124 F.3d 430 (3d Cir. 1997).
143.   *See id.* at 442.
144.   128 F.3d 398 (6th Cir. 1997).
145.   *See id.* at 404. *See also* Syncsort, Inc. v. Sequential Software, Inc., 50 F. Supp. 2d 318 (D.N.J. 1999).
146.   980 F. Supp. 1252 (M.D. Ga. 1997).
147.   *See id.* at 1258.

had never allowed alternative suppliers to supply the franchisees. Because Dairy Queen's conduct violated its franchise agreement and the franchisees' reasonable expectations, the franchisees were unable to estimate their costs before buying franchises and found themselves locked-in to the tying arrangement.[148]

Other courts have adopted the *Collins* approach and required a lock-in caused by a franchisor's behavior inconsistent with the franchisees' contractual expectations. These cases have dismissed claims where evidence of the lock-in did not exist.[149]

3. Recent Cases Examining the Rationale for Trademark Misuse

Recently, two district courts have critically examined trademark misuse defenses premised on broad assertions of violation of trademark policy. The first of these cases included an affirmative claim for relief based on the trademark misuse doctrine.[150] Juno Online, the plaintiff, alleged that Juno Lighting misused its trademark and committed business torts by trying to have Juno Online's Internet domain name "juno.com" canceled and by registering the Internet domain name "juno-online.com" for itself. Juno Online sought damages on its misuse claim.

The court considered the history of the trademark misuse doctrine. The court noted that courts in cases such as *Carl Zeiss* and *Phi Delta Theta* addressed misuse claims based on alleged antitrust violations, while other courts, such as the Supreme Court in *Clinton E. Worden & Co.*, applied the misuse doctrine without any showing of antitrust violation. The court finally concluded that even if trademark misuse could form the basis of an affirmative claim, the case before it was not the proper case in which to recognize it.

---

148. *Id.* at 1252.
149. *See, e.g.,* Little Caesar Enters., Inc. v. Smith, 34 F. Supp. 2d 459 (E.D. Mich. 1998) (summary judgment); Wilson v. Mobil Oil Corp., 984 F. Supp. 450 (E.D. La. 1997).
150. Juno Online Services, L.P. v. Juno Lighting, Inc., 979 F. Supp. 684 (N.D. Ill. 1997).

In 1998, a magistrate judge in the Northern District of Illinois extensively examined the trademark misuse doctrine and ultimately rejected the defendant's misuse claim.[151] In that case, Northwestern claimed that Ashland, one of the defendants, sold inferior knock-offs of Northwestern's gumball machines. Ashland argued that the trademark misuse doctrine was broad, preventing any trademark owner with unclean hands from enforcing its trademark. In addressing Ashland's claim, the court first looked to the patent misuse doctrine. The court found that a litigant may establish a misuse defense only when the intellectual property owner violates the policy underlying the specific intellectual property right at issue. For trademarks, the court concluded, a misuse defense would be viable only if the trademark owner were to misrepresent its product through its trademark.[152] As Northwestern had made no misrepresentations, the misuse defense failed; in the court's words, "[d]efendants' motion is based upon a phantom legal theory, and were it legitimate, the allegations presented would be entirely inapplicable to a claim of trademark misuse."[153]

4. Comparison of Trademark Misuse to Patent and Copyright Misuse

The appropriateness of importing misuse principles from patent or copyright law to trademark law depends on the extent to which the underlying policies of these two forms of intellectual property protection share common ground.

While patents protect novel ideas and copyrights protect original expression, trademarks protect against customer confusion. The theory underlying the grant of a patent or copyright is that the public is best served when inventors or authors are given a temporary period of exclusivity for their inventions or creations; however, that protection should be limited to that which is the inventor's or author's new contribution to society. Trademarks serve the public interest by facilitating "the public's

---

151. Northwestern Corp. v. Gabriel Manufacturing Co., 48 U.S.P.Q.2d 1902 (N.D. Ill. 1998).
152. *Id.* at 1908-09.
153. *Id.* at 1911.

ability to distinguish among competing products."[154] Only secondarily does trademark law protect individual interests such as a trademark holder's investment in the goodwill established by the quality of its goods or services.

Because of these differences between patent law and trademark law policies, misuse of patents and trademarks can have markedly different effects. As the *Carl Zeiss* court noted, "a sharp distinction must be drawn between the antitrust misuse defense in patent infringement suits, on the one hand, and trademark suits, on the other."[155] The magistrate judge in *Northwestern* concluded that "it is inappropriate to predicate trademark misuse upon the same anti-competitive practices which constitute patent misuse"[156] because the relevant considerations in a trademark use analysis have more to do with the significance that a mark has to the public than with the anticompetitive practices of stifling creativity and invention or preempting matter in the public domain. The need for any trademark defense beyond normal statutory defenses and the unclean hands doctrine would be extremely narrow, if a reason exists for it at all.[157]

Specifically, the goal of trademark law in preventing confusion and protecting the public against false designations of source or origin[158] counsels against adoption of a *Morton Salt* rule of unenforceability as against all unauthorized users of trademarks. In cases of counterfeiting or blatant unauthorized use, a *Morton Salt* approach might only confuse, rather than benefit, consumers. A more appropriate remedy for trademark misuse might be to limit relief to damages or the ability to terminate a particular license, or to predicate injunctive relief on termination of the

---

154. *Id.* at 1908.
155. Carl Zeiss Stiftung v. V.E.B. Carl Zeiss, Jena, 298 F. Supp. 1309, 1314 (S.D.N.Y. 1969).
156. *Northwestern*, 48 USPQ 2d at 1908.
157. *See* Chapter VIII, at nn. 34 & 61.
158. *See* James Burrough, Ltd. v. Sign of the Beefeater, Inc., 540 F.2d 266 (7th Cir. 1976). The *James Burrough, Ltd.* court stated, "In the consideration of evidence relating to trademark infringement therefore, a court must expand the more frequent, one-on-one, contest between-two sides, approach. A third party, the consuming public is present, and its interests are paramount . . . . A 'trademark' is not that which is infringed. What is infringed is the right of the public to be free of confusion and the synonymous right of a trademark owner to control his product's reputation." *Id.* at 274.

conduct, rather than to prevent injunctive relief against all unauthorized users.[159] A traditional misuse defense, if necessary at all, would seem appropriate only in two situations: (1) where the trademark owner's conduct has severely compromised the significance of a mark, or (2) where the trademark owner has wrongfully sought to assert exclusionary rights over generic words or functional features in a way that might substantially restrict competition in a relevant product or service market.

---

159. *See* RESTATEMENT OF UNFAIR COMPETITION (THIRD) § 31(e) (1995). *See also* Colt Beverage Corp. v. Canada Dry Ginger Ale, 146 F. Supp. 300, 303 (S.D.N.Y. 1956).

CHAPTER VIII

THE MISUSE DOCTRINE: ISSUES OF SCOPE AND REMEDY

by Mark Ostrau

The concept of misuse represents a long-standing tradition in U.S. law and has a certain intuitive appeal, particularly as applied to practices which contravene the purpose of rigorous Patent Office scrutiny of patent claims. Concerns that licenses could be used to allow patent holders to gain control over products not in themselves patentable or not having undergone the patent examination process were expressed in the early contributory infringement cases out of which the patent misuse doctrine grew.[1] Similar concerns about use of copyrights to suppress, rather than encourage, new expression underlie the copyright misuse doctrine.[2]

Yet the present misuse doctrine presents problems that might be expected for any rule based on intuition and developed in an era of extreme Supreme Court hostility to intellectual property. The scope of conduct covered by the misuse doctrine is broad, unpredictable, and has sometimes been applied on a per se basis to conduct that does not seem to be patent-extending, anticompetitive, or even particularly unfair. The doctrine stems to a large extent from pronouncements in a handful of Supreme Court patent cases from a quarter to more than half a century ago; these cases may provide outdated theoretical underpinnings for the doctrine, especially as applied to modern technology licensing or to copyrights and trademarks. Moreover, the doctrine, which involves the remedy of unenforceability against any infringer, seems in some situations extremely harsh, if not almost confiscatory, and can result in a windfall for infringers. The possible shortcomings identified by these

---

1. *See* Mercoid Corp. v. Mid-Continent Inv. Co., 320 U.S. 661 (1944); Morton Salt Co. v. G.S. Suppiger Co., 314 U.S. 488 (1942); Motion Picture Patents Co. v. Universal Film Mfg. Co., 243 U.S. 502 (1917).

2. *See* Alcatel USA, Inc. v. DGI Techs., Inc., 166 F.3d 772 (5th Cir. 1999); Lasercomb Am., Inc. v. Reynolds, 911 F.2d 970 (4th Cir. 1990).

criticisms arguably result in a doctrine that may overdeter dissemination and enforcement of intellectual property rights and underdeter infringement.

Debate about the misuse doctrine centers around two interrelated issues: (1) the conduct, if any, that should constitute misuse; and (2) the appropriate consequences of a misuse finding. Most criticism of the misuse doctrine involves the first issue and makes one or more of the following points. First, the case law may reflect outdated thinking about the market power that results from the exercise of patent or other intellectual property rights. Second, the doctrine, as applied on a per se basis, fails to take into account the procompetitive benefits of many licensing practices and thus covers practices that are competitively benign. Third, to the extent that the misuse doctrine embodies policies other than those inherent in the antitrust laws, there are no consistent standards for determining what is or is not misuse; the resulting legal uncertainty may discourage some socially beneficial licensing activities.

In addition to these criticisms about the definition of misuse, some additional criticism focuses on the consequences of a misuse finding in rendering a patent or copyright unenforceable, these consequences are said to be unduly harsh, discouraging innovation and the exercise of intellectual property rights.

The first three criticisms, dealing with the conduct that has been characterized as misuse, are summarized in section VIII.A of this chapter. Section VIII.B addresses the debate over what effects a finding of misuse should have. Finally, suggestions for refining the misuse doctrine to deal with these criticisms are set forth in section VIII.C.

A. Debate about the Elements of the Misuse Defense

1. The Presumption of Market Power

Some leading misuse cases rely expressly or implicitly on the arguably outdated presumption that the owner of intellectual property possesses market power.[3] However, legislative and regulatory

---

3.   *See, e.g.,* Senza-Gel Corp. v. Seiffhart, 803 F.2d 661, 665 n.5 (Fed. Cir. 1986) ("Commentators and courts have questioned the rationale appearing

developments, along with recent case law, have rejected this presumption. For example, Congress recently attempted to overrule case law upholding the patent misuse defense based on a presumption that patents confer market power.[4] Although this effort failed to succeed in its broader purposes, Congress did enact legislation requiring an independent showing of market power for misuse defenses based on allegations of tying or package licensing of patents.[5] Similarly, the Department of Justice and the Federal Trade Commission have stated in their *Intellectual Property Guidelines* that for purposes of determining whether antitrust enforcement action is necessary, they will not presume that intellectual property confers market power on its owner.[6]

Despite these views, misuse is not the only area of law to employ this presumption. Even in the antitrust context, the presumption that a patent or copyright confers market power, though abandoned by many lower courts, has never been repudiated by the Supreme Court.[7]

2. The Use of Per Se Analysis

The per se analysis applied to certain types of licensing arrangements under the present misuse doctrine is often criticized for failing to account fully for their beneficial effect. The notion that licensing has a number of procompetitive benefits has now become well accepted by the courts and is a fundamental premise of the *Intellectual*

---

in Supreme Court opinions dealing with misuse in view of recent economic theory and Supreme Court decisions in non-misuse contexts.");
J. Diane Brinson, *Patent Misuse: Time for a Change*, 16 RUTGERS COMPUTER & TECH. L.J. 357, 399-405 (1990).

4. *See* Richard Calkins, *Patent Law: The Impact of the 1988 Patent Misuse Reform Act and Noerr-Pennington Doctrine on Misuse Defenses and Antitrust Counterclaims*, 38 DRAKE L. REV. 175, 192-96 (1988-89).
5. 35 U.S.C. § 271(d)(5) (1988).
6. *See* U.S. DEP'T OF JUSTICE & FEDERAL TRADE COMM'N, ANTITRUST GUIDELINES FOR THE LICENSING OF INTELLECTUAL PROPERTY § 2.2 (1995), *reprinted in* 4 Trade Reg. Rep. (CCH) ¶ 13,132.
7. *See* Jefferson Parish Hospital Dist. No. 2 v. Hyde, 466 U.S. 2, 16 (1984); MCA Television Ltd. v. Public Interest Corp., 171 F.3d 1265 (11th Cir. 1999).

Property Guidelines.[8] Even in antitrust cases, most courts apply a rule of reason analysis to licensing arrangements in much the same way that other nonprice vertical restraints have been analyzed since *Continental T.V., Inc. v. GTE Sylvania, Inc.*[9]

3. The Absence of Consistent Standards

Misuse is often criticized for the lack of standards for determining what behavior is inappropriate. Much of this criticism is focused on whether the doctrine should or should not be closely tied to antitrust policies. A reason for applying antitrust-type analysis is the judiciary's experience with market power requirements and evaluation of different types of restraints, as well as the supposedly greater predictability that experience would afford; the counterargument is that misuse law implicates policy concerns beyond those of antitrust and is or can be made reasonably predictable.

a. The Role of Antitrust Principles

Although the early law was actually to the contrary, since at least the second *Mercoid* case in 1944, conduct constituting an antitrust violation has been recognized as a basis for invoking the misuse defense where the intellectual property contributes to the violation.[10] This view, taken to its extreme, suggests that misuse ought to use antitrust standards to determine the boundaries of competitive versus anticompetitive

---

8. *See* Windsurfing Int'l, Inc. v. AMF, Inc., 782 F.2d 995, 1001 n.9 (Fed. Cir. 1986) ("Recent economic analysis questions the rationale behind holding any licensing practice per se anticompetitive."); *see* U.S. DEP'T OF JUSTICE & FEDERAL TRADE COMM'N, ANTITRUST GUIDELINES FOR THE LICENSING OF INTELLECTUAL PROPERTY § 2.3 (1995), *reprinted in* 4 Trade Reg. Rep. (CCH) ¶ 13,132.

9. 433 U.S. 36 (1977). This is also the approach now taken to nonprice restrictions by the Federal Circuit. *See* C.R. Bard, Inc. v. M3 Sys., Inc., 157 F.3d 1340 (Fed. Cir. 1998); Mallinckrodt, Inc. v. Medipart, Inc., 976 F.2d 700, 708-09 (Fed. Cir. 1992).

10. *See* Mercoid Corp. v. Minneapolis-Honeywell Regulator Co., 320 U.S. 680 (1944).

conduct.[11] In the view of Judge Posner, "the antitrust laws as currently interpreted reach every practice that could impair competition substantially,"[12] and thus should be the basis for any misuse analysis based on economic or competition principles:

> If misuse claims are not tested by conventional antitrust principles, by what principles shall they be tested? Our law is not rich in alternative concepts of monopolistic abuse; and it is rather late in the day to try to develop one without in the process subjecting the rights of patent holders to debilitating uncertainty.[13]

Judge Posner argued that antitrust principles should serve at least as the basis for identifying new forms of misuse (if any) beyond those clearly identified by specific Supreme Court precedent.

According to this rationale, without a set of guiding principles such as those developed in the antitrust context, judges have the unfettered discretion to limit intellectual property rights based on their individual views of "competition policy" instead of operating within the structure of legislative or established judicial precedent. To address this concern, the 100th Congress considered legislation that would have required the finding of an antitrust violation to support a patent misuse defense.[14]

---

11. See USM Corp. v. SPS Techs., Inc., 694 F.2d 505 (7th Cir. 1982); *see also* Roger B. Andewelt, *Competition Policy and the Patent Misuse Doctrine*, 25 Pat. Trademark & Copyright J. (BNA) No. 604, at 41, 42 (Nov. 3, 1982) ("Since the antitrust laws are the appropriate vehicle for evaluating competitive effect, conduct should not be condemned as patent misuse on economic grounds unless the conduct is inconsistent with the antitrust laws."); William J. Nicoson, *Misuse of the Misuse Doctrine in Infringement Suits*, 9 UCLA L. REV. 76, 91 (1962) ("The concept of conduct not violative of the antitrust laws, but in some way violative of the policy inherent therein, can have no useful meaning whatever.").

12. *USM*, 694 F.2d at 511.

13. *Id.* at 512. *Accord* Saturday Evening Post Co. v. Rumbleseat Press, Inc., 816 F.2d 1191, 1200 (7th Cir. 1987); *Windsurfing*, 782 F.2d at 1001-02.

14. S. 438, 100th Cong., 2d Sess. (1988), provided that no patent owner would be deemed guilty of misuse unless the conduct being examined, "in view of the circumstances in which such practices or actions or inactions are employed, violate the antitrust laws."

While that legislation was not passed, courts such as the Federal Circuit have required proof of effects similar to those caused by an antitrust violation in determining whether conduct constitutes misuse.[15]

b. The Role of Nonantitrust Policy Concerns

Other courts, such as the Fourth Circuit in *Lasercomb*,[16] have not required such proof. While certain conduct violating the antitrust laws easily falls within the ambit of misuse, the doctrine originally evolved to further policies separate and apart from those furthered by the antitrust laws. Those policies include (1) competition policy covering conduct that does not result in an antitrust violation, (2) policies inherent in the patent or copyright laws, and (3) unclean hands. To critics of the doctrine, however, these policies, separately or together, have so far failed to provide a clear set of guidelines for determining precisely which practices promote or subvert these goals.

(1) Competition Policy
One problem with limiting the misuse doctrine to antitrust violations is that application of the sanctions associated with misuse, in addition to those sanctions associated with antitrust law, penalizes the holder of intellectual property more than holders of other property.[17]

Another problem is determining how and to what extent conduct involving the patent or copyright relates to the alleged antitrust violation. Under *Ansul Co. v. Uniroyal, Inc.*,[18] for example, misuse was not predicated on a licensing arrangement that violated antitrust law; rather, the mere fact of the patent's existence—and that it gave the patent holder the market power to engage in the allegedly unlawful conduct—sufficed to establish misuse. Therefore, even if limited to antitrust violations, the misuse doctrine often fails to require a meaningful nexus

---

15.   *See* cases cited at note 9.
16.   Lasercomb Am., Inc. v. Reynolds, 911 F.2d 970 (4th Cir. 1990).
17.   *See* Robert J. Hoerner, *Patent Misuse*, 53 ANTITRUST L.J. 641, 656 (1984).
18.   448 F.2d 872 (2d Cir. 1971).

between the intellectual property in suit and the alleged antitrust violation.[19]

While these arguments suggest that even a misuse doctrine limited to antitrust violations may go too far, others argue that a doctrine limited in this way does not go far enough, even if competition were the only relevant policy. There is no self-evident reason why antitrust policy should be the only relevant competition-based policy underlying the patent misuse doctrine. Practices that are not necessarily anticompetitive under the antitrust laws but that still have anticompetitive effects also may be undesirable and deserve to be deterred.[20]

Limiting misuse solely to conduct constituting an antitrust violation fails to address certain restrictive conduct that has a tendency to injure the competitive process. Strictly speaking, conduct violating the antitrust laws requires proof of each element of a claim under the Sherman Act, Clayton Act, or Robinson-Patman Act. Competition policy in the United States, however, encompasses other laws and principles. Conduct that violates any of the various restrictions against unfair competition—among them Section 5 of the Federal Trade Commission Act[21] and comparable state statutes[22]—as well as conduct

---

19.   See, e.g., Martin J. Adelman, *The New World of Patents Created by the Court of Appeals for the Federal Circuit*, 20 U. MICH. J.L. REFORM 979, 1003 (Summer 1987).

20.   This contention also has been made with respect to the copyright misuse doctrine. See, e.g., Ramsey Hanna, *Misusing Antitrust: The Search for Functional Copyright Misuse Standards*, 46 STAN. L. REV. 401 (1994).

21.   In *FTC v. Motion Picture Adver. Serv. Co.*, 344 U.S. 392, 394 (1953), the Court held that Section 5 of the Federal Trade Commission Act covers a broad range of anticompetitive conduct that might not violate the Sherman or Clayton Acts: "The 'unfair methods of competition,' which are condemned by § 5(a) of the Act, are not confined to those that were illegal at common law or that were condemned by the Sherman Act. . . . It is also clear that the Federal Trade Commission Act was designed to supplement and bolster the Sherman Act and the Clayton Act—to stop in their incipiency acts and practices which, when full blown, would violate those Acts, as well as to condemn as 'unfair methods of competition' existing violations of them." It must be noted that in recent years courts and the

that violates the spirit of the antitrust laws, is not necessarily a desirable use of intellectual property rights even if it may not technically meet all elements of an antitrust violation.

In *Transparent-Wrap Machinery Corp. v. Stokes & Smith Co.*,[23] the Supreme Court recognized that conduct that does not rise to the level of an antitrust violation may still contravene competition policy and, therefore, may support a misuse defense: "Though control of the unpatented article or device falls short of a prohibited restraint of trade or monopoly, it will not be sanctioned. . . . For it is the *tendency in that direction which condemns the practice* and which, if approved by a court either through enjoining infringement or enforcing the covenant, would receive a powerful impetus."[24] In short, limiting misuse to instances where an antitrust violation has been found leaves violations of other competition policies unredressed.[25]

Such a limitation creates significant practical concerns as well. Pursuing antitrust violations traditionally depends upon the attitudes, resources, and incentives of the government and private parties. The costs and uncertainties inherent in proving a rule of reason or

---

Federal Trade Commission have declined to extend Section 5 to conduct outside the Sherman or Clayton Acts in the absence of an actual showing of anticompetitive effects. *See generally* ABA SECTION OF ANTITRUST LAW, ANTITRUST LAW DEVELOPMENTS 559-63 (4th ed. 1997).

22. *See, e.g.*, California's Unfair Competition Act (CAL. BUS. & PROF. CODE § 17200 et seq.) (prohibiting "unlawful, unfair or fraudulent business practices"); Cel-Tech Communications, Inc. v. Los Angeles Cellular Tel. Co., 973 P.2d 527 (Cal. Sup. Ct. 1997) (statute applies to incipient antitrust violations or to conduct that violates policy and spirit of antitrust laws).

23. 329 U.S. 637 (1947).

24. *Id.* at 641 (emphasis added).

25. *See* Morton Salt Co. v. G.S. Suppiger Co., 314 U.S. 488 (1942). *See also* Zenith Radio Corp. v. Hazeltine Research, Inc., 395 U.S. 100, 136 (1969); Mercoid Corp. v. Mid-Continent Inv. Co., 320 U.S. 661, 667 (1944).

monopolization case would be likely to inhibit significantly the ability and incentive of an accused infringer to sustain a misuse defense.[26]

(2) Intellectual Property Law Policies

Apart from its effect on anticompetitive practices, the misuse doctrine originated to deter conduct that subverts the very policies the intellectual property grant was designed to achieve, as explained in Chapter I. It was because of the seriousness of this concern that the Supreme Court held in *Morton Salt*[27] that the intellectual property protection is suspended until the offensive conduct ceases.

In contract terms, the grant of exclusive, defined rights to an intellectual property holder for a limited term is consideration for creating and disclosing innovations that benefit the public.[28] With respect to patents, the Supreme Court has stated: "[T]he primary purpose of our patent laws is not the creation of private fortunes for the owners of patents but is 'to promote the progress of science and the useful arts.'"[29] Similar notions are at the foundation of copyright law: "The primary purpose of copyright is not to reward the author, but is rather to secure 'the general benefits derived by the public from the labors of authors.'"[30]

To achieve this socially beneficial end, the intellectual property laws attempt to strike a balance between protecting the intellectual property holder's exclusive rights, on the one hand, and encouraging access to

---

26. *See* Calkins, *supra* note 4, at 187; Troy Paredes, *Copyright Misuse and Tying: Will Courts Stop Misusing Misuse?* 9 HIGH TECH. L.J. 271, 297 (1994).

27. 314 U.S. 488.

28. *See* Hoerner, *supra* note 17, at 656; *see also* Hanna, *supra* note 20 (arguing that potential incompatibilities between antitrust and copyright policies support an independent misuse doctrine).

29. Motion Picture Patents Co. v. Universal Film Mfg. Co., 243 U.S. 502, 511 (1917).

30. MELVILLE B. NIMMER & DAVID NIMMER, 1 NIMMER ON COPYRIGHT § 1.03[A], at 1-66.7 (1999), *quoting* Fox Film Corp. v. Doyal, 286 U.S. 123, 127 (1932).

unprotected information to inspire further innovation, on the other.[31] Patent law seeks to achieve this balance by requiring delineation in the patent claims of the scope of what is and what is not covered by the claims in the language in the patent. These claims are closely examined by the government before being awarded.[32] Similarly, copyright protection covers only statutorily identified rights in a protected work.[33]

Patent and copyright laws further balance exclusivity and access to knowledge by limiting the duration of intellectual property protection. Indeed, the U.S. Constitution itself explicitly limits Congress to granting patent or copyright protection only for a "limited time."[34] Upon

---

31. *See* Bonito Boats, Inc. v. Thunder Craft Boats, Inc., 489 U.S. 141, 150-51 (1989) ("The federal patent system thus embodies a carefully crafted bargain for encouraging the creation and disclosure of new, useful, and nonobvious advances in technology and design in return for the exclusive right to practice the invention for a period of years. . . . The attractiveness of such a bargain, and its effectiveness in inducing creative effort and disclosure of the results of that effort, depend almost entirely on a backdrop of free competition in the exploitation of unpatented designs and innovations."); *see also* General Elec. Co. v. Wabash Appliance Corp., 304 U.S. 364 (1938); United States v. Dubilier Condenser Corp., 289 U.S. 178 (1933).

32. *See* Penwalt Co. v. Graver Corp., 284 U.S. 52, 60 (1931); *see also* Warner-Jenkinson Co. v. Hilton Davis Chem. Co., 520 U.S. 17, 29 (1997) ("Each element contained in a patent claim is deemed material to defining the scope of the patented invention, and thus the doctrine of equivalents must be applied to individual elements of the claim, not to the invention as a whole."); *Bonito Boats,* 489 U.S. at 151 ("To a limited extent, the federal patent laws must determine not only what is protected, but also what is free for all to use.").

33. *See generally* Note, *Clarifying the Copyright Misuse Defense: The Role of Antitrust Standards and First Amendment Values,* 104 HARV. L. REV. 1289 (1991).

34. This Patents Clause limitation does not apply to trademarks. Trademark protection is premised on the desirability of providing information about product origins and quality to consumers and is founded on the Commerce Clause, not the Patents Clause. Trademark law does not encourage or reward for its own sake technical or artistic innovation but rather fosters the development and consistent use of distinctive product

expiration of the statutory protection, the public has the unfettered right to use the intellectual property.[35]

Conduct that interferes with the unfettered use of ideas outside the scope or term of intellectual property protection tips the scales away from the ultimate goal of benefiting the public through innovation. This conduct is a "failure of consideration" or subversion of the assumption upon which intellectual property protection is based. With respect to patents, licensing restrictions giving the patent holder some control over trade in unpatentable goods or services arguably also conflict with the patent grant process itself.[36] Such restrictions may be seen as permitting circumvention of the examination process intended to limit protection to new, nonobvious, and useful inventions.[37]

---

symbols. It does not reflect the same balance of interests as do patent and copyright law, nor is there any statutory limitation on term of protection. Conduct that might offend trademark policy would include conduct that deceives consumers or perhaps the attempted assertion of trademark claims to functional or already widely used words or features; other policies that might apply, for example, to trademark tie-ins or covenants not to compete would be based on competition policy, not a trademark-extending policy similar to that in patent and copyright cases.

35. "The statute requires the patentee . . . to inform the public during the life of the patent of the limits of the monopoly asserted, so that it may be known which features may be safely used or manufactured without a license and which may not." *Penwalt Co.*, 284 U.S. at 60. *See, e.g., Bonito Boats*, 489 U.S. at 165 ("For almost 100 years it has been well established that in the case of an expired patent, the federal patent laws *do* create a federal right to 'copy and use.'").

36. Such licensing provisions may include attempts (1) to "recapture" elements not claimed in the patent or conceivably even rejected in the examination process, (2) to extend the temporal scope of the patent, (3) to squelch the ability or incentive of a licensee to make improvements or additions to the technology, or (4) to prevent a licensee from using the licensed technology as a springboard to a different and better technology.

37. 35 U.S.C. § 101 (1988). *See also Bonito Boats*, 489 U.S. at 146 ("Congress may not . . . authorize the issuance of patents whose effects are to remove existent knowledge from the public domain, or to restrict free access to materials already available."); Mercoid Corp. v. Mid-Continent Inv. Co., 320 U.S. 661, 667 (1944) (expanding reach of contract allows

Acts that place restrictions on previously unrestricted technology or expression, thereby inhibiting further innovation or creativity, also diminish the social value of a new innovation or creation. Thus, broad grantback requirements or noncompete provisions in an intellectual property license can prevent the licensee from producing or using other socially beneficial inventions competitive with the protected invention or hinder the development of sequential innovations and improvements.[38] Restrictive action not only diminishes social value but can result in affirmative public injury. For example, conduct inhibiting the free exchange of facts and ideas or suppressing new expression may conflict with the goals of the copyright laws as well as First Amendment values.[39]

The misuse doctrine has developed, in part, to discourage conduct that disturbs the balance in the dichotomy inherent in intellectual property law. By holding intellectual property protection unenforceable in cases of misuse, the doctrine preserves the social value of intellectual property protection. Antitrust doctrines and concern with competitive effects may be broadly relevant to this basis for the misuse doctrine, but they are by no means congruent with it. Thus, misuse might play a role in circumstances when antitrust would not, and misuse need be neither a redundant doctrine nor one bounded strictly by the contours of antitrust. As noted by Judge Posner and others, however, all aspects of the current misuse doctrine are not necessarily well correlated with the goal of deterring conduct that truly subverts the intellectual property system, and apart from the law passed by Congress with respect to patent-related

---

"private business" to "function as its own patent office and impose its own law upon its licensees").

38.   *See* James Kobak, Jr., *A Sensible Doctrine of Misuse for Intellectual Property Cases*, 2 ALB. L.J. SCI. & TECH. 1, 29-30 (1992), and *Intellectual Property, Competition Law and Hidden Choices Between Original and Sequential Innovation*, 3 VA. J. L. & TECH 6 at ¶ 28.5 (Fall 1998); *see also* Joseph Farrell, *Standardization and Intellectual Property*, 30 JURIMETRICS J. 35, 43 (1989).

39.   *Lasercomb Am., Inc. v. Reynolds*, 911 F.2d 970 (4th Cir. 1990), and its progeny reason that a broad covenant not to develop other software conflicts with the copyright goal of stimulating original expression.

tying contracts, well-defined standards for judging behavior are often lacking.

(3) Unclean Hands

The misuse doctrine is also based on the notion of unclean hands, i.e., that one seeking equity must come into court without itself being guilty of inequitable conduct. Equitable doctrines that favor the patentee run throughout patent law, and the patent misuse doctrine may provide a counterbalance to such doctrines.[40] For example, courts are given wide discretion to impart equitable principles in fashioning relief for infringement under 35 U.S.C. § 283; similarly, both the doctrine of contributory infringement and the doctrine of equivalents have their foundations in equitable principles.[41]

Anticompetitive effects are largely irrelevant under these doctrines. The test for infringement under the doctrine of equivalents reaches the same result regardless of the economic effect of the allegedly equivalent infringing product on the patentee's sales or profits.[42] Preserving the courts' discretion to limit enforcement of patents without requiring an extensive showing of effects on competition may be desirable to avoid results that are otherwise inequitable or injurious to public welfare.[43]

Even more so than with intellectual property law policies, however, unclean hands principles do not provide any guidance regarding what conduct is or is not misuse.[44] Unlike unclean hands-type conduct that is

---

40. *See* Robert Merges, *Reflections on Current Legislation Affecting Patent Misuse*, 70 J. PAT. [& TRADEMARK]. OFF. SOC'Y 793 (Dec. 1988).

41. *See id.*; International Visual Corp. v. Crown Metal Mfg. Co., 991 F.2d 768, 774 (Fed. Cir. 1993) (Lourie, J., concurring); Charles Greiner & Co. v. Mari-Med Mfg. Inc., 962 F.2d 1031, 1036 (Fed. Cir. 1992).

42. *See* Merges, *supra* note 40, at 797 n.5.

43. *See* Vitamin Technologists, Inc. v. Wisconsin Alumni Research Found., 146 F.2d 941 (9th Cir. 1945); City of Milwaukee v. Activated Sludge, Inc., 69 F.2d 577 (7th Cir. 1934) (stating that public policy is an important consideration when deciding on whether to grant or deny injunctive relief.)

44. As stated by Brinson:

    [W]hile the "unclean hands" maxim may provide the courts with their *power* to deny relief to patentees, the maxim does not tell

fraudulent or represents some other abuse of the judicial process, many of the practices subject to condemnation under the misuse doctrine "reveal nothing intrinsically evil; they are wrongful only if, on balance, they have a detrimental economic effect . . . [and] [t]herefore should be judged by the standards of antitrust law, not freewheeling equity."[45] Moreover, unlike traditional unclean hands, the misuse defense has been successful even with respect to activity of the patentee that does not relate to the allegedly infringing conduct at issue or the defendant in the case, but only to the intellectual property involved in the suit. The unclean hands doctrine alone does not fully support the current scope of the misuse doctrine.

B. Debate about the Penalty of Nonenforceability of Intellectual Property Rights

While many criticisms of the misuse doctrine, and legislative efforts to overturn it, have centered on defining the conduct that constitutes misuse, the severity of the remedy for misuse also has been the subject of debate. The remedy for intellectual property misuse traditionally favored by the courts prohibits *any* enforcement of intellectual property rights that have been misused, whether in the form of injunctive relief, damages, or contract royalties, until the misuse has been purged.

However, this rule has been considered unduly harsh, especially when extended to outright infringers of intellectual property who are unaffected by the conduct constituting misuse. The remedy overdeters the exercise of intellectual property rights, underdeters infringement, and penalizes intellectual property owners disproportionately as compared with other property owners. A more bounded remedy, such as unenforceability of contractual provisions or unenforceability for a

---

the courts whether the patentee's use of his patent is proper or contrary to the public interest. We lack, as Chisum has noted, a general theory for determining what licensing practices are *proper* exercises of the patent grant.

Brinson, *supra* note 3, at 372 (footnotes omitted), *citing* 4 D. CHISUM, PATENTS § 19.04[4] (1989).

45.   JAY DRATLER, JR., LICENSING OF INTELLECTUAL PROPERTY § 5.04[5], at 5-102 (1994).

defined period of time, might strike a more appropriate balance between the goals of encouraging innovation and deterring overreaching conduct.

1. Justifications for the Penalty

Since damages are unavailable, a penalty less stringent than unenforceability of the patent or copyright may not adequately deter the misuse. Any prospect of damages depends entirely on proving that the conduct constituting misuse is also (1) a violation of antitrust or other laws (2) for which damages are recoverable by the particular defendant bringing the claim. If the misuse rises to the level of an antitrust violation, a defendant claiming misuse may not have standing to seek damages resulting from the violation. Moreover, the substantial costs and uncertainties associated with a private antitrust suit make reliance on such suits tenuous. To the extent that a misuse defense is grounded in conduct that does not rise to the level of an antitrust or other violation for which damages are available, a damages-based remedy does not exist in the first place. The misuse remedy thus substitutes for damages in its deterrent and punitive effects.

Under this view, making the intellectual property right unenforceable may be necessary because an alternative such as merely refusing to enforce an offending licensing provision would still allow the patentee to retain any benefits of the offending conduct prior to the misuse challenge. The incentive to engage in prohibited conduct unless and until successfully challenged might therefore largely neutralize the deterrent effect of a lesser sanction. Also, factors such as the costs and delay of litigation and the potential loss of license rights can limit the likelihood that conduct constituting misuse will be challenged quickly, if at all.[46]

Another element of the misuse doctrine contributing to its severity is that any potential infringer can raise the defense, regardless of its connection to the conduct alleged to be misuse. On the other hand, if the patent misuse defense is limited only to those potential infringers who can prove that they suffered harm from misuse, the intellectual property

---

46.   *See* Calkins, *supra* note 4, at 187; Kobak, *supra* note 38, at 40-41.

owner could benefit from otherwise widespread acts of misuse.[47] Moreover, a standing requirement might inspire further undesirable conduct by the intellectual property owner. To avoid a misuse penalty, the intellectual property owner would have an incentive selectively to exclude the offending provision from license agreements with those persons more likely to challenge the intellectual property grant or protection, or to lessen the likelihood of challenge by offering more favorable license terms to such persons. No incentive to discriminate among licensees exists where the effect of a misuse determination is to bar all infringement claims, regardless of whether the alleged infringers are harmed by the misuse.

2. *Criticisms of the Penalty*

Intellectual property misuse can be considered a breach of the intellectual property holder's bargain or "contract" with the public, pursuant to which the public's obligation to respect the intellectual property is conditioned on the intellectual property holder's compliance with the policies underlying the intellectual property grant. Rescinding the "contract" by not enforcing the intellectual property disproportionately disadvantages the intellectual property owner, who can never recoup the intellectual property disclosed, published, or otherwise disseminated to the public in exchange for the intellectual property protection.[48] Under this view, nonenforcement is too great a deterrent, leading to underinvestment in new ideas or modes of expression and underutilization of intellectual property rights.

Moreover, nonenforcement of a patent or copyright is imperfect equity at best. The refusal to enforce intellectual property rights even against a willful infringer (at least until the effects of misuse are purged) may reflect too much reticence to protect the rights of the intellectual property owner with unclean hands. Critics argue that equity must run both ways, and that an infringer often itself has unclean hands or does

---

47.   *See* Mark A. Lemley, *The Economic Irrationality of the Patent Misuse Doctrine*, 78 CAL. L. REV. 1599, 1618-19 (1990); Kobak, *supra* note 38, at 38.

48.   *See* Hoerner, *supra* note 17.

not seem highly deserving of special protection, especially if the infringer is not even injured by the conduct constituting misuse.[49] In fact, making intellectual property rights unenforceable even against infringers and licensees who have not been subjected to the conduct constituting misuse results in a windfall to such infringers, whose risk of being enjoined or paying damages is reduced by the prospect of a misuse finding. The windfall is compounded by the fact that the infringer need not prove injury to have standing to raise the misuse defense. These characteristics create the potential for actually *encouraging* infringement: a prospective licensee faced with a restrictive provision may be better off using the intellectual property without a license and taking his chances armed with the threat of a misuse defense.[50]

Another criticism of the misuse remedy is that it unfairly subjects intellectual property owners to harsher penalties than are imposed on owners of other forms of property who have overstepped their permitted bounds. As one commentator has noted: "Patents are a form of property, 35 U.S.C. § 261, and except for forfeiture of personal property which is the instrumentality or fruit of a crime, even a convicted felon ordinarily retains ownership of his property and the right to exclude others from trespassing on it."[51]

A seller found to have illegally tied two products may be subject to damages and an injunction under the antitrust laws, but it does not forfeit all rights to sell those products.[52] On the other hand, a licensor found to

---

49.   *See* Data Gen. Corp. v. Grumman Sys. Support Corp., 36 F.3d 1147, 1170 n.43 (1st Cir. 1994) ("If copyright misuse is an equitable defense, a defendant that has itself acted inequitably may not be entitled to raise such a defense."); Atari Games Corp. v. Nintendo of America, Inc., 975 F.2d 832, 846 (Fed. Cir. 1992); Kobak, *supra* note 38, at 35-45.

50.   *See* Lemley, *supra* note 47, at 1615 n.107.

51.   *See* Robert J. Hoerner, *Patent Misuse: Portents for the 1990s*, 59 ANTITRUST L.J. 687, 700 (1991).

52.   This principle was stated forcefully in *M. Witmark & Sons v. Pastime Amusement Co.*, 298 F. 470, 480 (D.S.C., 1924), *aff'd*, 2 F.2d 1020 (4th Cir. 1924): "The Sherman Act does not make the party to an interstate monopoly an outlaw. It does not prevent such a party from asserting his rights in the courts. It does not give any person the right to trespass upon the rights of such party, or to deprive him unlawfully of his property."

have illegally used a patent in the same manner may be subject to damages and injunctive relief (based on an antitrust violation) *and* loss of its rights to enforce the patents and collect damages for infringement occurring during the period of misuse.

Similarly, the intellectual property misuse defense is effectively a general defense to a breach of contract claim, while an antitrust violation achieved with the use of real or personal property is not.[53] The misuse remedy thereby eliminates the intellectual property owner's right to defend its property against infringers.

Moreover, if intellectual property misuse is based on an antitrust violation and damages are awarded, the nonenforceability sanction acts as a double penalty, disproportionately deterring the exercise of intellectual property rights as compared with other property rights.[54] This discrimination against intellectual property owners reduces the value of intellectual property rights relative to other forms of property rights.

3. The Effect of the Ability to Purge Misuse

Some of the harsh effects of the misuse doctrine are ameliorated by the doctrine of purge, which permits a patent or copyright to regain enforceability once the practice constituting misuse has been terminated and its effects have been dissipated. As explained in Chapter I, some decisions have required very little by way of dissipation beyond cessation of a practice, while others have insisted on a great deal more; the intellectual property owner has no way of knowing whether a misuse has been purged without the expense and uncertainty of litigating the question.[55] Indeed, the lack of consistent guidelines for determining what constitutes a purge contributes to the uncertainty created by the misuse doctrine. Nevertheless, the doctrine of purge gives courts some

---

53. *See* Kelly v. Kosuga, 358 U.S. 516 (1959).
54. *See* Lemley, *supra* note 47, at 1617; Paredes, *supra* note 26, at 332-33. These points are more fully elaborated in Chapter V, outlining the economics principles thought to be most applicable to the misuse doctrine.
55. *See* Chapter I.J.

means of calibrating the penalty more closely to the harm, particularly if the courts define the requirements for purge at the time misuse is found to exist.

C. A Resolution

The criticism that the misuse doctrine is vague, uncertain, and even irrational as applied to certain conduct can be addressed by identifying the relevant policy concerns and more closely examining the behavior alleged to be misuse in light of such concerns. The other principal criticism of the doctrine—the harshness and inequity of the misuse remedy—can then be addressed in light of a more narrowly tailored doctrine.

1. Refining the Elements of Misuse

First, intellectual property policy rather than competition policy should primarily determine the types of conduct that warrant a misuse remedy. Antitrust law is always available to redress those "extensions" of intellectual property that cause competitive harm under the Sherman Act and other antitrust statutes. However, not all extensions that are undesirable from an intellectual property law standpoint are anticompetitive enough to warrant antitrust remedies; the misuse remedy should be applied in just such circumstances. Conversely, some practices that are anticompetitive may not be particularly troublesome as a matter of intellectual property policy; these practices should not be considered misuse.

In light of intellectual property law considerations, then, conduct constituting misuse should meet the following criteria:

1. *Undue Extension of Intellectual Property Rights:* The intellectual property owner has engaged in a practice—normally one restricting a licensee's activity—that "extended the scope" of its intellectual property.

2. *Conditioning:* The owner has conditioned the intellectual property license on a licensee's acceptance of the restriction.

3. *Coercion:* Using market power, the owner has coerced the unwilling licensee into accepting the restriction.

4. *Affirmative Justification:* The owner has failed to demonstrate a business justification for having insisted on the restrictive practice despite an opportunity to do so.

By requiring misuse conduct to meet criteria such as these, the misuse doctrine can maintain more effectively the balance of private and public interests inherent in intellectual property law. These criteria are also consistent with concerns expressed in *Mercoid*[56] and the early contributory infringement cases, as well as in the later per se misuse cases such as *Morton Salt*[57] and *Zenith*.[58] At the same time, they eliminate the arbitrary, counterproductive features of the doctrine identified in section VIII.A.

The same four criteria should be useful in determining copyright misuse as well as patent misuse. The *Lasercomb*[59] opinion, discussed in Chapter VII, correctly identified the copyright policies at stake but incorrectly relied on *Morton Salt*[60] to adopt a per se rule. It did not evaluate whether the copyright in suit conferred any coercive power, did not take into account the relevant differences between copyrights and patents, and did not consider any justification for the practice at issue in the case before it.[61] Because a copyright does not rely on precisely

---

56.   Mercoid Corp. v. Mid-Continent Inv. Co., 320 U.S. 661 (1944).
57.   Morton Salt Co. v. G.S. Suppiger Co., 314 U.S. 488 (1942).
58.   Zenith Radio Corp. v. Hazeltine Research, Inc., 395 U.S. 100 (1969).
59.   Lasercomb Am., Inc. v. Reynolds, 911 F.2d 970 (4th Cir. 1990).
60.   314 U.S. 488.
61.   For the reasons explained in 34, *supra*, trademarks do not implicate the same intellectual property concerns as patents or copyrights; and only conduct by which the trademark owner attempts to assert rights to generic words or functional features in the public domain could be said to be trademark-extending in the same way that a tie-in or post-expiration royalty provision in a patent license is said to be patent-extending. Any role for a trademark misuse doctrine would therefore be quite narrow. As noted in Chapter VII, use of a trademark as part of an antitrust violation is made a defense to incontestability of the mark by statute and may or may

defined and closely examined claims, and since the scope of most copyrights is more limited than the scope of most patents, a copyright misuse doctrine should, if anything, be applied more cautiously than a patent misuse doctrine.

a. Conduct Unduly Extending Intellectual Property Rights

The misuse claimant should first identify a practice by which the intellectual property owner appears to have obtained a benefit beyond that inherent in the scope of the intellectual property (as defined by the patent claims and the patent or copyright law mutatis mutandis). The following practices could satisfy this criterion: tying, package licensing, covenants not to compete (so-called "tie-outs"), total sales royalties, price fixing and minimum resale price maintenance after patent rights have been exhausted, and grantback provisions (primarily assignments or exclusive licenses back) that are unreasonably broad.

Field of use and customer restrictions and territorial limitations in intellectual property licenses, on the other hand, probably would not meet this requirement. Many postsale, nonprice restraints do not seem particularly intellectual property-extending; the antitrust rule of reason is sufficient to guard against their adverse effects. Moreover, the Federal Circuit's *Mallinckrodt*[62] decision suggests that some such restrictions on the use of patented products or processes may now be enforced under the patent laws.[63]

Conduct not subject to antitrust scrutiny also would be covered by this construction of misuse. For example, postexpiration royalty clauses or other efforts to extend a patent's term may or may not be particularly anticompetitive, but they have a patent-extending tendency. They could appropriately be characterized as misuse as long as the courts distinguish

---

not be regarded by the courts as providing a defense to a suit to enforce the trademark. *See* Chapter VII.B.

62. Mallinckrodt, Inc. v. Medipart, Inc., 976 F.2d 700 (Fed. Cir. 1992).

63. *See id.* at 709; *see also* James B. Kobak, Jr., *Contracting Around Exhaustion: Some Thoughts About the CAFC's Mallinckrodt Decision*, 75 J. PAT. [& TRADEMARK]. OFF. SOC'Y 550 (1993).

between coerced clauses and a royalty provision that simply provides a licensee an extended period to pay royalties that accrued during the life of the patent. On the other hand, discriminatory royalties are appropriately challenged, if at all, only under antitrust rules, not as misuse; those provisions allow an owner to maximize the reward for its intellectual property without extending the scope of an intellectual property right.

The automatic classification as misuse of any antitrust violation accomplished with the use of intellectual property should be discarded along with other per se rules. Any conduct that violates the antitrust laws should not automatically be misuse; it should receive independent analysis under the misuse principles described here to determine if it offends the relevant intellectual property policy.

b. Conditioning

A determination of misuse should require a "conditioning" of an intellectual property license on the licensee's agreement to the restrictive practice. Under this criterion, the misuse claimant would have to show that the intellectual property owner apparently offered the license combination on a "take it or leave it" basis. The intellectual property owner could rebut this proof with evidence that it offered the licensee reasonable alternative licensing or sales solutions.

c. Coercion

The misuse claimant also should have the burden of proving a separate "coercion" criterion, showing that (1) the intellectual property confers on the owner the ability to coerce, and (2) the intellectual property owner did in fact coerce the licensee. Specifically, the misuse claimant would ordinarily be required to prove that at the time of the licensing, the intellectual property holder had market power in the market for the protected technology. In addition, the misuse claimant would have to prove that the licensee was forced to accept a situation that it would not have accepted under other circumstances, i.e., that the licensee was unwilling to accept the objectionable practice but had no realistic economic choice to do otherwise.[64] The intellectual property holder would then have the opportunity to rebut this evidence by showing that the licensee's choice was voluntary, that the restrictive practice was mutually beneficial to both the licensor and the licensee, and that the practice was the product of a reasonable negotiation.

d. Affirmative Justification

Once the misuse claimant has made a prima facie showing of misuse under the first three criteria, the holder of intellectual property should be permitted to prove any special justification for the conduct. The burden of proof would shift to the holder, who must establish that it did not intend to employ the power of its intellectual property to extend its scope. Rather than having the courts apply a per se approach—and contrary to the dicta in cases such as *B.B. Chemical*[65] and *Mercoid*[66]—the holder would have an opportunity to demonstrate a reasonable business justification for its practice. A permissible justification would include a showing that the conduct in question represented a reasonable way to achieve a reward from the intellectual property not otherwise readily achievable. The relevant point in time for assessing reasonableness should be the time of contracting.

2. Tailoring the Remedy to the Harm

a. Better Defining the Elements of Purge

If the scope of the conduct to which the misuse doctrine applies were more specifically defined, as suggested above, the misuse remedy would apply only to seriously overreaching conduct, i.e., coercive, intellectual property-extending behavior without a business justification. In this way, much of the harshness and inequity of the misuse remedy would be mitigated.

---

64. This is the concept of "forcing" described by Justice O'Connor in *Jefferson Parish Hospital District No. 2 v. Hyde*, 466 U.S. 2, 37-38 (1984) (concurring opinion).
65. B.B. Chem. Co. v. Ellis, 314 U.S. 495, 498 (1942).
66. Mercoid Corp. v. Mid-Continent Inv. Co., 320 U.S. 661, 667 (1944).

Defining how, and in what period of time, the misuse might be purged, and doing so at the time misuse is determined, would further temper the misuse remedy. Under current misuse law, the intellectual property holder must bring another enforcement lawsuit to obtain a decision regarding the success of its attempts to accomplish a purge. A better practice would be for courts to define specifically the effects of the misuse and identify the action required of the intellectual property holder to ameliorate such effects at the time of the misuse determination.

b. Requiring a Nexus between the Enforcement Action and the Misuse

As noted in section VIII.B, the penalty of total unenforceability against all infringers imposed by the present misuse doctrine has been criticized because it overdeters the exercise of intellectual property rights, encourages strategic behavior by infringers, and may, at the margin, contribute to the temptation to infringe. To address this criticism, the misuse doctrine could be modified to require the misuse claimant to demonstrate "standing." The misuse claimant would have to demonstrate a nexus between itself and the misuse, either as a party to the contract containing the offending provision or because it is in some other way directly affected by the misuse.

c. Using Discretion to Limit the Penalty

To further address the overdeterrence factor, courts should consider the option of making unenforceable only the contractual provision deemed to be misuse rather than the intellectual property protection itself, thereby allowing the intellectual property holder to continue to enforce its intellectual property against other infringers. Such a sanction would allow the intellectual property holder to retain the benefits from the intellectual property, while limiting such benefits to those derived from the intellectual property itself (rather than from its misuse).[67]

---

67. *See* Kobak, *supra* note 38, at 35-45. This remedy is not without precedent. Courts have applied it in instances of patent misuse consisting of certain postsale royalty provisions, as well as no-contest clauses. *See* Brulotte v. Thys Co., 379 U.S. 29 (1964); Modrey v. American Gage &

Moreover, by selectively applying this sanction, the courts could tailor the severity of the remedy to the egregiousness of the conduct deemed to be misuse, as well as to the degree to which the misuse claimant's own hands are unclean.

D. Conclusion

The harshness and unpredictability of the misuse defense have been criticized over the years, but the doctrine need not be jettisoned in its entirety to meet criticisms. A more narrowly tailored doctrine could play a circumscribed but important role in achieving the balance between proprietary rights and access to material in the public domain mandated by the nation's intellectual property laws.

Mach. Co., 478 F.2d 470, 474-75 (2d Cir. 1973) (distinguishing between the portion of royalties in a license agreement that accrue after expiration, which are uncollectible under *Brulotte*, and the portion of royalties that accrue before expiration, which it held remain due and payable); Panther Pumps & Equip. Co. v. Hydrocraft, Inc., 468 F.2d 225 (7th Cir. 1972) (no contest clause is enforceable but not misuse preventing all enforcement of the patent).

TABLE OF CASES

A

C

F

G

N

O

P

Panther Pumps & Equip. Co. v. Hydrocraft, Inc., 468 F.2d 225 (7th Cir. 1972), 51, 110, 227

Paragon Podiatry Lab. Inc. v. KLM Lab., Inc., 984 F.2d 1182 (Fed. Cir. 1993), 68, 119

Peelers Co. v. Wendt, 260 F. Supp. 193 (W.D. Wash. 1966), 55, 89

Penwalt Co. v. Graver Corp., 284 U.S. 52 (1931), 212, 213

Peter Pan Fabrics, Inc. v. Candy Frocks, Inc., 187 F. Supp. 334 (S.D.N.Y. 1960), 178, 179

Phi Delta Theta Fraternity v. J.A. Buchroeder & Co., 251 F. Supp. 968 (W.D. Mo. 1966), 195, 199

Practice Management Info. Corp. v. AMA, 121 F.3d 516 (9th Cir. 1997), 31, 35, 47, 48, 82, 112, 151, 173, 174, 179, 180

PRC Realty Sys., Inc. v. National Ass'n of Realtors, Inc., 766 F. Supp. 453 (E.D. Va. 1991), *aff'd in part, rev'd in part, without op.*, 972 F.2d 341 (4th Cir. 1992), 47, 82, 83

PRC Realty Sys., Inc. v. National Ass'n of Realtors, 1992 Copyright L. Dec. (CCH) ¶ 26,961, 1992 U.S. App. LEXIS 18017 (4th Cir. 1992), 112, 172

Precision Instrument Mfg. Co. v. Automotive Maintenance Mach. Co., 324 U.S. 806 (1945), 68

Preformed Line Prod. Co. v. Fanner Mfg. Co., 225 F. Supp. 762 (N.D. Ohio), *aff'd*, 328 F.2d 265 (6th Cir. 1962), 32

Preformed Line Prod. Co. v. Fanner Mfg. Co., 328 F.2d 265 (6th Cir. 1962), 46, 189

Pressed Steel Car Co. v. Union Pacific Railroad Co., 270 F. 518 (2d Cir. 1920), 49

Professional Real Estate Investors, Inc. v. Columbia Pictures Industries, Inc., 508 U.S. 49 (1993), 66, 67

PSC Inc. v. Symbol Tech. Inc., 26 F. Supp. 2d 505 (W.D.N.Y. 1998), 26, 62, 66, 109

Q

qad, Inc. v. ALN Assoc., Inc., 770 F. Supp. 1261 (N.D. Ill. 1991), *aff'd*, 974 F.2d 834 (7th Cir. 1992), 67, 174, 175, 187

qad, Inc. v. ALN Assoc., Inc., No. 88 C 2246, 1992 WL142650 (N.D. Ill. June 11, 1992), 175

qad, Inc. v. ALN Assoc., Inc., 974 F.2d 834 (7th Cir. 1992), 67, 174

Q-Tips, Inc. v. Johnson & Johnson, 109 F. Supp. 657 (D.N.J. 1951), *modified*, 207 F.2d 509 (3d Cir. 1953), 60, 85

V

W

ABA SECTION OF ANTITRUST LAW
COMMITMENT TO QUALITY

The Section of Antitrust Law is committed to the highest standards of scholarship and continuing legal education. To that end, each of our books and treatises is subjected to rigorous quality control mechanisms throughout the design, drafting, editing, and peer review processes. Each Section publication is drafted and edited by leading experts on the topics covered and then rigorously peer reviewed by the Section's Books and Treatises Committee, at least two Council members, and then other officers and experts. Because the Section's quality commitment does not stop at publication, we encourage you to provide any comments or suggestions you may have for future editions of this book or other publications.

Defending Liberty
Pursuing Justice